FRAMING ROBERTO BOLAÑO

CW00819781

Poetry, fiction, literary history, and politics. These four cornerstone concerns of Roberto Bolaño's work have established him as a representative, generational figure in not only Chile, Mexico, and Spain, the three principal locations of his life and work, but throughout Europe and the Americas, increasingly on a global scale. At the heart of Bolaño's "poemas-novela," his poet- and poetry-centered novels, is the history and legacy of the prose poem. Challenging the policing of boundaries between verse and prose, poetry and fiction, the literary and the non-literary, the aesthetic and the political, his prose poem novels offer a sustained literary history by other means, a pivotal intervention that restores poetry and literature to full capacity. *Framing Roberto Bolaño* is one of the first books to trace the full arc and development of Bolaño's work from the beginning to the end of his career.

JONATHAN BECK MONROE is a former DAAD and ACLS Fellow and member of the IIEE's national Fulbright selection committee. He is the author of *A Poverty of Objects: The Prose Poem and the Politics of Genre* (1987) and *Demosthenes' Legacy* (2009), a book of prose poems and short fiction. Co-author and editor of *Writing and Revising the Disciplines* (2002), *Local Knowledges, Local Practices: Writing in the Disciplines at Cornell* (2006), *Poetry, Community, Movement* (1996), and *Poetics of Avant-Garde Poetries* (2000), he has published widely on questions of genre, writing and disciplinary practices, innovative poetries of the past two centuries, and avant-garde movements and their contemporary legacies.

FRAMING ROBERTO BOLAÑO

Poetry, Fiction, Literary History, Politics

JONATHAN BECK MONROE

Cornell University

CAMBRIDGE
UNIVERSITY PRESS

CAMBRIDGE
UNIVERSITY PRESS

University Printing House, Cambridge CB2 8BS, United Kingdom

One Liberty Plaza, 20th Floor, New York, NY 10006, USA

477 Williamstown Road, Port Melbourne, VIC 3207, Australia

314-321, 3rd Floor, Plot 3, Splendor Forum, Jasola District Centre, New Delhi - 110025, India

103 Penang Road, #05-06/07, Visioncrest Commercial, Singapore 238467

Cambridge University Press is part of the University of Cambridge.

It furthers the University's mission by disseminating knowledge in the pursuit of
education, learning and research at the highest international levels of excellence.

www.cambridge.org
Information on this title: www.cambridge.org/9781108735568
DOI: 10.1017/9781108633475

First published 2019
First paperback edition 2021

A catalogue record for this publication is available from the British Library

Library of Congress Cataloging in Publication data
NAMES: Monroe, Jonathan, 1954– author.
TITLE: Framing Roberto Bolano: poetry, fiction, literary history, politics / Jonathan Beck
Monroe.
DESCRIPTION: Cambridge ; New York, NY: Cambridge University Press, 2020. | Includes
bibliographical references and index.
IDENTIFIERS: LCCN 2019016370 | ISBN 9781108498258 (Hardback: alk. paper) | ISBN
9781108735568 (Paperback: alk. paper)
SUBJECTS: LCSH: Bolano, Roberto, 1953–2003 – Criticism and interpretation.
CLASSIFICATION: LCC PQ8098.12.O38 Z76 2020 | DDC 863/.64–dc23
LC record available at https://lccn.loc.gov/2019016370

ISBN 978-1-108-49825-8 Hardback
ISBN 978-1-108-73556-8 Paperback

For my wife, Alfie,

For all that was missing

Piu' di ieri, meno di domani

Contents

Acknowledgments

This book owes everything to my beautiful, brilliant, accomplished, resourceful, sagacious wife, Alfonsina (Alfie) Rechichi, whose love, counsel, and support for the past seven years have sustained me at every turn. The joy your way of being in the world makes possible in our life together inspires me every day. Your passion, loyalty, and friendship, your resilience and commitment, challenge me to be better than I could ever be without you. For all that, and more than I can say, I am eternally grateful.

To my mother, Josephine (Jodie) Beck Monroe, whose long life, good health, and example in all things continue to be such a blessing, and father, the Rev. Paul Eugene Monroe, Jr., deeply missed and gone these many years, thanks too for the strong foundation you have both given us, for all your love, support, and wisdom, your moral courage, intelligence, and integrity, your kindness and understanding, care and goodwill.

To Gabriel and Holly, my wonderful children, and their spouses Shelley and Marshall, to my precious grandson Dylan, this one's for you too, as always, with all my heart. I love you all and am so proud of who you are and all you do. To my sisters Lynn, Marcia, and Paula, their husbands Art, Luther, and Mac, to all the family's nephews and nieces, children, grandchildren, and great-children, my thanks go beyond words.

To Rosa and in memoriam Giovanni (Gianni) Rechichi, to Alfie's sons Mark and John Sabbas, to George and Grazia Svokos and their daughters Erin and husband Aaron, Elizabeth, and Alexandra, to Joseph and Suzanne Rechichi, sons John Joseph and Justin, thank you for welcoming me with such warmth and generosity into your awesome family as one of your own.

To all the incredibly bright, inspiring students in my seminars on "Poetry's Image," "Poetry and Poetics of the Americas," "Contemporary Poetry and Poetics," and "Postcolonial Poetry and the Poetics of Relation," thank you for your engagement and commitment to learning, for all I have learned from all of you on our shared voyage to the Unknown University.

Heartfelt thanks in particular, among my colleagues, to Edmundo Paz-Soldán, whose shared passion for Bolaño's work, encouragement, friendship, and support throughout the writing of this book are much appreciated, and to Edmundo and his co-editor, Gustavo Faverón Patriau, for publishing in the second edition of their edited volume *Bolaño salvaje*, in Spanish and under a different title, an earlier version of parts of what has since become this book's third chapter.

Special thanks, finally, to my editor, Ray Ryan, for his belief in the project and continuing professionalism and support, to Héctor Hoyos and Ignacio López-Calvo, for their extraordinarily generous, insightful, thorough contributions in reading the manuscript, to Edgar Mendez, for his always responsive, congenial role in moving the manuscript into production, and to Cambridge University Press for the privilege of bringing the book into being.

Abbreviations

WORKS CITED

ROBERTO BOLAÑO

Principal Works and Editions

English		Spanish	
AN	*Antwerp*	**A**	*Amberes*
AM	*Amulet*	**AMs**	*Amuleto*
BNC	*By Night in Chile*	**NC**	*Nocturno de Chile*
DS	*Distant Star*	**ED**	*Estrella distante*
MP	*Monsieur Pain*	**MPs**	*Monsieur Pain*
NLA	*Nazi Literature in the Americas*	**LNA**	*La literatura nazi en América*
SD	*The Savage Detectives*	**LDS**	*Los detectives salvajes*
TR	*The Third Reich*	**TRs**	*El Tercer Reich*
2666	*2666*	**2666s**	*2666*
UU	*The Unknown University / La Universidad Desconocida* (bilingual edition)		
WTP	*Woes of the True Policeman*	**SVP**	*Los sinsabores del verdadero policía*

Unpacking Bolaño's Library

Over the course of the two prodigiously productive final decades of his life and career, and with a growing sense of urgency, Roberto Bolaño developed an acute, sustained awareness that writers in all genres compete in the literary marketplace for the reader's increasingly distracted attention. That competition, which Benjamin saw Baudelaire was among the first to understand, takes place not so much within an anodyne "World Republic"—that utopian ideal—but rather, among "combative literatures" continually under siege, the lived reality of which may be aptly described as what Franco Moretti has called the "slaughterhouse," what Bolaño himself once called the "vast minefield" ("vasto campo minado") of literature.[1]

"A library is a metaphor," Bolaño remarks in "Literature Is Not Made from Words Alone" ("La literatura no se hace sólo de palabras"), "for human beings or what's best about human beings, the same way a concentration camp can be a metaphor for what is worst about them. A library is total generosity" ("Una biblioteca es como una metáfora del ser humano o de lo mejor del ser humano tal como un campo de concentración puede ser una metáfora de lo peor. La biblioteca es la generosidad total").[2] Within the frame of that shared understanding, this book traces the evolution of Bolaño's work and his emergence as a synecdochic, exemplary, generational figure bringing together into varied, mobile, complex constellations four pervasive and enduring, inextricably interrelated, overriding concerns: poetry, fiction, literary history, and politics. My central argument is that at the heart of Bolaño's poet- and poetry-centered novels, with all their formal, conceptual scope and range, is the history and legacy of the prose poem, that oxymoronic, antigeneric, utopian, genreless genre, as I have described it elsewhere, which played such a consistently integral, informing role in Bolaño's achievement.[3] Manifestly indebted in its form and structure especially to the prose poems of Baudelaire's *Le Spleen de Paris* (1869) and Rimbaud's *Une*

Saison en Enfer (1873) and *Illuminations* (1873–1875), Bolaño's first "novel," *Amberes* (2002, written 1980; *Antwerp*, 2010), which has been called the "Big Bang" of his work, remained of such importance to Bolaño throughout his career that he referred to it in his last interview, with Mónica Maristain shortly before his death in July, 2003—a year before the posthumous publication of his magnum opus, *2666*—as "La única novela de la que no me avergüenzo . . . tal vez porque sigue siendo ininteligible" ("The only novel that doesn't embarrass me . . . maybe because it continues to be unintelligible").[4]

My starting point is a fundamental question for the kinds of investigations Bolaño's work encourages among the growing legions of those he might call his fellow "literary detectives": How did his work evolve from the disjunctive a- and even anti-narrative "novel," *Antwerp*, a sequence of fifty-six numbered, individually titled prose poems only 119 pages long, in scale comparable to the fifty numbered, titled *Petits poèmes en prose* of *Le Spleen de Paris* (fifty-one counting the Preface to Arsène Houssaye)— each an average length of a half-page to several pages—to that most monumental of Bolaño's works, *2666*, a single novel in five parts (or is it five novels in one book?) that, while weighing in at a formidable 1,125 pages in the original (a mere 893 pages in Natasha Wimmer's English translation), concludes with the titled, two-page prose poem "Fürst Pückler" and its emphasis on the value of what it calls "small works" ("opúsculos"), "little books" ("libritos"), that can give "a rather decent idea" ("una idea bastante aproximada") of an entire era?[5] Tracking the development of Bolaño's diverse writing practices throughout his career, the chapters that follow explore the varied ways Bolaño's coming-to-terms with the relation between the prose poem and the novel, in particular, opens onto the politics of genre, literary history, and politics. Saturating his work with authors, texts, dates and venues of publication, numbers of pages of books, literary commentaries, annotated bibliographies, critical histories and receptions real and invented, Bolaño figures his literary and literary-historical materials not as mere decoration, but as integral matter for reflecting on the genres, forms, discourses, disciplines, and media, trajectories, structures, textures, and architectures, of their own construction.

As is clear from the steady stream of edited volumes devoted to Bolaño's work over the past decade, such concerns have proven pivotal for readers, poets, short-story writers, novelists, literary critics, and theorists throughout Europe, the Americas, and beyond. Understanding Bolaño as a writer in the most capacious sense of both Europe and the Americas in particular, my comparative approach emphasizes the extent to which his narratives circulate freely, as in *2666*, among the geopolitical and literary histories of all three continents. Complementing heuristically, prismatically, "Latin Americanist," "hemispheric," and "global" approaches, all of which, given the scope and range of Bolaño's work, have both their value and their limitations, my argument seeks to position his work especially in relation to questions not so much of a narrowly "personal" experience or identity, as of poetry, the novel, literary history, and politics as transnational concerns aligned with Bolaño's decidedly anti-parochial, cosmopolitan approach.[6]

Poetry, fiction, literary history, politics. These four pervasive, interlocking concerns are the cornerstones, I argue, on which the foundation of Bolaño's work and ever-broadening appeal is built. As his now increasingly "global"—or in Gayatri Spivak's specific use of the term, "planetary"[7]—reception attests, he has become in this sense a synecdochic figure, drawing both his admirers and detractors, as all synecdochic figures do, for writers of the final two decades of the twentieth century and the first few years of the twenty-first, not only in Chile, Mexico, and Spain, the three principal locations of his life and work, or in Latin America and the Spanish-speaking world more generally, but for what he himself called "all of Western literature" ("En fin, me interesa y creo que conozco un poco de toda la literatura occidental").[8]

Despite Bolaño's roots in Latin America, from his birth and residence in Chile to the age of fifteen through his nine years thereafter in Mexico, including his brief return to Chile in the year of the coup, his turn to the novel in the 1980s, following his move to Europe and eventually to Spain, demonstrates a perhaps initially surprising turn away from Latin American settings. While Latin America figures centrally during that period in Bolaño's poetry, the sense Bolaño conveys of himself at the time as a novelist is at least as European as Latin American.[9] Focused more consistently and pervasively on poetry, and on modern and contemporary poetry in particular, than on the novel, Bolaño found in the history and legacy of the prose poem a fulcrum for the construction of what he calls in a synecdochic passage of *Los detectives salvajes* (*The Savage Detectives*) "poemas-novela," what we may call his prose poem novels.[10] Situated within a lineage extending from Poe's detective stories through the prose poems of Baudelaire and Rimbaud and the prose poems and short fiction of Borges, Bolaño develops a prose-poetic literary-historical investigation of relations between poetry and fiction, and between poetry and the novel in particular, as well as between the literary and the non-literary, the aesthetic and the political.[11]

"The only exact knowledge there is," Benjamin writes in "Unpacking My Library" ("Ich packe meine Bibliothek aus"), quoting Anatole France, "'is the knowledge of the date of publication and the format of books.' ... Of all the ways of acquiring books, writing them oneself is regarded as the most praiseworthy method."[12] Tracing the development and arc of Bolaño's astonishingly prolific, varied work reveals four principal stages: 1) an extended early period from 1980 through 1989; 2) a transitional period between 1989 and 1993 culminating in the decision to assemble the collected verse and prose poems that would become *La Universidad Desconocida* (*The Unknown University*); 3) an intensely productive middle or late-middle period, from 1993 through 1998; and 4) a late, end-of-life period, from 1998 to 2003, with its explosive, final burst. Across all four periods, Bolaño explored literature's multi-layered histories in poetry and fiction on every scale, from the minimal to the maximal. Echoing the displaced, exiled stance of the opening prose poem of *Le Spleen de Paris*, "L'Étranger" ("The Stranger")—" – Ta patrie? /—J'ignore sous quelle latitude elle est située" ("'Your country?' / 'I am ignorant of where it is located'")—to which, along with Rimbaud's more disjunctive prose-poetic style, the structure and method of *Antwerp* are most deeply indebted, Bolaño speaks of himself in his 2002 preface as a writer without a country ("me sentía a una distancia equidistante de todos los países del mundo").[13] A reader and writer, we could also say, without a definitive, pre-defined genre, Bolaño was determined from the beginning to explore what with Baudelaire he would call the "voyage" of reading and writing (from the verse and prose poems "Le Voyage" and "L'Invitation au voyage" respectively), wherever that voyage might lead.[14]

Poetry

A certain view of poetry is at the heart of Bolaño's work—in his prose fiction, and in his novels most strikingly, no less than in his verse.[15] But what is that view, exactly? How consistent is it? How static or dynamic? In what respects does it remain constant over time? In what ways does it change throughout Bolaño's life as a writer of both poetry and fiction? At the core of Bolaño's view of poetry, I will argue, is the history and legacy of the prose poem, the prose poems of *Le Spleen de Paris* in particular, as well as, to a lesser extent stylistically (especially after *Antwerp*, Bolaño's most

Rimbaldian performance), those of Rimbaud (inspiration for his most prominent alter-ego, Arturo Belano), together the two synecdochic examples that shaped more than any other Bolaño's cultivation and development of the prose poem novel.[16]

Bolaño's early and enduring interpellation into what was called poetry in the specifically Chilean, later Mexican contexts of the 1950s, 1960s, and 1970s, and as more an aspiring young apprentice poet than writer of fiction, is perhaps most vividly on display in his innovative essay, "Carnet de baile" ("Dance Card"), the penultimate essay of *Putas Asesinas* (2001) and concluding essay, in Chris Andrews' translation, of *Last Evenings on Earth* (2006).[17] Composed of sixty-nine continuously numbered sections ranging from one to a dozen lines of prose each, "Dance Card" encapsulates Bolaño's struggle to free himself from the hegemony of the poetry of Pablo Neruda, more specifically the Neruda of the *Veinte poemas de amor y una canción desesperada* (*Twenty Love Poems and a Song of Depair*). Contrasting Neruda, whom he describes as in the end a "dignified courtier poet," with Rubén Darío, Walt Whitman, José Martí, Violeta Parra, Beltrán Morales, Rodrigo Lira, Mario Santiago, Reinaldo Arenas, and "poets who died under torture, who died of AIDS, or overdosed, all those who believed in Latin American paradise and died in a Latin American hell," Bolaño poses a series of questions with Neruda at their center that suggest the difficulty not only poets but all writers face in responding to specific historical, literary-historical situations: "Why didn't Neruda like Kafka? Why didn't Neruda like Rilke? Why didn't Neruda like De Rokha? 60 . . .. Do we have to come back to Neruda as we do to the Cross, on bleeding knees, with punctured lungs and eyes full of tears?"[18] Finding himself "unquestionably, Parrian" in his self-described "isolation" among the "Mexican poets he was hanging out with and swapping books . . . the Nerudians and the Vallejians," Bolaño returns to Chile in 1973 "to help build socialism," meeting along the way "with revolutionaries of various stripes," purchasing on his arrival two of Nicanor Parra's books, *Obra Gruesa* (*Construction Work*) and *Artefactos* (*Artifacts*), attending a conference of "awful" Chilean poets and being briefly arrested and released, a month after Neruda's death, before leaving Chile in January 1974, never to return, for Mexico City.

Appearing three decades later, in 2003, the year of Bolaño's death, as the penultimate text of *El gaucho insufrible* (*The Insufferable Gaucho*, 2010), the prose-poetic essay "Literature + Illness = Illness" provides a kind of literary-historical will and testament, a final rendering of accounts of Bolaño's influences and investments in both poetry and fiction.[19] In the essay's pivotal sixth section, "Illness and French Poetry," Bolaño focuses especially on the enduring legacy of nineteenth-century French poetry, which he argues has remained not only still vital but indispensable. Describing the French as "well aware" that "the finest poetry of the nineteenth century was written in France," Bolaño understands Baudelaire as the "point of departure" for that "great poetry" that "prefigured the major and still unresolved problems that Europe and Western culture were to face in the twentieth century": "Let's say that it begins with Baudelaire, reaches its highest volatility with Lautréamont and Rimbaud and comes to an end with Mallarmé ... really, with Baudelaire, Lautréamont, Rimbaud, and Mallarmé, there's plenty to be going on with."[20] Opening onto the global, planetary frames of the opening lines of "Le Voyage"—"The child enthralled by lithographs and maps / can satisfy his hunger for the world"—and including the line that gives *2666* its opening epigraph, Bolaño concludes: "Between the vast deserts of boredom and the not-so-scarce oases of horror, there is, however, a third option, or perhaps a delusion, which Baudelaire indicates in the following lines: 'Once we have burned our brains out, we can plunge / to Hell or Heaven—any abyss will do— / deep in the Unknown to find the *new*!' ('Au fond de l'Inconnu pour trouver du *nouveau*!').[21]

At the conclusion of its search for a cure to the illness that "afflicts not only our actions, but also language itself," Bolaño arcs back toward prose fiction by way of the transformative poetic practices of Baudelaire, Rimbaud, Lautréamont, and Mallarmé (the Mallarmé not so much of "Brise Marine" but of *Igitur* and its "Crise de vers") toward the prose-poetic, fictive, novelistic practices of Kafka in particular. In so concluding, Bolaño reaffirms a continuation of the voyage into the Unknown, and the search for an "antidote" to the splenetic "illness" of literature, through an oxymoronic, paradoxical reimagining of literature's scope and scale. While his pivotal commentary on the enduring value of nineteenth-century French poetry focuses on two interconnected verse poems by Baudelaire and Mallarmé, what is perhaps most striking and important about the commentary is its prose-poetic form. Like Benjamin, for whom Baudelaire is no less central, Bolaño limits his explicit commentary on Baudelaire's poetry, as does Benjamin's "On Some Motifs of Baudelaire" apart from its two final pages on "Perte d'auréole ("Loss of a Halo"), to the verse poetry of *Les Fleurs du Mal* (1857). Yet as with Benjamin, whose "One-Way Street," "Central Park," and "On the Concept of History" bear family resemblances as well to the prose poems of *Le Spleen de Paris*, Baudelaire's most profound influence on Bolaño manifests itself not in explicit commentary, but in the variety of prose-poetic, elliptically discursive forms that compose his innovative, heterogeneous writerly practice, a practice encompassing not only short fiction and poetry in verse and prose, but literary-critical, philosophical essays and "poem-novels" in prose. Benjamin's astute observation on Baudelaire's indirect absorption of Poe's detective stories describes perfectly his own reception, and absorption into his own varied writing practice, of the prose poems of *Le Spleen de Paris.*[22]

Fiction

"A library is total generosity" ("La biblioteca es la generosidad total").[23] Among the acts of generosity most prized in Bolaño's library were those of the author both Baudelaire and Julio Cortázar translated, whose encompassing strangeness and innovative legacy proved as pivotal to each, as also to Borges, as to Bolaño's own. Affirming the transnational, broadly comparatist character of his interests in literature of Europe and the Americas, and the early and enduring influence of Poe in particular, Bolaño remarks in his 2002 interview with Carmen Boullosa, "Reading is Always More Important than Writing": "I'm not one of those nationalist monsters who only reads what his native country produces. I'm interested in French literature . . . in American literature of the 1880s . . . As a teenager, I went through a phase when I only read Poe."[24] "The honest truth," Bolaño wrote in "Prólogo: Consejos sobre el arte de escribir cuentos" ("Prologue: Tips on the Art of Writing Short Stories"), his prose-poem-length preface (one-and-a half pages) to the collected short stories of *Cuentos,* "is that with Edgar Allan Poe we would all have more than enough good material to read" ("La verdad de la verdad es que con Edgar Allan Poe todos tendríamos de sobra").[25]

Acidly suggesting, by contrast, in the opening epigraph from Kafka for *The Insufferable Gaucho*—"So perhaps we shall not miss so very much after all"—that contemporary fiction may not live up to its hype, Bolaño turns in the collection's final essay, "Los mitos de Cthulhu" ("The Myths of Cthulhu"), from his affirmation of the transformative legacies of the poetry of Baudelaire, Rimbaud, Lautréamont, and Mallarmé at the center of "Literature + Illness = Illness"—as antidote for what ails contemporary literature in both poetry and fiction—to a frontal attack on the state of contemporary fiction in Latin America and in Argentina in particular.[26] Mapping the figures and scenes, affinities and antipathies, alignments and choices of contemporary fiction in Argentina with the kind of

explicit, sustained attention and taxonomic impulses that Bolaño had
previously reserved with few exceptions for modern and contemporary
poetry, "The Myths of Cthulhu" takes on the claim of "a critic by the
name of Conte" that "Pérez Reverte is Spain's perfect novelist .... the
most perfect novelist in contemporary Spanish literature," his "principal
quality" being, according to either Conte or "the novelist Juan Marsé,"
his "readability," a quality that makes him, in Bolaño's words, "not only
the most perfect novelist but also the most read. That is: the one who sells
the most books." Contemporary literature, he writes, "especially in Latin
America," and he suspects "in Spain as well," is defined only by "social
success: massive print runs; translations into more than thirty
languages ... dinners with the rich and famous ... and landing six-
figure advances."[27]

Taking his critique of Argentine literature to the heart of the canon in
a second essay from the same collection, "Derivas de la pesada" ("Vagaries
of the Literature of Doom"), Bolaño describes José Hernández's classic
2,316-line epic verse poem *Martín Fierro* (1872, 1879), in a formulation rich
with implication for his eventual abandonment of poetry as verse and
embrace of the prose poem novel, as "As a poem ... nothing out of this
world" yet "As a novel ... alive, full of meanings to explore."[28] Challenging
the work's centrality in Argentine literature, he writes that "If *Martín
Fierro* dominates Argentine literature and its place is in the center of the
canon, the work of Borges, probably the greatest writer born in Latin
America, is only a footnote." Finding it "odd" that Borges himself "wrote
so much and so well about *Martín Fierro*," Bolaño notes that "With Borges
alive, Argentine literature becomes what most readers think of as Argentine
literature," including such distinguished figures as Macedonio Fernández,
Bioy Casares, "who writes Latin America's first and best fantastic novel,"
and "Cortázar, best of them all." By contrast, "When Borges dies, everything suddenly comes to an end. It's as if Merlin had died ..."
Characterizing literature as "an armor-plated machine" that "doesn't care
about writers," Bolaño argues that "Literature's enemy is something else,
something much bigger and more powerful, that in the end will conquer
it."[29]

Recalling in "Encuentro con Enrique Lihn," the final essay of *Putas
Asesinas* (2001; "Meeting with Enrique Lihn," *The Return*, 2010), his 1999
dream of being taken to Lihn's apartment "in a country that could well
have been Chile, in a city that could well have been Santiago, bearing in
mind that Chile and Santiago once resembled Hell," Bolaño represents
Lihn, "a writer" he "had always admired," as a counter-figure to Neruda,

whose generous mentoring helped Bolaño begin to establish himself as a writer around 1981 or 1982, when he was twenty-eight years old, "living like a recluse in a house outside Gerona with practically no money and no prospects of ever getting any." Experiencing literature at that time as "a vast minefield occupied by enemies, except for a few classic authors" ("un vasto campo minado en donde todos eran mis enemigos, salvo algunos clásicos (y no todos)"), Bolaño initiated a correspondence with Lihn in which he described Chilean literature as "with one or two exceptions . . . shit." Projected by Lihn to become, in a letter he wrote to Bolaño in 1981–1982, one of the "six tigers of Chilean poetry in the year 2000," Bolaño recounts the fates of the other five (Claudio Bertoni, Diego Maquieira, González Muñoz, Juan Luis Martínez, Rodrigo Lira) that led all but Bolaño himself to become "Not so much tigers as cats . . . kittens of a far-flung province."[30]

For a writer whose work centrally involves the construction of a literary history by other means at the intersection of poetry and fiction, of the prose poem and the novel, especially one whose international reputation has been established much more on the basis not of his poetry (or at least not of his verse), but above all of his novels, it is striking how much less explicit attention he devotes, until late in his career, to writers and works of prose fiction. Described by Bolaño in "Sevilla Kills Me" ("Sevilla me mata"), the penultimate essay of *The Secret of Evil*, as the writer who "is or should be at the center of our canon" ("es o debería ser el centro de nuestro canon"), Borges is clearly a pervasive presence throughout Bolaño's work, not surprisingly the only influence to whom Chris Andrews, in *Roberto Bolaño's Fiction: An Expanding Universe*, and Héctor Hoyos, in *Beyond Bolaño: The Global Latin American Novel*, both devote full chapters. With Poe, Baudelaire, and Rimbaud, Borges is, so to speak, the center around whom Bolaño's orchestrated attack on the state of contemporary Latin American fiction revolves.[31] Addressing the question "Where does the new Latin American novel come from?" with a list of young authors he first assesses as "a promising scene, especially if viewed from the bridge," Bolaño concludes more pessimistically, but also realistically, by underscoring the extent to which all literature, not least the most contemporary, not least the most avant-garde, is in a continual process of becoming historical: "The river is wide and mighty and its surface is broken by the heads of at least twenty-five writers under forty, under thirty: How many will drown? I'd say all of them" ("¿Cuántos se ahogarán? Yo creo que todos").[32]

A Stroll through Literature

"The fact is," Bolaño said in his 2003 interview with Daniel Swinburn, "when I imagine a story or a novel or a play, whatever it might be, perhaps somewhat less with a poem, the first obstacle to overcome, the first problem to resolve is that of the structure, that is to say, the frame."[33] In approaching questions concerning poetry, fiction, literary history, and politics, questions of structure and form are for Bolaño a pivotal concern. As he writes in "Balas Pasadas" ("Spent Bullets"): "Every text, every argument requires its form. There are arguments or situations that ask for a translucent, clear, limpid, simple form, and others that can only be contained in forms and structures that are convoluted, fragmentary, resembling a fever or delirium or sickness. / Structure is never a superfluous resource."[34] The transformative legacy of mid- to late-nineteenth French poetry, and of the prose poem in particular, offers Bolaño a method, from *Antwerp* forward throughout his career, with which, if not to escape, then at least to get some distance from what Raymond Williams might call the familiar residual-dominant impasses of literature of the late twentieth century, in both poetry and fiction, if not globally, then at least throughout Europe and the Americas. It is in this enlarged, figurative literary-historical frame, reflecting the literal change of his writerly location from a Latin American to a European context, from Chile and Mexico to Spain, that we must understand the dreamscape exchange between Bolaño and Parra at the pivotal mid-point of Bolaño's prose-poetic, literary-historical autobiography, "A Stroll through Literature"—"Where are you going, Bolaño? he said. Far from the Southern Hemisphere, I answered" ("¿Adónde vas, Bolaño? decía. Lejos del Hemisferio Sur, le contestaba").[35]

In counterpoint to the three-part organization of Bolaño's monumental collection of his own poetry in verse and prose in *The Unknown University* (first assembled in 1993, published posthumously in full in 2004), which moves predominantly from verse (Part One) to prose (Part Two) and back to verse (Part Three), the structure of Bolaño's much more condensed poetry triptych, *Tres* (first assembled in 1994) moves in the opposite direction, from prose to verse and back to prose. Described by Bolaño as, along with *Antwerp*, one of his "two best books," *Tres* concludes—following the thirty-five page unnumbered prose poem sequence "Prosa del otoño en Gerona" ("Prose from Autumn in Gerona") and the 18-page verse poem "Los neochilenos" ("The Neochileans")—with "Un paseo por la literatura" ("A Stroll through Literature"), a modular, prose-poetic sequence of fifty-seven extraordinarily brief, numbered texts, generally a short paragraph averaging only three to six lines of prose, each of which features one of several dozen authors.[36] Taken together, the sequence's twenty-nine pages offer a radically elliptical literary-historical autobiography opening onto Bolaño's most cherished literary aspirations and apprenticeships—all but two of the fifty-seven texts begin, anaphorically, "Soñé que ..." ("I dreamed that ...")—a distillation of writers to whom he understood himself to be indebted, representing a range of genres and languages across Europe and the Americas.

Framed not by a poet, but by a novelist, and by a writer not from Spain or Latin America, but from France, "A Stroll through Literature" begins and ends with affectionate invocations of the French Oulipian Georges Perec. Given the tendency of Bolaño's literary-historical self-framing to draw more on poets than on novelists, these homages are significant. Signaling a special connection with a novelist whose procedures bear strong affinities to his own, the fifty-seven radically minimalist prose poems of "A Stroll through Literature" might be read in this sense as so many mini- or micro-novels recalling the explicit genre designation of Perec's *Life a User's Manual*, a book the author characterizes not as a (singular) "novel," but as "novels."[37] In the second numbered section of its prose-poetic, literary-historical autobiography, immediately following its initial homage to Perec, "A Stroll through Literature" situates Bolaño in terms that underscore Borges' continuing centrality: "We're underdone, father, ... like Latin American detectives lost in a labyrinth ...."[38] Halfway through its imaginary dreamscape—following references to, among others, "Enrique Lihn" and "a check from the Unknown University"[39] and "Aloysius Bertrand"[40]—the text includes two pivotal sections, the first ("26.") figuring a farewell visit at fifteen to Nicanor Parra's house, Parra's parting question, "¿Adónde vas, Bolaño?" ("Where are you going, Bolaño?"), and Bolaño's reply, "Lejos del Hemisferio Sur" ("Far from the Southern Hemisphere"), the second affirming his departure from the Southern Hemisphere ("en efecto, me marchaba del Hemisferio Sur") with now Vallejo's *Trilce* as "the only book" in his "backpack," its "pages" going up "in flames" at "seven p.m.," at which point he "chucked" the "scorched backpack out the window" (" ... en mi mochila el único libro ... (*Trilce*, de Vallejo) ... se quemaba. Eran las siete de la tarde y yo arrojaba mi mochila chamuscada por la ventana").[41] Suggesting the importance to Bolaño's prose-poetics of the challenging, oblique, opaque modernist Vallejo and of Bolaño's much-admired older contemporary, the playfully serious, seriously playful "anti-poet" Parra, sections 26 and 27 figure as well in their prose-poetic form

Bolaño's indebtedness to the "dream of a poetic prose" and the prose poems of *Le Spleen de Paris*. Inverting the structure of *Trilce*, the seventy-seven poems of which are all in verse apart from one near the end, the third from the last, which is almost in prose (almost but not quite right-margin justified), "A Stroll through Literature" includes among its numbered, untitled, single-paragraph poems only one near the beginning, the sixth, that is not in prose but in verse. Constructing a dream "labyrinth" of literary "Latin American detectives" as indebted to Poe and Baudelaire as to Borges, who like Bolaño cites more than he reads, it attests to Bolaño's indebtedness as well to *Trilce* and Parra's *Obra Gruesa* and *Artefactos* and their shared interest and investment in modular, combinatory poetic sequences, whether in verse or prose. Its single-paragraph numbered sections referencing in nearly all cases a single author, many consisting of only a single sentence of one to several lines, "A Stroll through Literature" offers a condensed, modular sequence of prose-poetic texts that further condense the prose poem form Baudelaire had himself conceived, at its inception as a condensation of the Poe short story, as by definition "*petit.*"[42]

Figuring the sheer "spontaneous combustibility" of a prose-poetic sequence that bursts in flames, Bolaño's jettisoning of a backpack that contains only *Trilce*, written almost entirely in verse, suggests as well, especially in the context of Bolaño's reply to Parra's question, Bolaño's trajectory from Mexico to Spain, which would come to enlarge his literary world "Far beyond the Southern Hemisphere" and Latin American and Spanish letters generally, beyond even Vallejo, Borges, and Parra, as vital as all three remained to him, to the more encompassingly European-American perspective that would define his work thereafter. Moving in the second half of "A Stroll through Literature," accordingly, through a series of wide-ranging references including Kafka, Mark Twain, Alice Sheldon, Anaïs Nin, Carson McCullers, Alphonse Daudet, Robert Desnos, Roque Dalton, Walt Whitman, Boethius, the Marquis de Sade, Pascal, Baudelaire, Marcel Schob, James Matthew Barrie, and Vallejo, concluding with his final invocation of Perec, the text continues to attest to the end to Bolaño's broadly transnational, comparatist range.

As central as a mapping of the history of modern and contemporary poetry is to Bolaño's fiction, and to his novels in particular, what is perhaps even more striking and surprising is the extent to which his explicit, sustained engagement with poetry as a novelist does not translate, really until the very end of his career, in Part V of *2666*, "The Part about

Archimboldi," into a similar level of fictional engagement with the history of the modern novel. When he does finally elaborate such an engagement, it is equally striking that it is not the modern novel in Spanish, whether in Spain or Latin America, that receives sustained explicit attention, but traditions of the novel in Germany and Russia. Writing within frames far removed from, yet in important respects analogous to the changing situation Baudelaire understood poetry faced in the mid-nineteenth century with the rise of the novel and the new mass medium of its day, the commercial newspaper, Bolaño saw with great clarity, in the last two decades of the twentieth century and the first few years of the twenty-first, that markets for poetry and fiction faced new threats, if also new opportunities.[43] Reversing the early modernist movement of poetry initiated by the prose poems of Poe, Baudelaire, and Rimbaud and codified by Pound's equation, "Dichten = condensare," Bolaño's "poem-novels" in prose move poetry back from the poem as monological, self-expressive lyric to the heteroglossic prose poem novel, the range of which extends from the condensed, disjunctive, elliptical, more-language-than-voice-based prose-poetic procedure of *Antwerp* to the fifty-plus narrators and seemingly endlessly multiplying prose-poetic journal and testimonial entries of *The Savage Detectives* and beyond. As revolutionary and challenging to the system of genres at the end of the twentieth century as Baudelaire's and Rimbaud's prose poems had been at the onset of modernism, Bolaño's prose poem novels free poetry from the shrunken ambitions and constraints that Bolaño slowly but in the end decisively recognized, largely through the manifest limitations of his own verse poems, had shackled poetry as self-expressive lyric.

The Prose Poem Novel as an Overturning of Scale

The prose poem's centrality to Bolaño's imaginary manifests itself throughout his career in a variety of ways: in his prose-poetic emplotments of brevity and intensity, not least in his most monumental works; his pervasive focus on poets, prose poets, prose poem novelists as characters and narrators; his lifelong investigations of the dialectics and dialogics of poetry and prose, their heteroglossic, cross-genre tropes and interdiscursive, intermedial turns. Central to my concerns in what follows are both the historical specificity of Bolaño's indebtedness to the modern prose poem's legacy and his sustained, self-conscious development of that legacy in his prose poem novels. I leave the term unhyphenated, like Baudelaire's "petits poèmes en prose," to emphasize the deliberate, oxymoronic non-adherence and resistance Bolaño's entire oeuvre offers, like *Le Spleen de Paris*, like *Une Saison en Enfer* and *Illuminations*, to processes of genrefication generally, the gentrification of genres leading to their discursive reification—what today some would call, without historical irony, their "branding"—what Jacques Rancière might call the policing of aesthetic regimes generally and in particular of poetry and the novel. The prose poem novel is in this sense for Bolaño not one hyphenated sub-genre among others, whether of "poetry" or "the novel," content to occupy its own circumscribed, self-limiting marketing niche, but its own in fundamental respects uncontain-able, diverse, potentially infinite project.[44]

In a pivotal moment near the end of *Amulet*, Bolaño affirms, through the "prophecies" of the self-described "mother of Mexican poetry," Auxilio Lacouture, a certain "non-power" of poetry not only not to "disappear," but to "make itself visible in another form" ("La poesía no desaparecerá. Su no-poder se hará visible de otra manera").[45] Envisioned while reading poetry in the women's bathroom of the Facultad de Filosofía y Letras at the Universidad Nacional Autónoma de México (UNAM), where she is hiding from soldiers occupying the University campus during the 1968 Tlatelolco massacre, Lacouture's prophecies figure Bolaño's investment in writing at the intersection of poetry, fiction, literary history, and politics. Inverting Baudelaire's understanding of the prose poem as by definition *petit*, a formula as indebted to Poe's association of poetry with brevity and intensity as Pound's equation of it with condensation, Bolaño's prose poem novels figure an overturning of economies of scale for poems and novels alike, a method at once formal and conceptual for constructing a prose-poetic literary history by other means. Against the dominant tendency to identify poetry almost exclusively with "lyric powers," Bolaño understood the prose poem's hitherto untapped oxymoronic, antigeneric, utopian potential to open poetry back out onto forms more promisingly capacious than what Charles Altieri has aptly called the self-expressive, first-person "scenic mode." Bolaño's prose poem novels elabo-rate an inclusive prose-poetic practice that challenges the policing of boundaries between verse and prose, as between poetry and fiction—Bolaño does not speak, through Auxilio Lacouture, of the non-power of lyric, but of poetry in its fullest sense.[46]

Responding in his 1983 novel, *Consejos de un discípulo de Morrison a un fanático de Joyce*, co-written with A.G. Porta, to Anthony Burgess' claim that *Ulysses* "lacks unity," Bolaño does not so much contest the claim as such as reframe it in terms of deliberate changes of narrative strategy from chapter to chapter. In wondering if the "exposition of different situations and characters" during the hours covered by the novel "doesn't justify that lack of unity and to a certain extent justify it," *Consejos* both affirms and instantiates the proto-Joycean, proto-Oulipian embrace of a variation of styles, in the manner of Raymond Queneau's *Exercises de Style* (1947, *Exercises in Style*), that informs Bolaño's writerly practice, along with its collaborative spirit, from the beginning.[47] A logical next step in Bolaño's development of the form of the prose poem novel for which *Antwerp* was already an emerging prototype, *Consejos* is divided, like *Antwerp*, into discretely titled, numbered sections of prose poem length, in this case with roman numerals. Expanding the scale of each its twenty-four sections from the average single-page length of the fifty-six numbered, titled texts of *Antwerp* to an average at the intersection of prose poem and short-story length between five and six pages, *Consejos* continues the dialectic in evidence as well in *Antwerp* between the prose poem's characteristic disjunctiveness, discontinuity, and modularity and the more traditional novel's expectations of narrative coherence, continuity, and development, now more markedly in the direction of the latter. No doubt owing to his collaboration with a writer whose ambitions more clearly lay at that point in both of their careers in the direction of the novel, Bolaño's own orientation still very much bound up with the desire to become a poet, the prose-poetic, literary-historical detective work of *Consejos* is oriented more in the direction of fiction and the novel than poetry (as verse).

Poe, Baudelaire, Rimbaud, Borges, Joyce. Among Bolaño's most enduring influences and indispensable precursors and influences, worthy competitors all for Bolaño's unspecified "Gang of Five," a starting line-up which, through Bolaño's own example, might convert even Jordi Carerera, the teenage basketball-playing son of a literature professor, from his hatred of literature, might even persuade him to admire poetry's, and the prose poem novel's, dazzling moves and intricate rhythms. Shaping the terms of his own reception as programmatically as any author could, Bolaño resumes and complicates Poe's, and Baudelaire's, and Rimbaud's resistance to the for a time seemingly inevitable, even tyrannical long march of the nineteenth-century realist novel, their combined attempt to nip in the bud the poetics and aesthetics of the novel's implacable *longue durée*. Aligning himself from the outset with the imperatives launched by his precursors to free poetry from its limiting equation with, and reduction to, verse, Bolaño encourages his readers, like Baudelaire, to come and go, to "cut wherever we please" ("Nous pouvons couper où nous voulons"), cultivating in his prose poem novels, even at their greatest length, a complex resistance to what Baudelaire called in his preface to

Le Spleen de Paris "le fil interminable d'une intrigue superflue" ("the interminable thread of a superfluous plot").[48]

At the heart of Bolaño's oeuvre, and thus of this study, lie questions at once literary-historical and political: Could what is called poetry not merely survive its fictive amplifications, incorporations, transformations, and reinventions in "poem-novels" in prose, but thrive in the diverse forms of his prose poem novels, his prose-poetic, fictive literary histories and politics by other means? Would poetry, as prose, Baudelaire's "miracle d'une prose poétique" ("miracle of a poetic prose"), burst poetry at its seams, at the ends of its lines, at the end of that enjambment Giorgio Agamben calls in *The End of the Poem* poetry's *sine qua non*—still as verse only, as if before Poe, before Baudelaire and Rimbaud, before Borges, as if separable from such prose-poetic, philosophical, literary-historical, historical, political practices as his own *Idea of Prose* and *The Coming Community* —as in the seemingly endless prose-poetic depictions, in *2666*, of the serial murders of women in "The Part about the Crimes," the catastrophic losses of World War II, including the Holocaust, in "La parte de Archimboldi" ("The Part about Archimboldi")?[49]

What could the fate of poetry be, in and as prose fiction, be in the hands of the implacable lover of poetry, yet famous novelist, Bolaño? While citations from actual verse poems are for the most part conspicuously absent throughout Bolaño's oeuvre, what Poe called the "poetic principle," which Baudelaire understood could apply just as well, even better to prose, is in Bolaño's work everywhere manifest. In this sense, especially, it seems fair to say that there is no harm done to poetry, that Bolaño's poetry-centered novels lead not to poetry's death, the sacrificial demise of the poet Cesárea Tinajero's notwithstanding, near the end of *The Savage Detectives*, but to what has been the goal of the prose poem's "novelization" of poetry, in Mikhail Bakhtin's sense of the term, all along, from Poe and Baudelaire forward, poetry's literal and figurative transformation in and as prose.[50] Not the death of poetry, that quintessence of the literary itself, then, but its continuous placing in relation among competing discourses and media which cannot and will not, now in the twenty-first century, let poetry rest.

Throughout Bolaño's poetry and fiction, from what he called his first "novel," *Antwerp*—a numbered sequence of fifty-six discrete, titled prose poems, more disjunctive and modular than narrative and linear—through the posthumously published *Woes of the True Policeman*, Bolaño's explores more consistently and pervasively than any other concern what we may call the narrative of poetic apprenticeship, what happens to aspiring young poets as they are drawn toward and into the "minefields" of poetry, of fiction, of literature, the embeddedness of their ambitions within literary-historical as well as historical, geopolitical contexts, the ways these contexts shape their choices, and the mutually overdetermined, mutually constraining impact of these contexts on each other, within specific sociohistorical situations and parameters. Only in the last few years of his life, as we shall see—coming to terms with his unexpected, belated fame not as the successful poet (in verse) he had long aspired to be, but as the celebrated novelist he became—in the fifth and final part of *2666*, "The Part about Archimboldi," does a similar reckoning with a novelist's apprenticeship come due.

The reduction of poetry to lyric is a relatively modern trope. As Bakhtin lucidly and forcefully made clear, the tendency to equate poetry with lyric, lyric with verse (with or without rhyme and/or meter), verse with first-person utterance (including "free" verse), and the first-person lyric with self-expression, is best understood as a historicizing description rather than an ahistorical, ontological claim. Against all attempts to dislodge this equation, both theoretical and practical, empirical evidence suggests that such a conflation remains dominant. Throughout his career, Bolaño understood the prose poem as a pivotal literary-historical intervention in the slaughterhouse or minefield of literature, the genreless genre that explicitly calls into question hierarchies of the literary and the non-literary. The prose poem novel, in Bolaño's hands, represents that minefield's implosion, the prose poem's maximal reversal, amplification, and overturning, at once its oxymoronic annihilation and its most capacious, manifold realization. Bolaño understands with Poe, Baudelaire, Rimbaud, and Borges, with respect to questions of genre, that scale is a work's foremost identity. Given that *"size is never just size,"* that as Moretti puts it *"small national markets"* are not *"scaled-down replicas of large ones, but different structures,"* and *"'strong' forms"* do not occupy *"more and more space, while 'weak' ones ... disappear altogether, thus drastically reducing the spectrum of possible choices,"* should the scale of a representation in a monumental novel like *2666* match the scale of a particular horror?[51] Or perhaps, by way of condensed contestation, invert it? If all literature, all art, is as Rancière has argued a matter of regimes of representation, where nothing is truly unrepresentable, is the accumulation of dozens of prose-poetic, proto-journalistic descriptions of the serial murders of women in "The Part about the Crimes" more or less effective than a single such representation?[52] What are the ethics of such accounts amplified to novel-length, extending even quite literally ad nauseum?

While a certain privilege accorded to poetry is an undeniably important feature of Bolaño's novels as much as his verse, I argue in what follows that poetry's hidden, underestimated "non-power" that "will not disappear, but make itself visible in another form" is not just one concern among others, but Bolaño's most sustained and pervasive concern. A dominant concern throughout his career, that non-power makes his work exceptional for understanding how poetry and fiction, poems and novels, tended to be conceived throughout Europe and the Americas at the historical juncture of Bolaño's writing. It is Bolaño's role, in this sense, as a synecdochic, exemplary figure of his generation's (and others') views of poetry and fiction, literary history and history, the aesthetic and the political, that has motivated my sustained inquiry into his work. My primary goal has been to track the dynamic relation his work maintains among the terms poetry and fiction, poem and novel. As crucial as these terms are, it would be a mistake, as Bolaño understands, to approach them statically and ahistorically rather than, as Bolaño does himself, historically and empirically, situationally.

Understanding that there are no guarantees as to any writer's next step, that we cannot know in advance any writer's or reader's literary and non-literary, aesthetic and political development, I approach Bolaño's sustained inquiry into the relation between poetry and fiction at once centripetally, with respect to questions of genre, and centrifugally, where the politics of genre opens onto the political in the broadest sense. My investigation has been motivated largely by the synecdochic ways Bolaño's prose poem novels test the limits of genre(s), of what Bakhtin calls "the system and hierarchy of genres," and more broadly the systems and hierarchies of discourses and disciplines on which poetry/fiction, poem/novel, verse/prose, prosaic/poetic, literary/non-literary, literary-historical/historical, aesthetic/political binaries depend. To the extent that poetry pursues self-isolating strategies in relation to other discourses, approaches to writing poetry that effectively constrain and contain it in misguided attempts to protect a certain "poetic," or "lyric," identity, it risks finding itself increasingly marginalized in relation to the novel's more inclusive dialogical, heterglossic capacities. Poetry's greatest hope thus continues to lie, paradoxically, in increasing openness to other discourses, that is, in embracing a certain non-identity.[53] Through the end of his life, Bolaño continued to pursue on a continuum of scales, from *Antwerp* to *2666*, poetry's defiance against its own irrelevance, working against its historically overdetermined constraints and limitations, resisting especially the autobiographical, first-person verse niche poetry had come to occupy. As Bolaño's prose poem novels illustrate at every level and on every scale, only as literature expands to be, as *Woes of the True Policeman* puts it, "open to the poetry of the world" ("abierto a la poesía del mundo"), only as it continues to investigate worlds at once literary and non-literary, prosaic and poetic, historical and philosophical in all their interdiscursive, interdisciplinary, intermedial dimensions, can it encompass the full range of possibilities Bolaño explores on the voyage from the known to the unknown university.[54]

Part One

CHAPTER I

"Undisciplined Writing"

Antwerp (Amberes)

Questions of genre, of the commodification of genres and of genres as commodities, of their specialization and marketability, questions central to the institutionalization of creative writing in the academy over the past several decades, preoccupied Bolaño early on when the idea of making a career out of writing appeared to him beyond reach. As he writes of his situation in 1981 in Barcelona in his preface to the 2002 publication of *Amberes* (*Antwerp*), "Anarquía total: Veintidós años después" ("Total Anarchy: Twenty-Two Years Later"): "I never brought this novel to any publishing house, of course. They would've slammed the door in my face ... The scorn I felt for so-called official literature was great, though only a little greater than my scorn for marginal literature. But I believed in literature: or rather, I didn't believe in arrivisme or opportunism or the whispering of sycophants ..."[1] An eclectic, unpredictable reader at the time, as throughout his life, Bolaño is already struggling, even before the birth of his children, to which he later attributed his drive to succeed monetarily, with the idea of poetry, of prose, of genre, as matters of economy and scale, a fundamentally economic issue in the most literal as well as figurative sense: "I didn't have children yet. I was still reading more poetry than prose ... One night I came up with a scheme to make money outside the law ... I felt equally distant from all the countries in the world. Later I gave up my plan when I discovered that it was worse than working in a brick factory."[2] Signaling his awareness from the outset of the extent to which the formal, figural economy of a text remains inextricably bound up with larger economic concerns and structures, with the articulation of discursive economies both literary and non-literary and the distribution of genres as commodities in the "marketplace of ideas" within the broader economy—an awareness Baudelaire and Rimbaud earlier shared with their resistance to certain economies of narration and description—the beginning of *Antwerp* sets up a sharp contrast between radically different economies, that of its epigraph, from Pascal, which situates the episodic texts to follow in relation to "eternity . . . the infinite immensity of spaces of which I know nothing and which know nothing of me" and the epigraph of the first, numbered, programmatically titled prose poem, "Fachada" ("Façade"), which recasts and reframes Pascal's literary-philosophical reflections in terms of the earth-bound, commercially driven space-time of David O. Selznick's 1939 blockbuster *Gone With the Wind*: "*Hollywood. Tara has no rooms inside. It was just a façade*" ("Tara no tenía habitaciones en su interior. Era sólo una fachada").[3]

Written in 1980 but only published in 2002 (its English translation not appearing until 2010), two years after the publication of *Nocturno de Chile* (2000, *By Night in Chile*, 2003) and a year before Bolaño's death, what Bolaño calls his first novel, the assemblage of consecutively numbered prose poems enigmatically titled *Amberes/Antwerp* has aptly been called, but without detailed tracking of its ripple effects, its full resonance and implications throughout what Andrews has called with Nora Catelli Bolaño's "fiction-making system," the "Big Bang of the Bolaño universe" (52).[4] While later works have garnered far more recognition, the significance of Bolaño's early experiments in the direction of the novel merits more than honorific attention. Composed of fifty-six short pieces in prose weighing in at a mere 119 pages (78 pages in Natasha Wimmer's translation), the book's structure and form resemble, in the length of each individual text as well as of the book as a whole, much less the structure and form expected of a novel than of such foundational prose poem sequences as *Le Spleen de Paris* and *Une Saison en Enfer* and *Illuminations*. Recalling Baudelaire's interest in the emerging genre of *faits divers* that had become, by the time he published his first twenty prose poems in 1862 in the journal *La Presse,* one of the featured forms of the medium of the newspaper then coming into prominence, not least through increases in circulation propelled by the serial publication of novels in newspapers, the concise verbal assemblages of *Antwerp* oscillate between representational and linguistically self-referential strategies, between what might be called vignettes or sketches and meta-fictional, meta-textual, meta-linguistic reflections on the type and genre of the texts themselves and the process of their construction.

Situated stylistically roughly halfway between the lucidly narrative, descriptive, at once referential and self-referential prose poems of *Le Spleen de Paris*, for which the transparent panes of glass of "Le Mauvais Vitrier" ("The Bad Glazier") might serve as synecdoche, and the more radically experimental, narratively and descriptively resistant opacities of Rimbaud's *Illuminations, Antwerp* remains fundamentally closer to the latter than the former.[5] A complex negotiation between the two, *Antwerp* remains the most Rimbaldian of Bolaño's books. While the more lucidly narrative, descriptive, referential and self-referential style of Baudelaire's prose poems would prove more influential and enduring, Bolaño's first "novel" retains in the end his highest estimation among his works precisely to the extent that it represented him at his most poetically, aesthetically uncompromising.

Recalling, in addition to Rimbaud's proto-cubist deconstructions, the demolition of the house of poetry with which Borges concludes *El Aleph* (*The Aleph*), *Antwerp* begins with a sense of late twentieth-century poetry's thoroughly mediated, intermedial, media-saturated environment, inseparable from its potential place on or off the market of literary and aesthetic value: "The mansion is just a façade—dismantled, to be erected in Atlanta. 1959 … 'It was just a façade'" ("La mansión sólo es fachada y la desmantelan para instalarla en Atlanta. 1959 …. «Era sólo una fachada.»").[6] Against the commonly held view that the purpose of a genre, of the novel especially, is to offer what E.M. Forster called "round" characters, *Antwerp* refuses from the outset any such comforting illusion, parodying such intended effects through the title of its second numbered section, "La totalidad del viento" ("The Fullness of the Wind").[7] Riffing on *Gone with the Wind* in a way that strips the film of its narrative pretensions and claims to such shared literary and aesthetic values as "substance" and "meaning," the second numbered text figures the relation between fiction and poetry as an economic issue at its core, a choice between commercial viability and textual, discursive freedom: "… and in the news Sophie Podolski is kaput in Belgium, the girl from the Montfaucon Research Center … 'So is Colan Yar after you too?' … The man sits at one of the cafes in the hypothetical ghetto. He writes postcards because breathing prevents him from writing the poems he'd like to write. I mean: free poems, no extra tax … 'The evening light dismantles our sense of the wind' … "[8]

Gesturing in the direction not so much of multiple plot lines as of multiple vectors, proferring and withdrawing, instantiating and deconstructing both "narrative" ("So is Colan Yar after you too?") and "poetic" ("'The evening light dismantles our sense of the wind' …") protocols and conventions, *Antwerp* demonstrates an awareness throughout that genre expectations are a literal and figural product of certain language games, a Wittgensteinian recognition that plays itself out explicitly in the third numbered text with the abstract-expressionist title "Cuadros verdes, rojos y blancos" ("Greed, Red, and White Checks"), where the word, that is to say the aesthetic materiality, of texts as well as of visual images, comes to the fore: " … the second game in a series. This game is called 'The Great

Triangle Escape' ... What he at first imagined was a screen becomes a white
tie, white words, panes whose transparency is replaced by a blind and
permanent whiteness ... The phrase 'The train stopped in a northern
town' distracts him ... The word 'shoes' will never levitate."[9] Establishing
from the beginning what emerges as one of its most sustained, characteristic
strategies, the text not only interrupts but in fact inscribes its own narrative
gestures, allusively and intertextually, in quotation marks, in ways that
call into question such traditional creative-writing categories as "voice,"
"plot," and "character," with explicit self-referential, meta-lingual attention to language as such, to the text as simultaneously constructing and
deconstructing itself, in a parodic "sequence" that does and does not add
up to (a or multiple) narrative(s), each possibility of which stands
(strands) at perpetual risk of remaining at loose ends in relation to its
narrative others.[10]

Nothing less, but also nothing more, than a game or series of games, the
brief, numbered prose texts of *Antwerp* share with Baudelaire's prose
poems, their closest intertexts along with those of Rimbaud's
Illuminations, a resistance to the novel's indulgence in description for its
own sake. The language-game status of literary genres does not mean that
they should not be taken seriously or trivialized. On the contrary, as
a Wittgensteinian understanding makes clear, such an awareness
encourages recognition of our own literary enchantments, the extent to
which, in the words of the title of the fourth numbered section, its
linguistic self-referentiality combines with a reference to the author himself, "Soy mi propio hechizo" ("I'm My Own Bewitchment"): "... Words
that drift away from one another ... I'm my own bewitchment ... The
language of others is unintelligible to me ... 'My name is Roberto
Bolaño' ..."[11]

As the prose poems of *Le Spleen de Paris* were inspired by the journalistic genre of *faits divers*, a genre resembling in length what we would
today call an op-ed, in both brief prose form and anecdotal content, so
too *Antwerp,* as it begins to settle, in the fifth numbered text, "Azul"
("Blue"), into a form of *reportage* with a more identifiable referential
intent that launches the text more decisively onto its primary trajectory,
a consistently invested yet detached, self-questioning exploration of the
parameters, protocols, and conventions of police procedurals, of detective fiction generally, and of the detective novel in particular:[12] "The
Calabria Commune campground, according to a sensationalistic article
in PEN. Harassed by the townspeople ... Six kids dead in the surrounding area ... 'Not from around here, that's for sure' ... The police

questioning the locals: 'I didn't do it,' says one . . ."[13] Recalling Bakhtin's distinction between the novel's characteristically dialogical, heteroglossic investments and poetry's more monological tendencies, *Antwerp* pursues, in the chronotope of the prose poem's brief, concentrated textual space, a consistently dialogic, heteroglossic self-questioning, a procedure that takes nothing for granted in its own construction and assumes the importance of its readers as, in effect, co-producers, not merely in piecing together a hermeneutic whole from identifiably cogent parts, but in making sense of the parts themselves.[14]

Appearing, reappearing in medias res, to be picked up again in the sixth and seventh texts, "Gente razonable y gente irrazonable" ("Reasonable People vs. Unreasonable People") and "El Nilo" ("The Nile"), characters (figures) resurface briefly, then drop just as suddenly from view, the literariness of the text's investments in question, the ambivalence of those investments, its only constant: "Sophie Podolski killed herself years ago . . . I'm alone, all the literary shit gradually falling by the wayside— poetry journals, limited editions, the whole dreary joke behind me now . . . A Belgian girl who wrote like a star . . ."[15] As the first numbered text's quotation of Selznick established from the outset, the literary itself has become inconceivable apart from its potential filmic adaptation. Thus, we read in "8. Cleaning Utensils" ("Los utensilios de limpieza"): "The two of them wept like characters from different movies projected on the same screen."[16] In keeping with its intermedial, intertextual understanding of how we have come to conceive of the fate of the literary, *Antwerp* figures a reciprocity of page and screen, of one as defined by and defining of the other, such that the two can scarcely be understood apart from each other.

The conjoined issues of narrative coherence and genre remain an open question: "I can't express myself coherently or write what I want . . ." ("9. A Monkey"; "Un mono"); "There are no police stations, no hospitals, nothing . . . The policeman . . . Someone started to clap" ("10. There Was Nothing"; "No había nada").[17] Oscillating between minimalist narrative and meta-lingual, meta-fictional, meta-textual gestures, *Antwerp* continually stages its own installments, its own suspension and recommencing, always with writing as much foreground as background, where the distinction between these in effect dissolves. While the text risks stalling out, leaving the reader in a perpetual state of uncertainty and potential anxiety, the outlines of what gradually comes into view as not merely a collection of prose poems but a "novel," as such, emerge with increasing clarity in the text's focus on "crime stories," on the possibility that the apparently inchoate assemblage of words, sentences, and quoted lines from unattributed sources piling up with each numbered section may yet yield, with the reader's active cooperation, a set of characters or at least figures referred to (with few exceptions—e.g., "Sophie Podolski," "Colan Yar," "Lisa") with generic designations (the "girl," the "writer," the "dwarf" or "hunchback," the "policeman," the "Englishman") involved in a serious plot, the murder of the six kids in the area surrounding the Calabria Commune campground.

In fact, while the text constructs, or the text's readers are at once free and not free to construct, such a "plot," to obey and disobey *"all* the rules" (*"todas* las reglas de construcción"),[18] its linguistically playful, narratologically challenged and challenging modalities are such that readers are likely to experience a certain tension between a "taxing" narrative (one not free not to add up to a story) and the idea it conveys of poetry, by contrast, as a non-commodifiable discourse unconstrained by market forces ("free poems, no extra tax" ["poemas gratuitos, sin ningún valor añadido"]), a discourse not subject to the instrumentalizing subjugation of language to the idea of a narrative, any narrative, any "plot" ("construcción") demands.[19] Torn between these two demands, between a certain pleasure and urgency of a "tax-free" poetic discourse and the in part scalable requirements of the marketplace that might make a work of verbal art saleable, *Antwerp* moves inexorably toward the genre Bolaño figures as most likely to offer the opportunity to pursue something like serious literary fiction without sacrificing the promise of a literal payoff, the genre of the detective novel, a promise for which *Antwerp* prepares the way and that Bolaño would be amply rewarded with the publication of *The Savage Detectives* (in 1998, eighteen years after the writing of *Antwerp*), the novel that would cement his reputation as a writer and bring fame and financial success.[20]

Antwerp reads, in this sense, as much as anything else, as a novel of self-conscious apprenticeship. Its principal narrative, notwithstanding its nominal, minimalist gestures to plot and characters, is that of becoming a writer and the choices and impasses, available and unavailable options for anyone trying to do so. With the novel's pivotal twelfth, numbered section, "Las instrucciones" ("The Instructions"), investment in this apprenticeship becomes increasingly clear: "Debía comenzar las pesquisas en los alrededores de un pueblo turístico ... Saqué del sobre las instrucciones ... Un par de hojas escritas a máquina con algunas correcciones hechas a mano ...'«Nuestras historias son muy tristes, sargento, no intente comprenderlas» ... ("I was supposed to start my investigation on the outskirts of a tourist town ... I took out the instructions ... A couple of typewritten sheets with handwritten corrections ... 'Our stories are sad, sergeant, there's no point trying to understand them' ...")[21] Alluding on one level to instructions for the speaker (earlier referred to in the first person, as we have seen, as "Roberto Bolaño") in his "investigation" of the Calabria Commune campground murders (as reported in "a sensationalistic article in PEN"), which emerged earlier as a prompt or pre-text for the text's halting, prismatic "unfolding," the "couple of typewritten sheets with handwritten corrections" that there's "no point trying to understand" suggest "instructions" for exploring the process of the text's own construction, a process that gives little to its readers that does not involve them in co-assembling "images" that "set off down the road and yet ... never get anywhere," where "Shit dripped from the sentences at breast height" along with "Stories about cops chasing immigrants" ("13. The Bar"; "La barra").[22] From "images" to "sentences" to "stories," the text's investigation is at its core an inquiry into the linguistic "elements" or materials constituting it at every level as it loops back on itself in the process of deciding what genre it wants to become. In naming itself explicitly a story of "cops chasing immigrants," it establishes itself as belonging to the "detective genre," a genre that opens increasingly, in Bolaño's hands, onto the rules governing its own textual economy.

Since genres can only be understood relationally, differentially, within sometimes overlapping, sometimes mutually exclusive systems and hierarchies of genres that are dynamic and in process, no individual text can coincide with itself, in any pure sense, as genre. The detective novel may thus stand, as Bolaño suggests in the nineteenth section, in close proximity to, and interwoven with, the genre "Romance Novel" ("Literatura para enamorados"): "I asked whether he really thought Roberto Bolaño had helped the hunchback just because years ago he was in love with a Mexican girl and the hunchback was Mexican too. Yes, said the guitarist, it sounds like a cheap romance novel ..."[23] Following this explicit positioning of genres in relation and corollary posing of the question of genre identity (with explicit reference again to the author "Roberto Bolaño," who understands, with the Borges of "Borges y yo," that his authorial, textual identity, as distinct from his autobiographical, personal identity, inheres in genre) the text has paved the way to announce a few numbered sections later, in "20. Sinopsis. El viento" ("Synopsis. The Wind"), what amounts to a gathering of the threads it has thus far assembled, not quite a third of the way through the text's 119 pages (Wimmer's 78), a succinct summary that counters the text's characteristic mode of dispersal: "Sinopsis. El jorobadito en el bosque ... un sudamericano ... Redes policiales ... El

escritor inglés habla con el jorobadito en el bosque ... Cinco o seis
camareros ... Comienzo del otoño. El viento levanta arena y los cubre"
("Synopsis. The hunchback in the woods ... a South American ... Police
dragnets .... The English writer talks to the hunchback in the woods ...
Five or six waiters ... Stirrings of fall. The wind ships up sand and buries
them").[24] As if more than anything else a set of notes, or an outline, to
remind the author himself of some common threads that might add up to
a coherent narrative, "Synopsis. The Wind" brings together the fundamental elements of a story that struggles to emerge as primary from the
act of writing in general, and the act of writing a detective story in
particular, in the form of a sequence of prose poems, as the text's real,
most urgently felt and considered, subject. From the "Synopsis" forward,
the pressures of writing, as it were, to spec, to the demands of a certain
audience Bolaño both does and does not want to please, emerge as the
text's central concern.[25] Voicing the concern, in "21. When I Was a Boy"
("Cuando niño"), that "'there isn't much aesthetics left in me'"
("«Bueno, supongo que ya poca *estética* queda en mí»"), and prefiguring
there and in "22. The Sea" ("El mar") the radically reductive schematics
for writing that would surface years later in the drawings of *The Savage
Detectives*, the narrator continues: "'The straight line is the sea when it's
calm, the wavy line is the sea with waves, and the jagged line is
a storm' ... 'nnnnnn' ... 'A little boat' ... 'nnnnn' ... 'nnnnnn' ...'";
"The straight line made me feel calm ... The wavy line made me
uneasy ...'"[26]

   Declaring in the text that follows that "Words are empty," and referring
to an "urge" that "propels poetry toward something detectives call perfection. Dead-end street" ("23. Perfection"; "Perfección"), Bolaño suggests
the extent to which, economic motives aside, he would have liked nothing
better than to produce, as Baudelaire put it with his own characteristic
ambivalence, irony, and trenchant affect in the prose poem, "Á une heure
du matin" ("One O'Clock in the Morning"), "a few beautiful verses."[27] Yet
Antwerp's "dead-end" aspirations lead to an increasing interpellation into
detective fiction as the most promising way to make a living from writing,
a way nonetheless itself not without difficulty: "The writer, I think he was
English, confessed to the hunchback how hard it was for him to write. All
I can come up with are stray sentences, he said, maybe because reality seems
to me like a swarm of stray sentences ... " ("30. The Medic"; "El
enfermero").[28] Recalling "the pronouncements of an English writer who
said how hard it was for him to keep his verb tenses consistent" and who
"used the word *suffer* to give a sense of his struggles" ("32. Calle Tallers";

"La calle Tallers"), as well as, in "35. A Hospital" ("Un hospital"), the imperative "Destroy your stray ['free'] phrases [or 'sentences']") ("«Destruye tus frases libres»"), the narrator arrives at the point of naming what his "problem," as an aspiring detective fiction writer, may be said to have been all along: "'Lonely words, people walking away from the camera' . . . I stopped at the fucking 'lonely words.' Undisciplined writing" ("Escritura sin disciplina") ("36. People Walking Away"; "Gente que se aleja").[29]

While "lonely words," "people walking away," *Antwerp* itself as "undisciplined writing," as non-commodifiable discourse, may pose problems for writers aspiring to adhere to the regime, at once aesthetic and commercial, of detective fiction, an adherence Bolaño embraced and resisted and chased, at the heart of *Antwerp* is the tension it enacts between the economic imperative of the detective novel, with all it requires as a popular commercial if also serious literary genre, and the "tax-free" counter-imperative of poetry, and of the prose poem in particular, in Stéphane Mallarmé's powerful formulation, as an arena within which to "cede the initiative to words," obeying no particular genre's agenda: "I can't be a science fiction writer because my innocence is mostly gone and I'm not crazy yet . . . Words that no one speaks, that no one is required to speak . . . writing that's stolen away just as love, friendship . . . " ("37. Three Years"; "Tres años").[30] The narrator's dreams of love and friendship that would not be "stolen away" notwithstanding, his dream of a non-instrumentalizing, non-commercial, tax-free writing remains haunted by the detective novel's conventional elements and expectations: "Dreaming of Colan Yar, police cars parked in front of a smoldering building, twenty-year-old criminals? . . . the nameless girl, with her guillotine mouth, strolling through the past and the future like a movie face . . ." ("40. "The Motorcyclists"; "Los motociclistas").[31] Against such prototypical genre elements linking fiction and film, the autonomy of love and of language, of language unfettered by narrative drive, remains, albeit in the threatened (or paranoid), anxious, economically disenfranchised figure of "The Bum" ("41. El vagabundo"): "Recuerdo una noche en la estación ferroviária de Mérida .... Aparecieron frases ... las frases literalmente aparecieron, como anuncios luminosos ... Letras blancas ... Pensé que el vagabundo podía ser un tipo violento. Frases. Cogí el cuchillo ... y esperé la siguiente frase ... " ("I remember one night at the Mérida train station. ... Phrases appeared ... just appeared, literally, like glowing ads ... like news on an electronic ticker. White letters ... I wondered whether the bum was dangerous. Phrases. I clutched the knife ... and waited for the next phrase ... ")[32] As *Antwerp* nears its conclusion, toward nostalgic, increasingly autobiographical remembrances of lost youth and love—"I'll probably never come back to the clearing in the woods, not with flowers, not with the net, not with a fucking book to spend the afternoons" ("45. Applause"; "El aplauso")[33]—the freedom affirmed by the phrase "Undisciplined writing" makes explicit Bolaño's resistance, in "47. No hay reglas ("There Are No Rules)"), to systems and hierarchies of genre, the rules of art, and the policing of aesthetic regimes: "... Toda escritura en el límite esconde una máscara blanca ... No hay reglas. («Díganle al estúpido de Arnold Bennet que *todas* las reglas de construcción siguen siendo válidas *sólo* para las novelas que son copias de otras.») ... Yo, también huyo de Colan Yar .... «Creo que lo único hermoso aquí es la lengua» ... «Me refiero a su sentido más estricto». (Aplausos.)" (".... All writing on the edge hides a white mask ... There are no rules." ('Tell that stupid Arnold Bennet that all his rules about plot only apply to novels that are copies of other novels.') ... I, too, am fleeing Colan Yar ... 'I'd say the only beautiful thing here is the language' ... 'I mean it in the most literal way' ... (Applause.)."[34]

The closer Bolaño gets to realizing the ideal of a commercially viable detective novel, the kind of novel the commercial fiction writer turned how-to author, "stupid Arnold Bennet," attempted to instruct aspiring authors to write, the greater the distance from the kind of tax-free text Bolaño aspired to write. As yet uncoerced by the market ("There are no rules"), yet already feeling acutely its pressures, the Bolaño of *Antwerp* aspires to write not "novels that are copies of other novels" but a genreless text in which he can affirm, without reserve, that "'the only beautiful thing here is the language' ... 'I mean it in the most literal way' ... (Applause.)" («... lo único hermoso aquí es la lengua» ... «Me refiero a su sentido más estricto». (Aplausos.)." It is in light of these sentences, in the most literal, strict sense, approaching the conclusion of *Antwerp*, that we must understand Bolaño's statement, near the end of his life, that it was the only "novel" that didn't embarrass him.

Accidents happen, and sometimes, as Bolaño suggests in the prose poem that gives the "novel" its title, these accidents, however real or absurd, are called "plots," sometimes, recalling such recent texts as Claudia Rankine's *Plot* and *The End of the Alphabet*, they may be "just" words, "just" sentences: "En Amberes un hombre murió al ser aplastado su automóvil por un camión cargado de cerdos ... «Cada palabra es inútil, cada frase, cada conversación telefónica» ... «Dijo que quería estar sola» ... En Amberes o en Barcelona. La luna. Animales que huyen. Accidente en la carretera. El miedo" ("In Antwerp a man was killed when his car was run over by a truck full of pigs . . . 'Every word is useless, every sentence, every phone conversation' . . . 'She said she wanted to be alone' . . . In Antwerp or Barcelona. The moon. Animals fleeing. Highway accident. Fear").[35] Brought around from this comical, detached, (auto-)referential invocation of the prose poem novel's title and its ambiguous, split location ("Belgium or Catalonia") to a sad autobiographical remembrance of a "secret sickness called Lisa . . . In the weave of a mysterious language whose words signify without exception that the foreigner 'isn't well'" and is "without much chance of writing epic poetry . . . sentences lacking in tranquility," the writer ". . . a dirty man . . . a waiter," his "jacket . . . also black" ("50. Summer"; "El verano"), *Antwerp* closes as it begins with an insistent situating of the act of writing, of the prose poem in particular, in an increasingly intergeneric, intermedial context dominated by film, by buildings that look "like warehouses out of gangster movies" ("52. Monty Alexander"). What "poems lack," says the narrator, echoing the freedom Baudelaire wished for his readers, "is characters who lie in wait for the reader" ("En todo poema falta un personaje que acecha al lector"); what they offer, instead, are "some sentences that were riddles that no one bothered to decipher" ("algunas frases eran jeroglíficos que nadie se daba el trabajo de descifrar"), sentences that might be enjoyed for their own sake, for the sheer, non-commodifiable pleasure of the riddle, unresolved.[36]

What drives detective fiction, by contrast, as *Antwerp*'s thoroughly meta-reflexive antepenultimate text makes clear, linking it more than any other literary genre to the commercial imperative, is the drive to compose and recompose plots that are copies of other plots, "novels that are copies of other novels," films that are copies of other films, in a never-ending procession and (re)appropriation, as "54. Los elementos" ("The Elements") suggests, of common generic materials: "Cine entre los pinos . . . Los espectadores miran la pantalla . . . Colan Yar, por supuesto . . . En el cine uno de los actores dijo «nos persigue un volcán» . . . Aparté la mirada de la pantalla . . . . el que huye de Colan Yar escribe una carta . . . Aeródromo clandestino. Espejos. Otros elementos" ("Movies under the pines . . . The spectators watch the screen . . . Colan Yar, of course . . . In the movie one of the actors said 'we're being chased by a volcano.' . . . I glanced away from the screen . . . the person fleeing Colan Yar writes a letter . . . Secret airfield. Mirrors. Other elements").[37]

Recycling such familiar, shared "elements" of commercial fiction and film, equal parts detective novel, science fiction, and adventure story,

Antwerp draws to its conclusion, in its fifty-fifth and penultimate piece, "Nagas," with a cinematographically overdetermined turn from the screen of the outdoor movie theater to the screen of the text itself, both equally projections of the author's and reader's mutual expectations and collaborations: "«No puedo escribir más» . . . En la pantalla aparecen los Nagas . . . Por las carreteras europeas condenadas a muerte se desliza el automóvil de sus padres. ¿Hacia Lyon, Ginebra, Brujas? Hacia Amberes? . . . Últimas imágenes . . . mientras un automóvil desconocida rueda al encuentro de una luminosidad mayor" ("'I've written all I can' . . . On the screen, the Nagas appear . . . Along the death-doomed European highways her parents' car glides. On the way to Lyon, Geneva, Bruges? On the way to Antwerp? . . . Final images . . . as a strange car moves to encounter a greater brightness").[38]

Underscoring the randomness of the text's "plot" ("construcción"), its accidental appearances and disappearances, the uneventful "napping" that leads, implicitly, to the generically scripted car crash bringing it to its (un)eventful end, at once obeying and disobeying the rules of the detective genre, where plot in effect equals violence, the text's ambiguous yet predictable ending preserves a final diegetic, non-diegetic "mystery." Are the "Final images" "in" or "out" of the film? At once blank canvas, screen, and page, the white sheet on which the film projects the final plot twist of a fatal car crash yields a final, fifty-sixth text, "Postscript" ("Post Scriptum"), that speaks to writing's more fundamental imperative: "De lo perdido . . . solo deseo recuperar la disponibilidad cotidiana de mi escritura, líneas capaces de . . . levantarme . . . Como esos versos de Leopardi que Daniel Biga recitaba en un Puente nórdico para armarse de coraje, así sea mi escritura. *Barcelona, 1980*" ("Of what is lost . . . all I wish to recover is the daily availability of my writing, lines capable of . . . lifting me up . . . Let my writing be like the verses by Leopardi that Daniel Biga recited on a Nordic bridge to gird himself with courage. BARCELONA 1980").[39]

Not the plot, but the writing. Not the fiction, but the narration. Not the story, but the telling. Not the characters, but the sentences. Not the voices, but the language ("the only beautiful thing here . . . I mean it in the most literal way"). Not an either/or choice between poems and novels, but poems and novels in prose. In *Antwerp,* Bolaño's closing homage to Leopardi notwithstanding, the "daily availability" of writing he seeks to recuperate, with a power like that of Leopardi's verses ("Como esos versos de Leopardi"), takes the form not of "Odes," nor of any other verse form, but of the prose poem, of Baudelaire's "petits poèmes en prose." Positioned roughly halfway between Baudelaire's *Le Spleen de Paris* and Rimbaud's *Illuminations*, and equally indebted to each, at once sequential and modular, narrative-anecdotal yet resistant to both narration and description, meta-textual and self-reflexive, *Antwerp* remains in the end Bolaño's most disjunctively Rimbaldian performance. Yet while the myth of Rimbaud as poet would continue, long after *Antwerp*, to play a central role in Bolaño's imaginary, especially through the doppelgänger "Arturo Belano" (whose name fuses Bolaño's own with the symmetrical beauty, "bel et beau," of Baudelaire and Rimbaud), stylistically and prose-poetically, the future would belong to Baudelaire. The rest is money.[40]

CHAPTER 2

Poetry as Symptom and Cure
Monsieur Pain

As the epic wing of possibilities for poetry migrated over the course of the nineteenth-century from verse to prose, both Poe and Baudelaire understood, at the moment of the rise of the bourgeois novel, that length was not merely a quantitative matter, that it was rather a defining, substantive, qualitative feature and a question of value in its own right, the question of brevity and intensity of effect being perhaps even the most important question for poetry, whether in verse or prose, as for literary value tout court.[1] Like the Poe of "How to Write a Blackwood Article," "The Poetic Principle," and "The Philosophy of Composition," the Baudelaire of the Preface of *Le Spleen de Paris* to Arsène Houssaye, of "Le Mauvais Vitrier" ("The Bad Glazier") and "À une heure du matin" ("One O'Clock in the Morning"), Bolaño understood, a century-and -a-half later, that the question of length, of scale, as value, remained integral to the growing separation, and attempts to bridge the divide, between "serious literary" and "popular" literature. Hence Bolaño's career-long interest, from *Antwerp* and *Monsieur Pain* through *Distant Star*, *The Savage Detectives*, *Woes of the True Policeman* and *2666*, in the prose poem and detective fiction, the continual quest for success both in the literary marketplace and in critical circles, to reach a popular audience while remaining skeptical, wary, even disdainful, of the popular and critical receptions such work might receive.[2]

Written in 1981–1982 and published in 1984 as *La senda de los elefantes* *[The Elephant Path]*, *Monsieur Pain* shares *Antwerp*'s interest in a form that would combine the brevity and intensity of the prose poem with the significantly more expansive, still relatively condensed narrative possibilities of the novella. Where *Antwerp* offers a paratactic, discontinuous mode of verbal collage and montage that requires active assemblage, a relationship to the reader that places it in the tradition of collections of prose poems, Baudelaire's and Rimbaud's in particular, *Monsieur Pain* represents a decisive step in Bolaño's career, following his first published

work's more disjunctive, experimental prose-poetic project, toward
a more continuous and in some respects (though not all) more conventional, traditional mode of narration. While the classic form of the prose
poem established by Baudelaire and Rimbaud, from a half-page to several
pages, shows up explicitly in the nine third-person biographical sketches,
each of prose-poem length, that make up the "*Epílogo de voces: la senda de
los elefantes*" ("Epilogue of Voices: The Elephant Track"), the status of
the concluding prose-poetic sketches as paratexts, supplements, addenda
to the preceding, intricately continuous first-person narrative of the title
character, with its oscillating intensities, that ultimately both includes
and excludes them, marks the extent to which poems—as brief, intense
verbal objects, in verse or prose—have begun to yield in Bolaño's oeuvre
to extended narratives that will increasingly come to define him as
a writer of prose fiction, above all, of novels.

Yet Bolaño was a writer of novels obsessed with poets and poetry, with
the relation between poetry and the novel, the hegemonic form of prose
fiction already figured by Baudelaire a century earlier, at the time of the
bourgeois novel's emergence, as poetry's primary competition, its nemesis
in the literary marketplace. In its title character's futile attempt to meet,
treat, and heal the novella's non-speaking, absent center, César Vallejo—
synecdochic figure of the most admirable of Latin American writers
transplanted to Europe, impoverished, suffering poet in both verse and
prose, the first of many future poet-protagonists in his fiction, real and
invented—*Monsieur Pain* picks up where *Antwerp* had left off in pursuing
investigations into the relation between poetry and prose that would come
to define Bolaño's *oeuvre*.[3]

Set in Paris in 1938, *Monsieur Pain* takes place during the nine days
leading up to Vallejo's death on April 15, primarily the five days from
April 6 to April 11, concluding in its final pages with the day after his
April 19 funeral at Montrouge Cemetery organized by the Communist
party and attended by "the leading Communist intellectuals and sym-
pathizers-Jean Cassou, Louis Aragon (who delivered a speech 'in the
name of the International Association of Writers'), André Malraux,
Tristan Tzara and Jean-Richard Bloch; among the Latin Americans was
the Cuban poet Nicolás Guillén."[4] Supplementing this condensed time-
frame, the nine prose-poetic biographical sketches of "Epilogue for
Voices" extend the work's historical frame of reference from 1858,
the year Baudelaire began moving away from the verse poems of *Les
Fleurs du Mal* toward the prose poems of *Le Spleen de Paris* he would first
publish in *La Presse* in 1862, to 1985, the year after the initial publication

077

of *Monsieur Pain*, a connection suggested by the epigraph from Poe's "Mesmeric Revelation" with which the novel begins.

Concerning questions of genre, "Mesmeric Revelation" contains in nuce Poe's most consequential response for poetry and poetics, in "The Poetic Principle" and "The Philosophy of Composition," with implications as well for prose fiction that would prove foundational both for Baudelaire's invention of the modern prose poem and for Bolaño's cultivation of the prose poem novel. The literary-historical importance of these two revolutionary essays, so pivotal and indispensable to Baudelaire's transition from poems in verse to poems in prose, can hardly be overstated as a watershed moment with the furthest reaching effects for the birth of modernism. Without question two of the most important essays of the past two centuries on poetry and poetics in particular, and on genre in general, they radically challenge the reductive equation that remains uncontested in Poe's third, much more conventional essay—significantly not called "The Rationale of Poetry," but "The Rationale of Verse"—the common confusion at the core of Bolaño's prose poem novels.[5]

Signaling his dual indebtedness to Poe, as inventor of the detective genre, and to Baudelaire, Poe's admirer, translator, and commentator, as inventor of the modern prose poem, the passage has as its precise intertext the piece with which Baudelaire launches, immediately following the Preface to Arsène Houssaye, the *Petits poèmes en prose* of *Le Spleen de Paris,* "L'Étranger" ("The Stranger"). Carving out in their dialogical forms and procedures a space perfectly poised between verse and prose, and between poetry—no longer identified, since Poe, exclusively with verse—and fiction, the two texts together mark the preoccupations with poetry and prose, with fiction and detective fiction, that will shape Bolaño's career. Reaching across the Atlantic for an epigraph from Poe that can't help but recall Baudelaire, *Monsieur Pain* frames its narrative about Vallejo's last days in Paris, establishing in one stroke the literary and geographical coordinates of Bolaño's work throughout his career.

While the pronounced turn toward (especially) Chilean and Mexican and more broadly American settings in Bolaño's work from the early 1990s through his death in 2003 led to his growing international reputation as the preeminent novelist of his generation in the Americas, in the 1980s, by contrast, from *Antwerp* and *Monsieur Pain* through his first full-length novel, *El Tercer Reich* (*The Third Reich*, written 1989), Bolaño established himself as a writer with a decidedly European orientation. As crucial as Poe and Baudelaire would prove to be in the shaping of Bolaño's oeuvre, his focus on Vallejo's last days in *Monsieur Pain* attests to his strong identification with the poet, who had found his way to Paris as Bolaño himself had done in the first year following his arrival in Europe before settling in Barcelona. Like Vallejo, dying poet, specter of the potential death of poetry, who over the course of the novella never speaks, whom neither Monsieur Pain nor the reader ever encounter directly, and from whose powerful poems not a single line is quoted—as is the case with Bolaño's poet-protagonists, with few exceptions—Bolaño becomes a figure of haunting transatlantic connections that are both there and not there, displaced and refracted. In keeping with the narrative's hallucinatory articulations of space and time, its twin dream logics of condensation and displacement, what we learn of Vallejo, we learn obliquely, indirectly, in part through the mediation of the two shadowy, detective-like figures identified as Spanish-speaking on the first page and as "the two Spaniards" on the page after Vallejo's identity is revealed, one "dark," one "thin," who track Monsieur Pain.

In offering a bribe to Monsieur Pain not to attempt to heal Vallejo with the expertise they attribute to him, acupuncture, the two Spaniards set up an initial frame, in keeping with the epigraph from Poe's "Mesmeric Revelation," for the novel's investigation of literature and the arts (as we shall see including film), of the aesthetic as such, as at once illness, symptom, and talking cure.[7] In its striking anticipation of Freud's *The Interpretation of Dreams*, including Freud's preoccupation with the question of whether the hermeneutics of psychoanalytic interpretation could establish itself as science rather than as (mere) art, the essay provides a template for Monsieur Pain as a figure whose "nervous instability" ("desarreglos nerviosos") allows Bolaño to explore relations, at once physical and psychological, individual and social, among poetry, fiction, pain, and illness. Its succinct, dialogical, prose-poetic form and core concerns prefigure much that *Monsieur Pain* will pursue at multiple levels in the specific literary-historical, aesthetic, and political context of late 1930s Paris, the Spanish Civil War, and the run-up to World War II.[7]

The comically yet fatally prosaic illness of which Vallejo is said to be dying mysteriously, in *Monsieur Pain*, is "hiccups" ("el hipo")[8] (rather than malaria, as is thought to have been most likely), an affliction of the larynx, hence of breathing and (dis-)articulation, that may prove a serious condition yet may also seem a bad joke, provoking laughter as the symptom, the synecdoche, of an inability to regain control of breathing, of eruptive, disruptive (non-)utterance, as it were of both *langue* (native-tongue-become-foreign) and *parole*. Evoking, in the trope of the hiccup, the

Freudian nexus of conscious-unconscious articulation, of wit and *Witze*, of involuntary puns, unwitting jokes, and slips of the tongue—as in the title's play on French bread, English pain—Bolaño signals from the outset the novella's investment in the serious play of signification. The stakes and implications of this serious play, with its intricate plotting of language's (self-)referential functions within oscillating and interpenetrating frameworks, are as bound up with questions of psychoanalysis, history, and politics, as these three intractably interrelated terms are, according to the narrative's unfolding, with the interplay of poetry, poetics, and narrative.[9]

Recalling Borges, Breton's *Nadja*, and Aragon's *Le Paysan de Paris*, *Monsieur Pain*'s innovative, labyrinthine form and structure appear at first glance to be easily divisible into a curiously asymmetrical hybrid of two distinct forms: 1) a single, continuous novella-length narrative, uninterrupted by subtitles or chapter divisions, followed by 2) the nine prose-poem length texts of "Epilogue for Voices," all of which bear as their titles the names of characters in the preceding narrative.[10] In their strikingly disproportionate lengths (116 and 17 pages in the original, respectively), these two forms stage a further evolution of Bolaño's inquiry into the relation between poetry and the novel.[11] While the difference in length is understandable to some extent merely in terms of the supplemental, paratextual status of the latter as "Epilogue," the nine synoptic, retrospective and proleptic prose poems closing the novella demonstrate a residual continuation of the investment in the form on display in *Antwerp*, completed only a year earlier. The affinities and differences, continuities and discontinuities in this regard between *Antwerp* and *Monsieur Pain* recall the importance of reading Bolaño's works in the context of their original dates of composition and publication. While *Antwerp* is arguably best understood less as a "novel" than as a parodic assemblage of prose poems, *Monsieur Pain* marks a pivotal transition toward the former. While the brief, prose-poetic texts of the "Epilogue" are all in service of the preceding narrative, providing succinct closure to it while expanding its frames and range of reference, it is the narrative "proper," from which the "Epilogue" both is and is not separable, with and without which it is and is not complete, that clearly dominates both in length and substance. It is ironic, yet fitting, in this regard, as an indication of Bolaño's lingering and enduring attachment to the prose poem as form, even as his investments were evolving increasingly toward the novel, that *Monsieur Pain* bore as its original title not the name of the character at the heart of its intricate, extended, novelistic yet still prose-poetic narrative, but "The Elephant Track," subtitle of an "Epilogue for Voices" (with its explicit focus on language), composed entirely of nine relatively autonomous, self-contained, individually titled prose poems.

The question of form in *Monsieur Pain* thus emerges as more complex than a mere two-part division might initially suggest. For while the not-quite-complete, more-or-less-self-contained 116-page narrative that precedes the "Epilogue" might appear to be, by comparison, a comparatively continuous whole, it proves to be, on the contrary, radically discontinuous formally, affectively, and conceptually.[12] Focusing in its first 114 pages on the five days from April 6 to April 11, 1938, coming quickly to a close with only three pages devoted to the nine days thereafter (April 11 to April 20), followed by the expanded time-frame opened onto by the birth- and death dates included under character names that serve as titles for the nine prose poems making up the "Epilogue"—prose poems in the form of obituaries, or vice versa—the text's chronology is straightforward enough. Within this relatively straightforward temporal frame, however, the narrative logic of what transpires is decidedly non-linear, constructed, in prototypically Freudian fashion, according to the associative logic of dreams—ever proximate, in the popular as well as literary imagination, to what is called poetry—thus inviting a psychoanalytic mode of interpretation.

Segmented into twenty-one sections by twenty white spaces of short-paragraph length (five lines in the original, six in the English translation—five of which are preceded by a demarcation of three dots not included in the Spanish), *Monsieur Pain* proceeds in comparatively short bursts of prose along a continuum from one-and-a-half to (by far the longest) twenty-eight pages. Together, these consistent disruptions break up the first-person "stream" of narrative into a dream-like collage that does not merely reflect but simultaneously constructs and unhinges, articulates and disarticulates the dissociative state—at once real, imaginary, and symbolic; referential and self-referential—of what he calls his "nervous instability."[13] Recalling Monsieur Pain's instructions to a taxi driver to head toward "Place Blanche" ("la plaza Blanche," with its Mallarméan play on the terror of the act of writing, on facing the abyss of "la page blanche"), the white spaces punctuating the prose blocks of *Monsieur Pain* provide a structure and rhythm, like the city blocks Pain continually navigates on foot and by taxi in Paris, for the reader's experience of navigating the text, gaps like those Bolaño refers to in the prose-poetic synopsis of the "Epilogue," just over a page in length, summarizing the life of Monsieur Pain's unrequited love-interest, Marcelle (Madame) Reynaud: "Sometimes when she remembered ... Pierre Pain, a poet whose work she had never read, not a line ... the gaps in any story, gaps that slowly close as years go by, narrowing, becoming less significant, not so much gaps as blanks."[14] In this, the novel's first reference of any kind to Monsieur Pain as a poet, in the final sentences of the first part's extended narrative, on the last page preceding the "Epilogue," only eight pages from the book's conclusion, Bolaño signals the central role poetry would continue to play in his fictive imaginary.[15]

Thus, the prose-poetic, dream-like associative structure of *Monsieur Pain*, with its paragraph-length white spaces between each section for the reader to "slowly close," not as "years" but as pages "go by," doubling Pain's psychically disoriented, disorienting journey. That journey takes him above all through his own mind; the streets of Paris; his apartment building; a restaurant with his friend and unrequited, would-be lover, Madame Reynaud; the "Clinique Arago," where Vallejo is said to be dying of hiccups; a nightmare "labyrinth ... reminiscent of the Clinique Arago with its circular corridors"; Vallejo's room at the hospital; a Surrealist nightmare of an "eccentric café ... The Forest"; giving way the next morning in the clear light of day to "Raoul's café," where there's news of "the war in Spain" and Nazis; followed by another nightmare in a "warehouse full of useless junk" ["almacén de trastos inútiles"]. From there, Pain finds himself in a movie theater where a film, *Actualité* ("Current Reality," "Current Events") is showing; then back in the hospital, lost and unable to find Vallejo's room. Recalling in its unpredictable paths the "crossing" of "innumerable relations" ("croisement de [leurs] innombrables rapports") in "enormous cities" ("villes énormes") to which the Preface of *Le Spleen de Paris* attributes the necessity and urgency of the prose poem, the journey ends, finally, in the street in "despair" with Pain, the very figure of Baudelaire's "quelque mauvais poète" ("some bad poet"), the generic poet "X" or "Z" in "Perte d'auréole" ("Loss of a Halo"). It is only on hearing from Madame Reynaud of Vallejo's death, a day after Aragon's speech at Vallejo's funeral, that Pain learns the great Vallejo, his former "patient," whose illness and suffering he could not cure, was himself a poet, "although not at all well known, and very poor."[16]

In the course of elaborating these primary scenes, *Monsieur Pain* opens onto a handful of oscillating, overlapping, interrelated narratives: 1) Monsieur Pain's unrequited love for Madame Reynaud; 2) his relationship as former student, mentee and, in effect, analysand to the eighty-year-old former mentor and confidant, M. Rivette, figure of the patient, laconic analyst Pain calls on to confide in (literally calling him on the telephone) at moments of nervous crisis concerning his unrequited love for Madame Reynaud, his sustained monologues eliciting patient (non-)responses—figured by literal ellipses (" … ")—minimal exchanges recalling the prototypical dynamic of the talking cure; 3) Monsieur Pain's fantasy (non-)relationship to M. Vallejo as acupuncturist entrusted with curing him by Madame Reynaud and Madame Vallejo—with whom he visits him only once (having been bribed in advance by the "two Spaniards" to stay away from him) until competing authorities, the esteemed "real" doctors at the Clinique Arago's, Lejard and Lemière (playing on the Spanish "lejos," or "distant" and French "lumière," "light" but also the brothers Lumière, pioneers of modern cinema), prevent further access to Vallejo; 4) Pain's distanced, all-but-completely oblivious relation to the Spanish Civil War, filtered through his encounter with his former World War I acquaintance turned Fascist, "Pleumeur-Bodou" (playing on "plumes," "flâneur," and "Baudelaire") at the showing of the film *Actualité* (a film whose protagonists, Michel and Pauline, offer a displaced cinematic version of the relationship Pain desires with Madame Reynaud); and finally, 5) Pain's at once Poesque, Baudelairean, Bretonian, Borgesian struggles with and against a solipsistic reality variously represented as a "labyrinth, architecturally reminiscent of the Clinique Arago with its circular corridors," "dream-corridors" where he is unsure if he is there "of [his] own free will" or if "some external force [is] holding [him] in that place," "where … nightmares … dreams" have "all the features of a … radio transmission," where his "dream-world," like "a private radio station …" opens onto a "hell of voices … a kind of empty reading room, which at some point [he] identified as [his] own brain."[17]

Figuring centrally in its complex of interlocking narratives and their dismantling of conceptual binaries (inside and outside, sleep and wakefulness, mind and matter) is the question of language, a question, as Bolaño's narrative understands, at the heart of aesthetic, psychoanalytic, economic, philosophical, and political investigations. Hence the narrative's intricate punning, its *Witze*—following the insights and methods of *The Interpretation of Dreams* and *Jokes and Their Relationship to the Unconscious*—of "Pain" as English "suffering" and French "bread"; of "Clinique Arago," "argot," and Aragon; of "Place Blanche" and "page blanche"; of "the word *engaged*" in the context of the character "Jules Sartreau" (playing on Sartre); its commingled investigations of the physical and psychic that lead Pain, "an amateur ["un aficionado"] … of Edgar Allan Poe," to say his "nerves are not the best" when he "meant to say my optic nerve. ("9. No estoy muy bien de los nervios. / Mi intención había sido decir del nervio óptico").[18]

At the heart of the narrative's complex of interrelated, ultimately inseparable concerns is Vallejo's status as a pivotal figure in the history of twentieth-century poetry, linking French, Spanish, and South American strands of Surrealism with the Spanish Civil War, the ideological struggles between fascism and communism, and the trajectory of the Surrealist movement, as elaborated in Breton's *First* (1924) and *Second Manifestoes* (1929), from Freud to Marx.[19] Situating the narrative's fictive world within a context at once literary, aesthetic, historical, and political, a procedure characteristic of Bolaño's oeuvre thereafter, *Monsieur Pain* begins, following its epigraph from Poe's "Mesmeric Revelation," with the specific geographical, temporal, historical referent "PARIS, 1938." Yet while the narrative provides a place and date with which to anchor our reading, made more precise by the (native-French-speaking) narrator's opening phrase, "On Wednesday the sixth of April, at dusk, as I was preparing to leave my lodgings," followed by the second paragraph's reference to "two men . . . [who were] speaking Spanish, a language I do not understand, and wearing dark trench-coast and broad-brimmed hats, which . . . obscured their faces," the first reference to the Spanish Civil War does not occur, significantly, until roughly a quarter of a way through, even then without quite naming it, through the introduction of a character by the farcical, paronomastically named "Pleumeur-Bodou," who is said not to have gone away to join not the "International Brigade" but rather "the other side," meaning "The Fascists."[20] While the narrative refers explicitly some twenty-five pages later to "news . . . about the war in Spain . . . and new weapons that we hadn't known in the Great War" (in which Monsieur Pain served) as well as to "Nazis" and the "damned Germans . . . testing out their arsenal," broader historical, political frames of reference remain subordinated, in the first half of the novella, to a psychoanalytic frame figured most centrally by the "Clinique Arago" to which the narrative tells us Vallejo was admitted on March 24, 1938.[21]

The story to which Monsieur Pain gives shape is not the one he would wish to tell. Wounded veteran of the Great War, in love with a woman who doesn't return his affection, he is living through a nightmare—like Vallejo, whose death in the novel by hiccups both is and is not a sick joke—from which he is unable to awake. Unlike Vallejo, he will be neither beloved nor read. Aragon will not give a speech at his fictional funeral. As we learn in the entry about him with which the "Epilogue" concludes, he will die in 1949, at fifty-seven, only a few years after World War II. The narrative takes place nine years earlier, when he is forty-eight, on the eve of the War; he is a palm and tarot card reader, veteran illusionist of "every kind of esoteric practice" (Poe's, Mesmer's) in cabarets and circuses without a pension, unknown and alone except for a "poor orphan" he befriended and mentored, in whose arms he later dies in the "manager's office at the Cabaret Madame Doré."[22]

What accounts for this harsh narratological conclusion? In the end, whatever sympathy the reader has for him despite his own great self-pity, Monsieur Pain is what his name says he is. Unknown and forgotten as a would-be healer of Vallejo, yet mythologized as such in Bolaño's fictive imaginary, Pain is also a figure of the failed poet. As such, he eerily prefigures Bolaño's own relative lack of success as a poet, both in terms of the limited publication and circulation of his poetry during his lifetime and the comparatively minimal recognition his poetry received—the full collected poems assembled between 1990 and 1994 that would be *The Unknown University*—a deeply embittering fact of Bolaño's life that stayed with him to the end, despite his fame as a novelist, as the four sardonically titled verse poems "Mi carrera literaria" ("My Literary Career"), "La poesía chilena es un gas" ("Chilean Poetry Is a Gas), "Horda" ("Horde"), and "La poesía latinoamericana" ("Latin American Poetry") attest.[23]

Like Bolaño's much later *Amuleto* (1999, *Amulet*, 2007) and *By Night in Chile*, the two texts it most resembles and anticipates in its first-person condensed yet sustained narration, *Monsieur Pain* presents the reader, in its own segmented, prose-poetic fashion, with an intricate form of figuration and representation inseparable from its conceptual, affective, psychoanalytic, philosophical, social, historical, political, economic, narratological stakes and implications.[24] Divided into fourteen numbered chapters of fairly normative length, *Amulet* presents on first glance a comparatively accessible, reader-friendly novelistic structure that belies the novel's complexity. While the dominant temporal, historical frame of *Monsieur Pain* is, by contrast, relatively straightforward—moving forward, as we have seen, from April 7 to April 20, 1938 (at times interweaving succinct back-story glances), through the Epilogue's inclusive birth and death dates and updates of the fates of nine of its characters—its primary challenge to the reader lies largely in the complex task of (re)assembling the text's twenty-one resolutely segmented, disarticulated component parts. Both in themselves and in relation to one another, these parts entangle the text's readers in the daunting task of weaving together a coherent narrative, a process of suturing, of healing, of curing a text focused on "individual" illness— Vallejo's "hiccups," Pain's "nervous instability"—understood as at once physical, psychological, and social.

Where the narratological challenge of *Amulet* involves making sense of unstable, temporal, historical, mythological frames of reference, with unpredictable leaps among past, present, and future, *Monsieur Pain* moves primarily, like *By Night in Chile*, from past to present to future. But while *Monsieur Pain*'s white spaces and the segmented structure of the former require active assemblage into a coherent narrative, the continuous stream of narration of *By Night in Chile* requires readers to work in the opposite direction, actively segmenting the text into discrete individual scenes to allow narrative comprehension. With its intensely calculated, intricately constructed, hallucinatory effects, *Monsieur Pain* provides a template for the personal and political negotiations of the title character's first-person-narrator counterparts in *Amulet* (Auxilio Lacouture) and *By Night in Chile* (Sebastián Urrutia Lacroix) that will prove integral to Bolaño's approach to questions of poetry and poetics, of history and literature, of language and politics: "Absorbed in my own problems once again ... How could I describe, or understand, my experience in the warehouse? Had it been a hallucination due to my own nervous instability, or some kind of inscrutable apparition? Was the imitated hiccupping a parody or a premonition? I had claimed that there was a plot to assassinate Vallejo, did I really believe that? ... Yes, I did."[25]

As Bolaño suggests in this passage, in the voice of Monsieur Pain, the "warehouse" and "nervous instability" can only be understood, like the real, the symbolic, the imaginary, as mutually constitutive and defining, temporally and historically situated terms. Interwoven with the story that emerges "on screen" in the film *Actualité*, Plumeur-Bodou's attack on Monsieur Pain gives way to Monsieur Pain's resigned acceptance of his "spectatorship," the "safe position" of non-engaged, political cheerleading: "'Fine ideas, young man,' I said. Fine ideas, Fascism must be stopped.'" Confined in the end to the "circular and semi-circular corridors" of his solipsistic imagination, determined only "not to ask any questions," Monsieur Pain figures the complicity and resignation of a disengaged life. Separated from the history and politics of his time ("not knowing what to do, or where to turn in the chaotic struggle against fascism"), from the Resistance from which he hears "not a word," and for which he has "ceased to exist," he is reduced to "conscientiously reading palms, palms stained with blood, the palms of killers and sinister whores, of spongers and black marketeers" for a club owner "jailed for collaboration."[26]

The issue of authority, as of joint responsibility and engagement between authors and readers, figures early on in *Monsieur Pain* in the anxiety the narrator feels and expresses concerning his credibility as an acupuncturist—who is himself a poet—to cure Vallejo's curious, and comical, illness. "He's dying," of "hiccups," Madame Reynaud tells Monsieur Pain, "No one knows why; it's not a joke. You have to save his life."[27] Confronting the expertise of Lejard, the Clinique Arago's "famous specialist" and "leading physician," concerned that Lejard's colleague, "the eminent Doctor Lemière," who "never had much time for charlatans," wouldn't tolerate his presence in his patient's room, and imagining further the two Spaniards who have been following him as less like "doctors or medical students" and "more like gangsters in training," Pain repeatedly expresses feelings of insecurity about being entrusted to diagnose and cure Vallejo's illness.[28] Yet as much as Pain fears being considered a charlatan and a quack by the narrative's emblematic figures of medical and scientific prestige, Lejard and Lemière remain as perplexed as the acupuncturist-poet narrator about the causes of Vallejo's symptoms. "'All his organs are in perfect working order!'" says Lemière. "'I can't see what's wrong with the man.'"[29] Lemière's inability to identify a reason for Vallejo's mysterious condition opens onto a confusion between physical and psychic causes, between "neurology" and "psychoanalysis," the "hard" science of the "brain" and the ghostly, spectral pseudo-science of mind, spirit, Soul.[30]

Disappointed, accordingly, with the limitations of his "friendship" with Madame Reynaud, with conversations "never broaching our feelings or political convictions, or at least not hers,"[31] Pain figures the narrative's pivotal conflict between art and science, or what amounts to the same, as the description of the film *Actualité* has it, between science and love.[32] At the heart of this conflict is Vallejo, the poet-patient whose illness can't be cured, figure of poetry as a non-commercial art in the service of love, as counter to the authority of science in the service of the marketplace. From the Vallejos' poverty, to Monsieur Pain's expired pension and conflicted acceptance of two thousand francs not to treat him; to Monsieur Pain's reference to "[Raoul's wife] doing the day's accounts or reading a novel" and conflation of his "Professional ethics!" with being a "pimp" and "the oldest profession"; to the proto-Surrealist Leduc brothers Monsieur Pain runs into in the "eccentric café" called "The Forest," who lack money to escape to practice their art in New York; to the "labyrinth" of "Our life in … the Great Market" and the "warehouse full of useless junk," the condition of "modern art" is framed by demands of the general economy, an economy inextricably bound up with questions of expertise and authority.[33]

At the center of Bolaño's imaginary in addressing these demands, in *Monsieur Pain*—"anchored," as the title character puts it in a moment of referential fervor, continuing the illusion of the possibility of explicit reference "in the *real world*" ("en el *mundo real*")—is Vallejo as an emblematic figure of poetry's status as privileged yet marginal, heralded yet little read, honored yet neglected, a cultural "hiccup," a "dying" art that can hardly compete with the advances of science, the "Great Market," and the machinery of war.[34] "It is difficult / to get the news from poems," one of Bolaño's favorite U.S. American poets, William Carlos Williams famously wrote, "yet men die miserably every day / for lack / of what is found there."[35] Restricted, in the immediate post–World War II literary economy of Sartre's *What Is Literature?* (*Qu'est-ce que la littérature?* 1948), to the status of a linguistically self-referential cultural treasure, poetry must content itself, in contrast to prose fiction, the capaciously referential genre of a *littérature engagée,* with being decorative but disengaged, non-instrumentalizing but without consequence, a synecodochic example of "useless junk."[36] Vallejo, of course, contra the self-absorbed Monsieur Pain, thought otherwise: "me encontré departiendo con tres muchachos … y hablaban de mujeres y política. Filosofamos, afirmaban …. / frases fragmentadas sobre el fascismo y la guerra" ("I had fallen into conversation with three young men … talking about women and politics. We're philosophizing, they declared …. / fragments of sentences about fascism and the war … ").[37] Followed by the eruptive inclusion immediately thereafter, roughly halfway through the narrative, of the only thing resembling verse in the whole of *Monsieur Pain,* "un cartel escrito a mano que decía: *Lulú / Insoslayable / Soledad / Pitones / Sexo / Verdadero*" ("a hand-written sign that read: Lulu / Unavoidable / Solitude / Horns / Sex / True"), the explicit reference to "fragments of sentences about fascism and the war" recalls playfully yet seriously, as does the following line's encoded reference to the Spanish Civil War ("—Pitones? ¡Pitones de toro! ¡Pero eso es España! ["Horns. Bull's horns! But that's Spain!"]], the elliptical political poetics of Vallejo, a poetics that embraced the intricate possibilities of linguistic self-referentiality along with the full range of referential "screens," frames, and functions on display in Bolaño's narrative, including both *Monsieur Pain*'s disjunctive narrative collage and the nine prose-poetic synopses that make up the "Epilogue."[38] Through the comical yet serious figure of Vallejo's absurd passing, dying of "hiccups" yet "anchored in the *real world,*" as in the symbolic and the imaginary, *Monsieur Pain* affirms Bolaño's belief in the continuing capacity of poetry, whether in verse or in prose, no less than fiction, no less than literature and the arts generally, if not to cure then at least not merely to "confirm," in the closing words of *Monsieur Pain,* "[our] attendance, [our] humble but punctual spectatorship," but to offer instead some resistance as needed, as active co-participants to help stage, and engage, the urgent issues and questions of its time, of Vallejo's, of Bolaño's, of our own.[39]

CHAPTER 3

The Novel's Regimes Made Visible
The Third Reich (El Tercer Reich)

Twenty-eight years after the fall of the Berlin Wall and the end of the Cold War, a generation after World War II, the 2010 posthumous publication of Bolaño's *El Tercer Reich* (*The Third Reich*, 2011) offered a powerful belated reminder of the extent to which those legacies posed a seemingly unsurpassable challenge to the literary, historical, political imagination, the challenge of that most terrifying of global scenarios that bore the appropriately playful yet deadly serious acronym "MAD" for the apocalyptic endgame known as "mutually assured destruction."[1] Turning the unrepresentable horrors of the historical Third Reich into *The Third Reich*, adolescent board game and novel—of beach vacations, of boredom, of the boredom of beach vacations and beach novels—twin occupations of no real world consequence apart from the petty, insular careers of those few male "geeks" obsessed with playing and writing about it, Bolaño's trope of gaming anticipates at the time of its writing, in 1989, the same year Timothy Berners-Lee invented the World Wide Web, the omnivirtualization and simulacrization of the age of the Internet on the threshold of the post-Cold War era.[2]

Written in the form of a first-person diary from an unspecified year in the *longue durée* after World War II, *The Third Reich* tells the story of a young German, Udo Berger, first encountered vacationing in Spain with his girlfriend Ingeborg at the end of summer at a generic seaside hotel, "Del Mar," on or near the Costa Brava, a setting that suggests, like the seaside campground in *Antwerp*, the town of Blanes, near Barcelona, Bolaño's home for over two decades and virtually the entirety of his adult writing career.[3] Unfolding chronologically from Berger's first day at the hotel on August 20 to his departure on September 25, with one entry on September 30 following his return to Stuttgart and a final brief entry from there on October 20, the novel consists of: 1) twelve consecutively dated entries from August 20 to 31, followed by 2) twelve from September 1 to 12, which together account for roughly the first two-thirds of the novel,

3) twelve more thereafter including eleven for the last half of September (1 through 14 and 17 through 30), and the final, brief dated entry for October 20, and 4) three additional entries by season, alluding respectively to the spring, summer, and fall/winter of 1942 in lieu of September 13 (date of the beginning of the Battle of Stalingrad, the turning point of the Eastern Front), 14 (titled "Anzio. Fortress Europa. Omaha Beachead"), and 15. Interwoven with these entries, between "Spring of 42" and "Autumn of 42. Winter of 42" are seven non-dated entries: "With the Wolf and the Lamb" ("Con el Lobo y el Cordero"), named after two relatively minor characters Berger gets to know at the Del Mar; "My Favorite Generals" ("Mis Generales Favoritos"); "Ingeborg" and "Hanna," updating two major characters from the first half of the novel between the two final dated entries, for September 30 and October 20; and "Von Seeckt," "Frau Else," and "The Convention" ("El Congreso"), referring respectively to one of Berger's competitors as a player of the eponymous boardgame; "Frau Else," the older woman and owner of the Del Mar with whom Berger pursues an affair that is never consummated; and a much-anticipated gaming conference in Paris that ends the novel with Berger's complete disaffection from the world of competitive gaming from which he had drawn a sense of his own value and importance, both as a player and as a writer who specialized in writing about the games he played. Taken together, the thirty-six dated entries (12+12+12) from August 20 to October 20 amount to one day for each year of the author's life at the time of writing (1953–1989).

From this brief summary, it will be clear that *The Third Reich* exhibits the intensely self-referential, metafictional style that characterizes Bolaño's writing generally. Written in 1989, seven years before the publication of *La literatura nazi en América* (1996, *Nazi Literature in the Americas,* 2008) and *Estrella distante (1996, Distant Star,* 2004), *The Third Reich* commemorates in effect the end of the Cold War period in which Bolaño had until then lived his entire life.[4] As so to speak, in the language of "war games" that provides the novel's central trope, the Cold War offered a totalizing world-view that froze all its inhabitants in a timeless time between the atrocities of the *Nazizeit* and the seemingly unvisualizable time, until the sudden fall of the Wall in 1989.

If everything real in the age of the Internet has become virtual—WWW displacing WWII, forty-five years after the fall of the Third Reich, as the pivotal frame of reference for the first generation since the end of the Cold War—as in Bolaño's hands everything real always already was and is in the process of becoming fiction, so fiction represents a virtually unavoidable process of becoming aware of itself, every poem a meta-poem, every novel a meta-novel, as synecdochic of what a poem, a novel, should be. In play at every level from beginning to end, the central associative chain real=fiction=metafiction represents the underlying logic governing not only the particular rules of the historical Third Reich, where human subjects were treated as objects in every possible way to be manipulated at will for the most dehumanizing of purposes, but the aestheticizing complicity of a novelist's decision to turn the historical Third Reich into Third Reich the boardgame that lies at the heart of *The Third Reich* the novel.[5] The novelist "Roberto Bolaño" confronts, through Berger, his central protagonist and doppelgänger, the spectacle of the novelist's obsession with the unrepresentable (in 360 pages, the Holocaust nowhere explicitly appears) as seen through the eyes of a narrator whose anti-social, narcissistic self-absorption, resembling that of the title character of Bolaño's preceding novel, *Monsieur Pain*, is exposed from the opening pages in his expressions of self-satisfaction and feelings of superiority over his lover and traveling companion, the woman he calls the love of his life, Ingeborg, the "angel."[6]

As if taking its cue from Roland Barthes' famous piece in *Mythologies* (1957), "L'Écrivain en vacances" ("The Writer on Holiday"), a more precise intertext for which could hardly be found, *The Third Reich* offers the fiction of a roughly two-month period, from August 20 to October 20—a mythology of the act of writing as a novelist, as if the ramblings of Berger's diary and the hyper-constructedness of Bolaño's novel were coincident with each other and of the same genre—a fiction that would conflate the actual time of writing of the novel with the period of time for which the novel claims to account.[7] Like Goethe's *The Sorrows of Young Werther*, with its cognate structure of first-person, dated entries in epistolary form, the first-person novel-as-diary *The Third Reich* chronicles the hopeful beginnings of a new love affair, or rather of two love affairs, one requited, with Ingeborg, which eventually fails, and another, with Frau Else, which develops only to a certain point and is never consummated.[8] Like Werther, Goethe's twenty-four-year-old protagonist, Berger, Bolaño's twenty-five-year-old protagonist, doppelgänger, author, and gamer, is a writer on holiday. Werther/Berger resonate with each other both phonically, through the off-rhyme of their names, and semantically, through the literal meaning of Berger, "shepherd," which translates Werther's literal pastoral context to the beaches near the Costa Brava. As Bolaño's beach vacationers echo Goethe's idyllic peasants, including memories from Berger's family vacations at the Del Mar as an adolescent, ten years earlier, of a young girl named Lotte, recalling Werther's

Charlotte, so Goethe's Fräulein B is recast as Bolaño's Frau Else. As Carlos Wieder will later recall in *Distant Star* the recurrence of fascism under Pinochet, Berger opens onto the Romantic lens of pre-Nazi Germany—moving backward from *Nazizeit* to *Goethezeit* in a way that anticipates as well Part V of *2666*—invoked through Berger's nostalgic recitation of the concluding poem of Goethe's *West-östlicher Divan: Buch des Sängers* (1814–18), "Selige Sehnsucht" ("Holy Longing").[9] Where Goethe was twenty-four, like his protagonist, when he wrote *Werther*, from which he later distanced himself in light of the novel's fatal reception throughout Europe, inducing numerous readers to imitate Werther's suicide, Bolaño wrote *The Third Reich* when he was thirty-six. As Charlotte's fiancé, Albert, is eleven years her senior, and Berger ten years older than he was when he vacationed with Lotte in his adolescence, so Bolaño is eleven years older than his protagonist, Berger, who is ten years older, when he falls in love with Frau Else, than he was when he first met her as a fifteen-year old vacationing at the Del Mar. Along with the intertextual fun Bolaño is having with these resonances between the two novels, there is the crucial difference that his more mature—or disillusioned, almost cynical—perspective brings to his representation of the novel's central characters and issues. Recalling the dramatic oscillation of personal and political narratives, private and public histories, in *Madame Bovary*, Bolaño structures *The Third Reich* around an accelerating alternation between Berger's two love stories—roughly divided between Ingeborg in the first half of the novel and Frau Else in the second half, with a gradual shift from one to the other—and the increasingly intense game of *The Third Reich* Berger plays over the latter half of the novel with the enigmatic, beach-bum character known as El Quemado ("The Burned One"), a figure of trauma, as his name suggests, pointing both to the horrors of World War II and the genocide of native Americans ("El Quemado ... reminds me of Atahualpa, the Inca prisoner of the Spaniards who learned to play chess in a single afternoon ... / "And the burns on his body ...?" / "Jackpot!").[10]

As suicide links Goethe's Werther and Flaubert's Emma, so does its specter haunt *The Third Reich* in the figure of Charly, another German vacationer at the Del Mar, whom Berger and Ingeborg get to know with his girlfriend, Hanna. Although Charly doesn't appear to be the type to commit suicide and would seem to have no motive for doing so, the question is raised when he dies under mysterious circumstances while windsurfing. His disappearance and death then serve as the central plot device for Bolaño to develop an interest that pervades his later fiction: the

detective story. While the related investigation registers by the end of the
novel as a mere subplot of subordinate interest to the love affairs between
Berger–Ingeborg and Berger–Frau Else and the increasing focus on
Berger's game, even to Berger's relationship to Conrad, back in Stuttgart,
it builds on another character with resonances to *Werther*, the fictional
popular investigator ("investigador") named Florian Linden, whose detective novel Berger is distractedly reading as *The Third Reich*, the novel,
begins. As Berger's diary of his stay at the hotel Del Mar on the beach near
the Costa Brava recalls *Werther*'s epistolary account of his stay in the
fictional village of Wahlheim, so the detective Florian Linden recalls that
Werther, following his suicide by pistols Lotte has sent him at his request,
is buried under a linden tree, which figures prominently in *Werther*'s
letters.

While effects of the real, of fiction, and of metafiction are interwoven
throughout *The Third Reich*, the question arises as to whether one or the
other of the three terms might be said to have the upper hand, whether one,
in effect, superimposes itself, placing the other two terms under erasure and
surpassing them in importance. Characteristically, Bolaño brings together
references to all three, as in the following passage's invocation of diegetic
and non-diegetic materials: "In my day, if a woman gave me the brush-off,
I would have nothing else to do with her, even if she was Rita Hayworth.
Do you know what these papers mean? Yes, they're copied from war
books ... but I didn't suggest any of this to El Quemado. (I would have
recommended Liddell Hart's *History of the Second World War* ... or
Alexander Werth's *Russia at War*)."[11] While the juxtaposition of such
diverse elements is certainly in some measure a goal, or the whole game,
which Bolaño relishes in and of itself, not only in *The Third Reich* but
throughout his oeuvre as a whole, the novel invites us to consider whether
the outcome of any particular iteration of the game called "novel reading,"
depending perhaps on each reader's genre-orientation, among other fac-
tors, might result in the privileging of one element over another. While
some readers may be drawn, like Ingeborg, to the popular detective fiction
of Florian Linden, whose work Berger disdains for its lack of seriousness,
and thus to the detective story at the heart of *The Third Reich*, others, more
inclined to non-fiction, may prefer the manifestly referential, historical
allusions that receive increasing emphasis as the game between Berger and
El Quemado heats up. Still others may attribute greater value to the
metafictional self-consciousness of Bolaño's intertextual play. Bolaño himself finally might figure, by example, as the reader who encourages readers
to engage on as many different levels as possible, with the greatest possible

diversity of audiences for fiction, such that the desire to be popular (which Berger, writer of specialist articles on the war games he himself plays, disdains in Linden) and the desire to reach even elite, erudite audiences in certain fields (literary criticism, military history) may be seen as continuous with each other rather than mutually exclusive.

As great a love for erudition as Bolaño displays in his consistent shaping of his work as literary history and politics by other means, he owes his remarkable success at least in part to his literal and figurative investment in the detective genre. Heir especially to Poe and Borges in working across a full range of genres in mutually generative relation, he poses consistently the question of the relation between poetry and prose, a question at the heart of the triptych of poet- and poetry-centered novellas he wrote and published in the final four years of the twentieth century: *Distant Star, Amulet,* and *By Night in Chile.* As *Antwerp, Monsieur Pain,* and *The Third Reich* had already begun to make clear between 1980 and 1989, Bolaño understood that such questions of genre were opening increasingly, and unavoidably, onto diverse media, encompassing not only texts but, more broadly, games and screens.[12]

Although poetry figures less centrally in *The Third Reich* than is generally the case in Bolaño's work, it emerges in places to play a pivotal role in the novel's cross-genre, intermedial imaginary, particularly in how it envisions the relation between logic and literature, instrumentality and human fulfillment, gamesmanship and the pursuit of meaning. Where the language and logic of the prose genres on display in the novel—Florian Linden's popular detective fiction; the specialist, meta-prose of Conrad, Berger, and others in their circle; the historiographic works with which Berger hones his skills at playing Third Reich—all share approaches to questions of language and genre that align them with the kinds of linguistic instrumentality Martin Heidegger's "The Question Concerning Technology" argues against. Like Heidegger, the Nazi sympathizer, and despite Berger's insistent claim that he is not himself a Nazi, is in fact "antinazi,"[13] Berger views poetry in a way that conforms to Heidegger's own positioning of it as the discourse of a certain transcendence.[14]

Throughout the novel, most notably in the lines from Goethe quoted earlier as the novel is drawing to its conclusion, poetry appears in its familiar role as the anti-discourse of "games" in general and of war games, and *The Third Reich*—both the game and the novel, and the novel as game in particular.[15] Thus, in a pivotal dialogue early in the novel between Berger and El Quemado:

Ignoro qué impulso me hizo confesarle que pretendía ser escritor. El Quemado . . . dijo que era una profesión interesante . . . .

—Pero no de novelas ni de obras de teatro —aclaré . . .

—¿Qué?

—¿Poeta? . . .

—No, no, por supuesto, poeta no.

Aclaré . . . que yo no despreciaba en modo alguno la poesía. Hubiera podido recitar de memoria versos de Klopstock o de Schiller; pero escribir versos en estos tiempos, como no fueran para la amada, resultaba un tanto inútil, ¿no lo veía él así?

—O grotesco —dijo el pobre infeliz, asintiendo con la cabeza . . . .

—Escritor especializado —dije—. Ensayista creativo.

Acto seguido hice a grandes trazos un panorama del mundo de los *wargames*, con las revistas, las competiciones, los clubes locales, etcétera . . . .

—Es un deporte en alza —afirmé.

El Quemado rumió mis palabras . . .

—Una vez leí algo de gente que juega con soldaditos de plomo —dijo— . . .

—Si . . . Como el rugby y el fútbol americano. Pero a mí los soldaditos de plomo no me interesan demasiado . . . Prefiero los juegos de tablero.

—Tú sobre qué escribes.

—Sobre cualquier cosa. Dame la guerra o la campaña que quieras y yo te diré cómo se puede ganar o perder, qué fallos tiene el juego, en dónde acertó y en dónde se equivocó el diseñador, cuál era el orden de batalla original . . .

I can't remember what made me confess that I wanted to be a writer. El Quemado . . . said that it was an interesting profession . . .

"But not of novels or plays," I explained . . .

"What?

"Poet?" . . .

"No, no, definitely not a poet."

I explained . . . that I in no way scorned poetry; I could have recited from memory lines by Klopstock or Schiller. But to write poetry in this day and age, unless it was for the love object, was a bit pointless, didn't he agree?

"Or grotesque," said the poor wretch, nodding . . .

"Specialized writer," I said. "Creative essayist."

On the spot, I sketched in broad strokes a picture of the world of war games, with all its magazines, competitions, local clubs, etc. . . .

"It's a sport on the rise," I said.

El Quemado mulled over the words . . .

"I did read something about people who play with little lead soldiers," he said . . . .

"Yes . . . Like rugby and American football. But I'm not very interested in lead soldiers . . . I prefer board games."

"What do you write about?"

"Anything. Give me any war or campaign and I'll tell you how it can be won or lost, the flaws of the game, where the designer got it right or wrong, the correct scale, the original order of battle . . ."[16]

In the running analogy the narrative pursues between the world of war games and the literary worlds of poetry and the novel, Great Writers and Great Generals are interchangeable: "If El Quemado had the slightest knowledge or appreciation of twentieth-century German literature (and it's likely that he does!) I'd tell him that Manstein is like . . . Celan. And Paulus is like Trakl, and his predecessor, Reichenau, is like Heinrich Mann. Auderian is the equivalent of Jünger, and Kluge of Böll."[17] As the reference to Celan as well as Grass suggests, Bolaño does not ultimately distinguish between the games of fiction and poetry.[18] While advocates of poetry may want to affirm its value as an anti-instrumentalizing discourse, its social utility inheres, to the limited extent society grants it utility, as both Barthes and Bolaño understand, though Bolaño more cynically, precisely in the oxymoronic, paradoxical attribution of what we may call a use beyond use, its status, in other words, as the discourse that exemplifies the Kantian "purposiveness without purpose" more than any other, what Bolaño calls in *Amberes/Antwerp* "poemas gratuitos, sin ningún valor añadido" ("free poems, no extra tax").[19] The flipside and downside of this logic, however, is figured in the central role Goethe plays in *The Third Reich* as the author of both *The Sorrows of Young Werther,* the key intertext for its knowing participation in a certain genre of prose fiction, and the poem "Selige Sehnsucht," the four quoted lines from which open onto the laconic, potentially devastating judgment, as much Bolaño's as Berger's, of the sentence immediately following: "Todo inútil" ("All for nothing").[20]

The "holy longing" evoked in Goethe's poem, the same longing that results in Werther's suicide in Goethe's novel, is understood by Bolaño to be poetry's particular domain, the domain of Neruda's *Veinte poemas de amor y una canción desesperada* and of poetry generally as invoked in the following passage, where poetry once again arises as a topic of conversation between Berger and Quemado:

—Sigues visitando la biblioteca, Quemado?
—Sí.
—¿Y sólo sacas libros de guerra? . . .
—¿Y qué clase de libros sacabas antes, Quemado?
—Poemas.
—¿Libros de poesía? Qué hermoso. ¿Y qué clase de libros eran ésos?
El Quemado me mira como si estuviera frente a un paleto:

—Vallejo, Neruda, Lorca . . . ¿Los conoces?
—No. ¿Y aprendías los versos de memoria?
—Tengo muy mala memoria.
—¿Pero te acuerdas de algo? ¿Puedes recitarme algo para que me haga
una idea?
—No, sólo recuerdo sensaciones.
—¿Qué tipo de sensaciones? Dime una.
—La desesperación . . .
—¿Ya está ¿Eso es todo?
—La desesperación, la altura, el mar, cosas no cerradas, abiertas de par en
par, como si el pecho te explotara.
—Sí, entiendo. ¿Y desde cuándo has dejado los poemas, Quemado?
¿Desde que empezamos el Tercer Reich? Si lo llego a saber, no juego.
A mí también me gusta mucho la poesía.
    —¿Qué poetas te gustan?
—A mí me gusta Goethe, Quemado.
Y así hasta que llega la hora de marcharse.
"Are you still going to the library, Quemado?"
"Yes."
"And you only borrow books about the war?" . . .
"So what kind of books did you borrow before, Quemado?"
"Poetry."
"Books of poetry? How nice. What kind of poetry?"
El Quemado looks at me as if I'm a bumpkin:
"Vallejo, Neruda, Lorca . . . Do you know them?"
"No. Did you learn the poems by heart?"
"My memory is no good."
    "But you remember something? Can you recite something to give me an
idea?"
"No, I only remember feelings."
"What kind of feelings?" Tell me one."
"Despair . . ."
"Nothing else? That's all?"
"Despair, heights, the sea, things that aren't closed, things that are part-
way open, like something bursting in the chest."
    "Yes, I see. And when did you stop reading poetry, Quemado? When we
started Third Reich? If I'd known, I wouldn't have played. I like poetry too."
"Which poets?"
And so on until it's time to leave.[21]

Equally celebrated, as Bolaño would have liked to have been, for both his
prose and his poetry, Goethe nevertheless figures in *The Third Reich*, in the
aftermath of the historical Third Reich, the utter futility of both. In *The
Third Reich,* war games, as a kind of counterfactual history, or fiction,
nonetheless come down on the side of the victors. Thus, confessing his

ignorance about "what will happen after the fall of Berlin ("—¿Qué sucederá después de la caída de Berlín?" / Confesé mi ignorancia"), and discovering that Frau Else's husband "looked like Don Quixote. A weakened Quixote, ordinary and terrible as Fate" ("El marido de Frau Else ... se parecía al Quijote. Un Quijote postrado, cotidiano y terrible como el Destino"), Berger concludes with the recognition that "The game ends with Decisive Victory, Tactical Victory, Marginal Victory, or Stalemate, not with trials or stupid things like that," that it's "a game of strategy ... of high strategy" ("—El juego termina con Victoria Decisiva, Victoria Táctiva, Victoria Marginal o Empate, no con juicios ni estupideces de ese tipo ... / —Es un juego de estrategia ... de alta estrategia"), and that "After all, Berlin—the one true Berlin—fell some time ago, didn't it?" ("—Total, Berlín, el único y verdadero Berlín, cayó hace tiempo, ¿no?").[22] Whether in verse, or prose, or prose poem novels, the rules of the literary game, like all other games, are determined by those who triumph. As if figuring capitalism's reduction of writers of all literary genres to the role of what have come to be called "cultural workers" and "content providers," Berger returns from his writer's idyll near the Costa Brava to the prosaic condition of an everyday wage laborer, a condition of such diminished value as to make it impossible for Berger to persuade himself after all that literature offers the form of escape, of rescue, of transcendence and redemption from adolescent boredom he had hoped the combination of love and writing would allow him to leave behind: "Have I come up in the world too? Absolutely. Back then I hadn't met Ingeborg and today we're a couple; my friendships are more interesting and deeper ... I'm financially independent; I'm never bored now ... I don't think it's an exaggeration to say that my life has never been better. / Most of the credit goes to Ingeborg. Meeting her was the best thing that ever happened to me."[23]

While love and writing appear aligned in these pages from the novel's opening chapter, the tension between them that plays itself out in Berger's self-absorbed, ever-increasing obsession with writing and/as gaming reaches its conclusion in the novel's final, disillusioning chapter, "El Congreso" ("The Convention"), where Rex Douglas's triumph at the gaming conference in Paris coincides with Berger's ultimate defeat and fall back into obscurity, a fate that eventually drives a wedge between the lovers. From the more mature, if more cynical, perspective of Bolaño's authorial perspective at the age of thirty-six, the most hopeful aspect of the novel's conclusion lies in what does not happen, in the fact that unlike Werther, Berger does not surrender to (poetic) despair and commit suicide when his affair with Ingeborg ends. Instead, in the third of eight individually titled prose poems at the novel's conclusion—the same recourse to the form of the prose poem that concludes *Monsieur Pain*—the relationship between the two former lovers turns from tragic to comic. Though devoid of a lover's passion, their reconciliation arrives nonetheless at a kind of lover's discourse that the oxymoronic, hybrid form of the prose poem—neither instrumentalizing prose nor "useless" poetry—figures and represents. Concluding formally in a way that resembles neither the novel form of *Werther* nor the poetry as verse of "The Holy Longing," and with Berger's sadder but wiser farewell to *The Third Reich*, both the game and the novel, Bolaño offers the reader the hope of embracing ambivalence, of an acceptance of being, as the title of his posthumously published *Entre paréntesis* (*Between Parentheses*) suggests, in-between.[24]

While the accommodations Bolaño makes in *The Third Reich* to more familiar, popular, marketable modes of novelistic narration place it in these respects among the least experimental, more conventional of his works, its rendering of convergent regimes of the aesthetic and political merits the reader's full attention. The central questions it raises through its rewriting of *Werther* about the legacies of German romanticism—questions Bolaño will take up again extensively in the German context of Part V of *2666*—echo in the instrumentalizing reproduction, circulation, and distribution of ready-made commercial genres of all kinds that increasingly organize and shape aesthetic experience according to familiar marketing niches across all media. In its resistance to, but also complicity with, the futility of novelistic gamesmanship, the literary, intermedial game *The Third Reich* both embraces and contests an instrumentalizing, commodifying aesthetics. Betting against the writer's cardinal sin of boredom, Bolaño's work continually risks an over-production of fiction, of counterfactuals, which he understands have little chance of resulting in the outcome "loser wins"—as in a literary history not written by and for the victors—though that hope may be said to drive his work continually, even relentlessly.[25]

In the end, in *The Third Reich*, as Germany loses again to the Allies, and Berger to El Quemado, the novel suggests, in Berger's disaffected return from the wargames conference in Paris, that literature may prove little more than an affair of insider trading for the production of a few evanescent, and some more enduring, stars, like Rex Douglas, the gamer's Goethe or now even, in the industry that has grown up after his death, with a consummate irony he would be the first to recognize and acknowledge, Bolaño himself. For every Douglas, every Goethe, the novel suggests, billions of Bergers—and *Bürger*, citizens—slave away at monotonous, low-paying, routinized wage labor. To the question of what literature could possibly be for, of what use it might be in the face of such personal, individual catastrophes as the loss of a great love, or a love unrequited, or the horrors of World War II, *The Third Reich* offers its sobering answer: not much, maybe nothing, but a sharpened awareness, perhaps of difficult questions, a sense of complicity, even futility, of tedium and ennui, but also of compassion and the shared struggle to make sense of it all that is every writer's and reader's challenge. In the end, at least, in the two final, disillusioned pages of "El Congreso," the last of the eight succinct, individually titled prose poems with which *The Third Reich* concludes, we have not Werther, not Emma, but Berger and Ingeborg, accepting that the end of the affair (anticipating the "relief" ["alivio"], near the end of *2666*, of giving up literature) doesn't have to be a catastrophe, that love in any genre, in poems, in novels, in prose poem novels, doesn't have to be a zero-sum game, that it can sometimes yield to friendship, as tragedy to comedy, Werther's sorrows to Berger's laughter, the anticipatory laughter of a Blochian "Noch-Nicht" ("not-yet") that may be literature's most utopian gift of all. The rest is history.[26]

Part Two

CHAPTER 4

Poetry at the Ends of Its Lines
The Unknown University (La Universidad Desconocida)
Nazi Literature in the Americas (La literatura
nazi en América)

Poetry's lineages are multiple. In this sense poetry, which has no singular, single identity *an sich,* may be said not to exist, or to exist only in its varied, often conflicting, ever-changing forms. Typically offered as mere description, theories of poetry and poetics, as of literature and the arts generally, tend to open, implicitly if not explicitly, onto programmatic prescription. The proofs are, quite literally, in the poems. Selection and combination, description and prescription, narratives and norms, canonical or avantgarde, conservative or experimental, in Raymond Williams' terms residual, dominant, or emergent, emerge as inseparable. To take several of the past century's most enduringly synecdochic examples of critical commentary and theoretical reflection on poetry and poetics, where Benjamin's privileged examples among poets are Baudelaire and Brecht, Roman Jakobson's "Linguistics and Poetics" is drawn to Valéry, Hopkins, and Poe (his poetry, not his fiction), Adorno's "Lyric Poetry and Society" to Mörike and George. However rich and full of implication their explanatory power, their capacity to account for what has already occurred and what is currently within view, all theories of poetry, of fiction, of literature, of the arts, have their histories, as well as their unknowable futures. Bound by what Rancière might say the past and present have not yet made visible, their ability to police, much less to prescribe what will happen next remains at best partial, provisional, we might also say fortunately, happily, incomplete, in the process of becoming historical.[1]

The multiple births and deaths of poetry, its ceaseless renewals and declines, are not singular events. They occur and always have, as Bolaño knew and helped make visible, all the time. Every line, every poem, is both a death and a new beginning. One step, (in)finitely (in)divisible, a *longue durée,* a journey, into what Bolaño calls, in the title of his posthumously published collected poems, *La Universidad Desconocida* (*The Unknown University*).[2] That, for Bolaño, is poetry. And has nothing necessarily to do, though it might yet still, and always, have something to do, with what are called lines, that is to say with enjambment, as the synecdochic, proto-typical poet's apprentice Juan García-Madero knew, in *The Savage Detectives*—the novel of poetic apprenticeship that had the consummate irony of establishing Bolaño, after all his years of aspiring to be recognized for his poetry, more as a novelist than as a poet—even as he found his way through to seeing poetry otherwise, as Bolaño puts it only a year later in his other novel of poetic apprenticeship in Mexico City, *Amuleto* (*Amulet*), "de otra manera" ("by other means," "in another form").[3]

In the dozen categories that make up the fantastical literary-historical taxonomy that is Bolaño's *La literatura nazi en América* (*Nazi Literature in the Americas*), Bolaño offers a structure for a book that is, like *Antwerp*, not a novel in any traditional sense, but a collection of meta-short-story prose poems or meta-prose-poem short stories reflecting the static political state of exception of Latin America under Pinochet and other right-wing dictatorships of the 1970s through the early 1990s, concluding with the aerialist poet Carlos Ramírez Hoffman, who becomes in *Distant Star* that figure of historical staticity and repetition, of the eternal recurrence of the same fascist nightmare, Carlos Wieder, a figure Bolaño works through at once aesthetically and politically to the other side of 1989 and the Pinochet regime.[4] Where poetry, including the prose poem, in *Nazi Literature*, finds itself in Chile, Argentina, and elsewhere in Latin America enacting and emplotting with sardonic playfulness the holding pattern of Latin American dictatorships, in *Distant Star*, through the figure of Carlos Ramírez Hoffman, transfigured as Carlos Wieder, Bolaño figures the prose poem's transformation into a fully realized novel that suggests, in the form of its content and the content of its form, as both history and literary history by other means, what Fredric Jameson called in *The Political Unconscious* "imaginary solutions to real problems."[5]

The Unknown University represents at least the belated possibility, previously unrealized during his lifetime, that Bolaño, an author best known as a novelist, may at last garner some greater measure of recognition as a poet, not only as a writer fully invested in poetry who wrote auto-biographically inflected novels in which so many of the protagonists, as well other characters, are poets and/or poet-critics, and in which poetry is central, but also as an author who himself wrote poetry. The collected poems assembled in *The Unknown University* were in this sense a long time coming for a novelist for whom it might be said that nothing is of greater concern than the fate of poets and of poetry. The long delay in publishing the collected poems assembled in *The Unknown University* raises several vexing questions: Why did it take so long? Now that we have them, what do we make of them? Given the pervasive interest in modern and contemporary poetry manifest in Bolaño's fiction, and in his novels in particular, and the extent to which it offers a kind of literary history by other means, including a richly parodic interest in systems of literary classification and literary-critical taxonomies, how should we understand Bolaño's efforts and contributions as a poet? How should we situate his own poetry? In relation to which poets, movements, schools, styles, and conceptual, theoretical, philosophical orientations, which aesthetic and political ideologies, does he position himself, and how, to what ends? What is the relation, in short, between the poetry and poetics Bolaño explores in his fiction—his novels in particular—and his own poetic practice? What relation does that practice have to what he calls in *The Savage Detectives* "poem-novels" in prose, or prose poem novels?

In addressing these questions, it is helpful to situate the chronological history of Bolaño's poetry publications in relation to the novels that would eventually prove the primary source of his growing reputation. As Carolina López notes in her "Breve historia del libro" ("Brief history of the book") at the conclusion of *The Unknown University*: "Around 1993, Roberto set about organizing and classifying his poetry. A few months earlier, they had diagnosed his illness. Lautaro was only two. The manuscript entitled *The Unknown University* dates to this period and was the origin for the book published here."[6] Traced by López to the same year, 1993, as Bolaño's first collection of short stories, *La pista de hielo* (*The Skating Rink*), the manuscript that was "the origin for the book published" under the same name, only posthumously, twenty-four years later, is composed with only a few exceptions of poems written in the first fifteen years of Bolaño's only marginally successful efforts to establish a career for himself as a writer.[7]

The manuscript Bolaño began assembling in 1993 published posthumously by Anagrama in 2007 as *The Unknown University* thus marks a pivotal moment in his career. In its turning away from the writing of poetry in the more conventional sense and toward the intensive, sustained, still poet- and poetry-centered focus on the writing of poem-novels in prose that would dominate the final decade of his writing life, Bolaño's career bears an uncanny resemblance, in its roughly fifty-year time frame and change of trajectory, to that of Baudelaire, with its similar turn from poetry in and as verse to poetry in and as prose, from the verse poems of *Les Fleurs du Mal* (at 36, in 1857) to the prose poems of *Le Spleen de Paris* (through his death in 1867, at 46). Yet where Baudelaire's late turn from verse to prose remained in the realm of condensation, to the prose poem defined as "petit," Bolaño's most consequential late turn proved to be not to the prose of the short story, for all his achievements in that genre, but to the prose-poem-inflected architectures of his poet- and poetry-centered poem-novels in prose (144). In what retrospectively was a watershed moment that brought closure to his lifelong aspirations to gain recognition primarily as a poet, the assemblage of verse and prose poems brought together under the title *Fragmentos de la Universidad Desconocida* (Fragments of The Unknown University) in 1993, the year of his first short-story collection, signals a shift in the direction of prose that would prove almost unimaginably generative over the course of his final decade, bringing him the literary recognition and celebrity he had come to understand were far less likely to come to a writer of poetry than to a writer of prose, particularly novels.

By 1993, when Bolaño "set about organizing and classifying his poetry," a period during which, as López remarks "A few months earlier, they had diagnosed his illness" and "Lautaro was only two," the relative paucity of recognition, rewards, and remuneration for his proven dedication to the writing and publishing of poetry had become unmistakable. While Bolaño was chosen in 1992 and 1994, respectively, in López's words, "as winner of several prizes" for poems eventually published in *The Unknown University*, specifically the "Rafael Morales Prize, Talavera de la Reina, 1992, with 'Fragments of the Unknown University'" and the "City of Irún Literary Prize, 1994, with 'The Romantic Dogs,'"[8] and while the section of *The Unknown University* called "People Walking Away" ("Gente que se aleja") had already been published "with small variations, as *Antwerp* by Anagrama in 2002," by 1993 Bolaño clearly perceived that his career as a poet, for all his love of poetry, was not likely to yield the results he had hoped for either in realizing his literary ambitions or in his ability to provide financially for himself and his young son.[9]

It is fitting in this sense that López's introductory "Note from the author's heirs" begins with Bolaño's retrospective "Mi Carrera Literaria" ("My Literary Career*")—"October 1990"* / ("Unpublished poem from a notebook that contains some of the poems found in *The Unknown University*")—and its list of "Rechazos de Anagrama, Grijalbo, Planeta [. . .] de Alfaguara, / Mondadori. Un no de Muchnik, Seix Barral, Destino . . . Todas las editoriales" ("Rejections from Anagrama, Grijalbo, Planeta . . . from Alfaguara, / Mondadori. A no from Muchnik, Seix Barral, Destino . . . All the publishers"), its first-person self-description as "Escribiendo poesía en el país de los imbéciles / . . . pero escribiendo" ("Writing poetry in the land of idiots . . . / but writing").[10] While Bolaño's "organizing and classifying" of his poems has yielded a three-part structure that proceeds loosely, though not exclusively, in the chronological order of the poems' composition, the first, relatively late poem López provides as an entry point for *The Unknown University* opens onto one of a handful of kinds of poems that tend to occur throughout the collected poems most frequently. Applying to Bolaño's own poetic practice, beyond the book's division into three untitled parts of roughly equal length, the classificatory impulses on display at the beginning of his posthumously published *Woes of the True Policeman*, begun in the late 1980s, the decade of his primary investment in writing poetry in and as verse, in Juan Padilla's queer poetic taxonomy, and later in Óscar Amalfitano's satirical "Notas de una clase de literatura contemporánea: El papel del poeta" ("*Notes from a Class in Contemporary Literature: The Role of the Poet*"), we might identify five major types of poems distributed throughout *The Unknown University*: 1) *meta-poems in verse*—by far the most common, predominantly autobiographical, along the lines of "Mi carrera literaria," bearing on Bolaño's poetic ambitions, including what Amalfitano calls, in a clear gesture of pedagogical parody, "the role of the poet," and engaging specifically with questions concerning what poetry is, what it means to write it; 2) *autobiographical verse poems*—the next most common, in which meta-poetic references are either altogether absent, minimal, and/or subordinated to more "personal" matters; 3) *detective-genre poems in verse*—often with an intermedial frame of reference, far less common than types 1 and 2, in fact far less common than readers of Bolaño's prose might expect, yet clearly of special importance for his fiction; 4) *intermedial verse poems*—poems in which images of visual media, especially cinema, television, and screens of various kinds, figure prominently; and finally, out of sequence in terms of their pivotal placement at the heart of the tripartite division of the collected poems, 5) *prose poems*—comparable in importance to 1 and 2, typically both the most thoroughly meta-poetic as well as, in their frames of reference, the most thoroughly intermedial of the poems of *The Unknown University* in its entirety.[11]

Reflecting Bolaño's gradually dwindling investment by the end of the 1980s and early 1990s in cultivating a literary identity for himself as a poet—or more specifically as a writer of poetry narrowly conceived of as reducible to verse—the distribution of the 312 poems collected in *The Unknown University* decreases across its three parts from 136, to 102, to 74, respectively. While not adhering to a strict chronology of dates of composition, Part III both foreshadows and announces as well, in its 74 poems, all in verse the impending shift henceforth in Bolaño's literary investments from poetry in and as verse to poetry in and as prose with a pronounced interest in detective fiction. Resuming in effect of the combination already present over a decade earlier *in nuce* in *Antwerp*, the apprentice prose poem detective novel that resurfaces in its entirety, in López's words, "with small variations," in Part II, at the very heart of *The Unknown University*—Bolaño underscores its pivotal importance to his imaginary, both literally and figuratively, under the title "People Walking Away."[12]

While the structural arc of *The Unknown University* thus suggests a circular movement from verse to prose and back to verse, the conceptual arc moves from the first part's manifest early embrace of poetry as verse by Bolaño, the aspiring young poet, through the second part's questioning and dismantling of that investment in Bolaño's turn to poetry in prose, to the third part's parting resumption of a commitment to poetry as verse in the mode of a nostalgic yet determined farewell. Where Parts I and III figure Bolaño's early commitment to and eventual, more mature, "turning [or "walking"] away" from, poetry *as* verse exclusively *in* verse, the pivotal and decisive Part II—the part that anticipates and prepares the way most consequentially, at once formally and conceptually, for Bolaño's extraordinarily productive decade ahead—figures a near total domination of poetry in prose. Of the five titled sections that make up Part II, the first, second, and fourth are composed entirely of prose poems. Comprised of only three short poems totaling a mere four pages, only Part II's tellingly titled third section, "Iceberg," is exclusively in verse. Like the first, second, and fourth sections, the fifth and final, 34-page section of Part II, "Manifiestos y posiciones" ("Manifestos and Positions"), is entirely in prose apart from three verse poems on contemporary poetry in Latin America, totaling a mere four pages, "La poesía chilena es un gas" ("Chilean Poetry Is a Gas"), "Horda" ("Horde"), and "La poesía latinoamericana" ("Latin American Poetry"), all of which preface the parodically titled text that follows with an ill-humored, lacerating irony.[13]

Following quite logically on the argument with and farewell to poetry as verse that is *The Unknown University*, Bolaño published the condensed prose-poetic fiction of *Nazi Literature*, his first book since assembling the collected poems in and around 1993 (which remained unpublished until four years after his death), only three years later, in what would prove to be the breakthrough year of his career, 1996, along with what is arguably his first fully realized novel, *Distant Star,* a companion text to *Nazi Literature* that is also in fundamental respects, developmentally, narratologically, already its sequel. A true collection precisely to the extent that it knowingly lacks or suppresses the novel's expected narrative drive, remaining reso- lutely static, it stages and bears witness to the aesthetic and political aporias of Latin America in the 1970s and 1980s, the formative years of Bolaño's nascent literary career.[14] Its texts stand accordingly not, as the vast majority of Bolaño's later, most impactful and consequential work will, at the intersection of poetry, or more specifically of the prose poem, and the novel, but of the prose poem and the short story, an intersection that allows readers, in the spirit of Baudelaire's preface to *Le Spleen de Paris*, to "cut wherever we please," a mode of reading aligned with Baudelaire's dedica- tion to Arsène Houssaye of his book as what he calls "le serpent tout entier" ("the whole serpent"), in this case precisely, in Bolaño's corresponding, historically reconfigured gesture, the book called *Nazi Literature in the Americas*.[15]

In 1996, only three years after what López describes as "years of work and struggle, but above all years of work" failed to result, as they would for the remainder of Bolaño's life, in publication of the collected poems of *The Unknown University*, the publication of the condensed, prose-poetic fic- tion of *Nazi Literature* and the novel *Distant Star* set Bolaño's career on a path that would not so much leave poetry behind as carry it forward by incorporating it as the central preoccupation of his prose fiction, particu- larly of his novels, through the astonishingly productive final decade of his life.[16] As always for Bolaño, questions of form and structure, no less important in the collected poems than in his prose fiction, are indispen- sable and informing. Much of the force of *Nazi Literature* inheres in its classificatory form and structure, an approach to such questions that takes on the most powerful significance in light of the Nazi fetishization of purity and classificatory systems that led to the systematic annihilation of others judged racially, sexually, ideologically, and otherwise inferior and impure. Figuring in the first years after the fall of the Berlin Wall the collapse of the Latin American dictatorships of the 1970s and 1980s, *Nazi Literature* offers both in the form of its content and in the content of its form not so much imaginary solutions to real problems as a knowingly static representation of aporetic conditions at once literary and historical, aesthetic and ideological, that seemed in the years leading up to the end of the Cold War to have no exit.

Described as having most likely launched his career "in 1970 or 1971, when Salvador Allende was president of Chile," the protagonist "Carlos Ramírez Hoffman / Santiago de Chile, 1950—Lloret de Mar, Spain, 1998" unlocks the door to Bolaño's return to his early years in Chile before moving with his family to Mexico at the age of fifteen, his brief return and incarceration in the early days of the Pinochet regime, and the focus on poetic apprenticeships, that would become such a defining feature of his prose poem novels, most notably in what amounts to a tetralogy of prose poem novels of poetic apprenticeship published between 1996 and 2000.[17] Still calling himself "Emilio Stevens" (suggesting a Latin American Wallace Stevens), Ramírez Hoffman is first introduced as attending "the writing workshop run by Juan Cherniakovski," precursor of the figure "Juan Stein" in *Distant Star*.[18] Soon developing into an avant-garde poet whose "first poetic act" is observed from "the La Peña detention center" by a prisoner "called Norberto, who was going mad," when the plane Ramírez Hoffman is piloting begins writing "a poem in the sky," Ramírez Hoffman is the fictional protagonist through whom Bolaño returns to the Chilean context of his own brief incarceration, on his brief return from Mexico, and the poetic and political choices apprentice poets faced in Chile, Mexico, and elsewhere in Latin America in the years leading up to and after the coup.[19]

Recalling the schematic poetic choices represented by the workshops of Cherniakovski and García in its closing long-short-story/short-novella, "The Infamous Ramírez Hoffman" (as of Stein and Soto *in Distant Star*), *Nazi Literature* organizes the portraits of its thirty invented authors—all of whom, apart from "Carlos Ramírez Hoffman," range from prose-poem to condensed short-story length—into a baker's dozen of categories. Limited to portraits of only one (two categories), two (seven categories), three (two categories), or four (two categories) authors each, the taxonomic structure of *Nazi Literature of the Americas* resists easy classification. Framing the book's twelve organizing categories—excluding the anomalously lengthy "Carlos Ramírez Hoffman"—"The Mendiluce Clan" and "The Fabulous Schiaffino Boys" organize their five authors clearly enough in terms of kinship structures, an approach shared more figuratively with the eleventh category, "The Aryan Brotherhood," which has only one member, "Thomas R. Murchison." Significantly, the literal kinship structures in both cases figure a competition between genres that manifests itself in the form of sibling rivalry. Fighting, and winning his fight, with his sister poet, Luz, "over control of the family magazine, Juan Mendiluce is a novelist who goes on to "crusade against the lack of feeling in the contemporary novel . . . francophilia, the cult of violence, atheism and foreign ideas," denouncing the stories of " Cortázar . . . and Borges" (so central for Bolaño) as "parodies of parodies."[20] Where Juan Mendiluce is a novelist and his sister, Luz, is a poet, and where Italo Schiaffino is a poet, his brother Argentino (who moves from Argentina to the United States) is a novelist. Suggesting the containment of poetry by and in the novel that will prove to be Bolaño's path over the last decade of his life and career, the chiasmus of the first and twelfth texts with respect to genre figures the complex negotiations between the aesthetic and the political that are at the heart of *Nazi Literature* and Bolaño's work as a whole.

Of the remaining ten categories, three are organized explicitly around affiliation by genre, the fifth and tenth devoted to two poets each from Latin America and the United States, respectively, "*Poètes Maudits*" and "North American Poets," and the seventh, mid-way between, to three novelists, the Americans "J.M.S. Hill" and "Zach Sodenstern" and the Guatemalan-American "Gustavo Borda," under the category of "Speculative and Science Fiction." Of the remaining six categories, the second, "Itinerant Heroes or the Fragility of Mirrors"; fifth, "Wandering Women of Letters"; and sixth, "Two Germans at the Ends of the Earth," all figure conditions of exile and geographical displacement, conditions of obvious resonance for Bolaño (as in "Itinerant Heroes and the Fragility of Mirrors"), placed both literally and figuratively at the heart of the book's structure. More difficult to cluster around a single classificatory concept or methodology, the remaining three categories—"Forerunners and Figures of the Anti-Enlightenment," "Magicians, Mercenaries and Miserable Creatures," and "The Many Masks of Max Mirebalais"—the third, eighth, and ninth, respectively, focus on authors associated with temporal-historical as well as ideological-philosophical positioning and affiliation—including what we might call after Horkheimer and Adorno a dialectic of anti-enlightenment ("Precursos y antiilustrados," in the original)—with truth, illusion, in this case including the play of alliteration, misery, and what might be considered marginal occupations; and with fictive illusion and the production of multiple identities ("The Many Masks of Max Mirebalais").[21]

Underlying these overlapping yet irreducibly diverse categories of subordinate classification are two dominant categories that link all thirty imaginary authors together, the ideological affiliation of being a Nazi and the geographical, geopolitical affiliation of being from one or another of the Americas. Of the seventeen countries with which the thirty authors portrayed have a primary or significant identification, whether through birth, travel, or immigration, twelve are in the Americas (Argentina, Brazil, Chile, Colombia, Cuba, Guatemala, Haiti, Mexico, Peru, Uruguay, Venezuela, and the United States), five are in Europe (France, Italy, Germany, and Spain), and one is in Africa (Uganda). Of these, by far the most are associated with Argentina (8), Germany (7), and the United States

(9). The remaining countries are associated with only one (Cuba, France, Guatemala, Haiti, Mexico, Peru, Uganda, Uruguay), two (Brazil, Colombia, Spain, Venezuela), or three authors (Chile). (Not included are the dozens of imaginary authors, publications, and publication venues mentioned briefly in the thirty-one-page "Epilogue for Monsters," which is composed of "1. Secondary Figures"; "2. Publishing Houses, Magazines, Places"; and "3. Books"). With birth and death dates for its thirty imaginary authors ranging both as far back as 1880 and as far forward as 2021, *Nazi Literature* spans a time frame at once historical and literary-historical that suggests the tenacity, if not intractability and ineradicability, of a Nazi ideology, imported from Europe, that has continued to shape and inform the aesthetics and politics of the Americas for a period envisioned as encompassing roughly an entire century and a half of modern and contemporary literature across all genres, including both poetry and the novel.

Of the thirty authors represented, concluding with the avant-garde sky-writing poet Ramírez Hoffman, roughly two-thirds are exclusively or primarily identified as poets. While a handful of the authors identified primarily with poetry—"Ignacio Zubieta," "Jesús Fernández-Gómez," "Pedro González Carrera," "Franz Zwickau," "Thomas R. Murchison," whose "narrative poetry" he calls "broken novels" ("novelas quebradas")[22] —are attributed with writing at least one (usually short) novel, the remaining ten—excluding the Brazilian writer of massive, and massively unread, philosophical critiques, Luiz Fontaine Da Souza—are primarily if not exclusively identified with the writing of novels. The structuring genre dynamic of *Nazi Literature*, developed both formally, in the book's dominant prose-poetic form, and conceptually, in a hierarchical distribution between the two major genres that has poets outnumbering novelists by two to one, stages anew Baudelaire's fundamental insight that poetry's principal literary rival would not prove to be the short story, in the manner of Poe, of which the prose poems of *Le Spleen de Paris* offer a calculated condensation, but the novel, the increasingly popular, increasingly hegemonic literary form in relation to which Baudelaire understood all poetry would in future be measured.

But again what, for Bolaño, is poetry? In *Nazi Literature*, most crucial to observe in responding to this question is the virtually total indifference it displays to any particular poetics as a determining criterion of poetic value.[23] The gallery of imaginary poets and novelists assembled in *Nazi Literature* thus throws into question claims for a coherent, much less intrinsic (not necessarily situational) relation between poetics and ideology, aesthetics and politics.[24] From a perspective at once historical and literary-historical, aesthetic and political, an aspiring writer's interpellation into poetry, or the novel, or both, or neither, carries within it the risk of inconsequence, as Bolaño knew better than anyone, never more pressingly or with greater certainty, as he came to see clearly in the 1990s, than in the emerging post-Gutenberg era, the age of digital media. In relation to which, Bolaño's investments in poetry, in the novel, no less than those of the "Monsters" of *Nazi Literature*, as he knew very well, remain decidedly old school. In the devil's quadrangle of *Nazi Literature in Americas* dominated by authors associated primarily with Argentina, Chile, Germany, and the United States, the fear inscribed on every page is that attempts to differentiate and align aesthetic, ideological, and political choices may matter little or not at all. Author of "*The New Spring*," a book described as "Part travel narrative, part philosophical memoir … that reflected on the state of the world, and the destinies of Europe and America in particular, while warning of the threat … Communism posed to Christian civilization," the tone-setting Argentinian Nazi and literary matriarch "Edelmira Thompson de Mendiluce"—married to a German philosopher from whom she takes her last name, "mendacious-light"— who felt, like Baudelaire before her, "that she had found a soul mate in Poe," thus finds inspiration in the radical, prose-poetic hybridity of a text like Poe's "The Philosophy of Furniture" for "her finest work, *Poe's Room* (1944), which prefigured the *nouveau roman* and subsequent avant-garde writing, and earned the widow Mendiluce an eminent place in the panorama of Argentinean and Hispanic letters."[25] In a similarly antigeneric, genre-resistant, genre-defying mode, in the context of poetry scenes specific to the United States, "Rory Long," one of the two "North American Poets," writes "letters, plays, songs, television scripts and movie screenplays, unfinished novels, stories, animal fables, comic-strip plots, biographies, economic and religious pamphlets, and above all poetry, in which he blended all the foregoing genres," trying to be "impersonal … experimented with oral poetry" and ultimately putting "[Charles] Olson and his father, but not poetry, behind" to publish "a successful collection of short stories, poems, and 'thoughts' entitled *Noah's Ark*)," devoting himself thereafter to "spreading his message in the Southwest" until "one midday in March 2017, when a young African-American man named Baldwin Rocha blew his head off."[26]

Whether purifying or hybridizing the "language of the tribe," adopting conservative or experimental styles and strategies, or both, Bolaño's gallery of invented authors suggests—like so many of its Borgesian interexts, among them *Historia universal de la infamia* (1935), *Historia de la eternidad*

(1936), "Deutsches Requiem" (1949), and *El Aleph* (1949)—the becoming historical of any and all (and not only or exclusively Nazi) aesthetic, ideological, and political perspectives and positions, the sobering implication that each finds its way sooner or later to oblivion in the strictest, most irreducible sense, regardless of approach, methodology, system, or style.[27] Yet the questions at hand, in a fundamentally historical as well as literary-historical sense, arguably the most pervasive questions throughout Bolaño's oeuvre, remain: If all styles, all systems, are "frauds," what is the truth, and enduring value, of what is called poetry, as of novels, as of literature? What do these terms include and exclude? How are they to be defined, and with what implications and consequences? If all styles are frauds, what is not style, not fraud?

While each of Bolaño's works approaches and responds to these fundamental questions in its own way, the parodic yet serious, prose-poetic taxonomic classifications of *Nazi Literature* reframe the arc of *The Unknown University* and its dominant dialectical (or parodically dialectical, or negative- or anti-dialectical) progression (or should we say merely movement) from verse to prose and back to verse in terms at once stylistic, ideological, and geopolitical, terms that open the predominantly autobiographical focus of the collected poems onto larger historical and literary-historical frames. Responding to, and no doubt inspired by, the changed historical and literary-historical situation created by the fall of the Berlin Wall and the beginning of the end of the Pinochet regime in 1989–1990, *Nazi Literature* and *Distant Star* represent a decisive advance in Bolaño's work, not only in his commitment to honoring and pursuing his love of poetry in prose, but to a recognition of the extent to which poetry, understood not only as verse but as autobiographical verse, has profound aesthetic ideological consequences in its potential to constrain individual authors from engaging with larger historical, economic, and geopolitical, as well as more narrowly literary-historical, forces.

Having begun his collected poems with an epigraph from Baudelaire's "Sonnet pour s'excuser de ne pas accompagner un ami à Namur" that speaks to his own lack of recognition as a poet, followed by an opening section of verse poems tellingly titled "The Snow-Novel," Bolaño reprises and updates, through Part II's reconfiguring of the prose poem novel *Antwerp* as the (now titled but unnumbered) prose poem sequence "People Walking Away" and its other prose-poetic texts—"Tres textos" ("Three Texts"), "Nel, majo" ("Fat Chance, Hon"), "El inspector" ("The Inspector"), "El testigo" ("The Witness"), "Prosa del otoño en Gerona" ("Prose from Autumn in Gerona"), and "Manifiesto mexicano" ("Mexican Manifesto")—the transformative gesture of the prose poems of *Le Spleen de Paris* as a way to move through and beyond the impasses and limitations of contemporary Latin American poetry and of contemporary poetry more generally.[28] Echoing in that context, in "Chilean Poetry is a Gas," "Horde," and "Latin American Poetry," Baudelaire's equally splenetic, disillusioned attacks on the poetry of his own period, attacks from which Baudelaire, like Bolaño, did not exempt himself, the three final verse poems of Part II offer in effect a final leveling and dismissal of contemporary scenes of poetry as verse, to which the whole of *The Unknown University* is bidding farewell.[29] Moving from the predominantly autobiographical, meta-poetic poems of Part I, all of which are in verse, to the more impersonal, experimental poems of Part II, all but nine pages of which are in prose, and returning, finally, in an increasingly nostalgic, elegiac mode, to the autobiographical farewell-to-verse poems of Part III, Bolaño stages a dialectic of verse and prose poetry in which the former registers as authentic, not fraudulent, precisely to the extent that it remains invested in, subject to, constrained by, the association of poetry as verse with first-person, autobiographical utterance, an association the prose poems of Part II call into question and dismantle, from their position quite literally at the book's core, looking both forward and back. Together with the handful of detective-genre verse poems in Part III that they effectively reframe in advance as prose, the "Three Texts" with which Part II begins both resume and prepare the way for Bolaño's decisive turn from poetry in and as verse to poetry in and as prose. Saying in effect to the former, in the words of the title of the first of the three texts, "Fat Chance, Hon," Bolaño announces in the second and third of the "Tres textos" ("Three Texts"), "El inspector" ("The Inspector"), and "El testigo" ("The Witness"), a resumption of his work at the intersection of the prose poem and the detective novel, already on display from the beginning in *Antwerp*, which would continue to evolve over the course of his final decade as the signature achievement of his career.[30]

As the beginning of Part One suggests in its movement from the epigraph by Baudelaire figuring a lack of recognition for poetry as verse to the first section called "The Snow-Novel" (all of the poems of which will prove nonetheless to be in verse), Bolaño understands with Baudelaire that where the short story, in the manner of Poe, may be considered, especially in the more condensed form of the prose poem, as aligned with poetry, by virtue of their shared emphasis on intensity and unity of effect, poetry's true competition in the literary marketplace is not fiction in general but the novel—precisely because of the capaciousness its sustained length allows. It is the novel, not the short story, that is increasingly, from the mid-nineteenth to the end of the twentieth century, poetry's principal literary rival. It is the novel, as Bolaño's understands Baudelaire was the first to articulate, in his preface to *Le Spleen de Paris*, with which poetry must engage to survive, an imperative that novelists, including Bolaño, know is not reciprocal and does not work in reverse.

Poetry in verse, too, had always been about more, for Bolaño, than the merely personal, always about a desire to be in some sense representative, to speak for and about his generation, as he writes in "Autorretrato a los veinte años" ("Self-Portrait at Twenty Years"), for the "thousands of guys like me, baby-faced, / or bearded, but Latin American, / all of us, / brushing cheeks with Death"[31]—even as he wants to lay claim to that distinctive authorial voice that is not a style but a direct presentation of an authentic self so often conceived, especially since the Romantic period, as the essence of poetry. As his first-person speaker suggests in the fourth poem of Part I, symptomatically titled "Ésta es la pura verdad" ("This Is the Honest Truth"), such a conception of poetry risks reducing literary ambition to sentimental self-absorption, complex historical questions to solipsistic self-congratulation. Embracing a poetics of guilelessness, of "straightforward" utterance that extends beyond himself to others, he writes, in "Las pelucas de Barcelona" ("The Wigs of Barcelona"): "Sólo deseo escribir sobre las mujeres / de las pensiones del Distrito 5 / de una manera real y amable y honesta" ("I'd just like to write about the women / of the District 5 boarding houses / in a way that's real and kind and honest ...").[32] Yet as the "Wigs" of the title suggests, guile, artifice, style, as the "Many Masks of Max Mirebalais" also attests, is everywhere, unavoidable. His first poems "copied from Aimé Césaire" having met "with a rather negative reception from certain intellectuals in Port-au-Prince, who openly mocked the young poet," the aspiring Haitian poet Mirebalais thus demonstrates in his "next exercises in plagiarism ... this time the poet imitated was René Depestre."[33] Figuring the extent to which an identity poetics and politics are bound up with questions of style, Mirebalais's subsequent "years of poetic labor" see his works and noms-de-plume multiply in strikingly self-canceling, contradictory ways—"(von Hauptman the bard of the Aryan race, a fanatical mulatto Nazi; Le Gueule the model of the practical man, Mirebalais the lyrical poet, the patriot, calling forth the shades of Toussaint L'Ouverture, Dessalines and Christophe, while Kasimir celebrated négritude, the landscapes of the fatherland and mother Africa, and the rhythm of the tam-tams)."[34] Perceiving "Literature, as it had been conceived in the nineteenth century" as having "ceased to be relevant to the public," and observing that "Poetry was dying. The novel wasn't, but he didn't know how to write novels" ("La literatura, en su soporte decimonónico, ya no interesaba a la gente . . . La poesía se estaba muriendo. La novela todavía no, pero él no sabía escribir novelas"), Mirebalais has nights when he cries "with rage."[35]

While Bolaño positions the predominantly autobiographical stance of the poems of *The Unknown University* throughout in relation to a wide range of poets from Europe and the Americas, one of those to whom his (non-)poetics bear the strongest affinity, not surprisingly, is the apparently guileless, intensely casual style of the American poet Frank O'Hara. From such poems of an O'Haraesque personalism, to the more overtly political autobiographical stakes of a poem such as "Ernesto Cardenal y yo" ("Ernesto Cardenal and I"), to the poems advising his son Lautaro near the end of Part Three's concluding section, "A Happy Ending," to "*Read the old poets*" —"ridiculous and heroic / The old poets / . . . and take care of their books"—the collected poems cultivate a consistent *style* of their own in interweaving autobiographical self-reference with self-conscious literary-historical positioning in relation to poets with whom Bolaño aligns or distances himself along a continuum of affinity and antipathy.[36] Appearing not only in Part III of *The Unknown University* but as the title poem of the slim volume of forty-three poems, all in verse, almost all drawn from Parts I and III of *The Unknown University*, first published in 1993 as *Los perros románticos: Poemas 1977–1990* and reissued in 2000 as *Los perros románticos: Poemas 1980–1998*, the title poem "The Romantic Dogs" announces a for Bolaño familiar, programmatic poetics of the underdog, the dispossessed, the *maudits*, which is also, from a literary-historical perspective, a poetics in keeping with the autobiographical turn of Romanticism that has contin-ued to dominate how poetry is conceived, perceived, and practiced throughout Europe and the Americas for the past two centuries. In this respect, despite and in contrast to the prose-poetic experimentalism of *People Walking Away/Antwerp*, the verse poems of Parts I and III of the collected poems are aligned consistently and predominantly with the more traditional poetic practices and stylistic features of the first-person, auto-biographical, image-based, anecdotal, free-verse lyric that gained ascen-dancy over the second half of the twentieth century and remained dominant in poetry for Bolaño's generation through his death in 2003. In this more conservative sense too, in his verse poetry, in contrast to the more radical poetics of his prose poem novels, Bolaño was a profoundly generational figure, in the former more symptomatically, preserving famil-iar, received forms even as he recognized and figured their limitations, in the latter more indexically, pointing the way to new, more capacious, forms.

In turning his energies and commitments from 1993 onward decisively away from verse poetry in the direction of the prose poem novels to come, Bolaño opened onto a far more inclusive form that allowed him to come to terms, in a way the autobiographical free-verse lyric had not, with the complex political, historical, and literary-historical forces and legacies, including the pre- and post-histories of the Pinochet regime and *Nazi Literature,* of aesthetics and politics in Europe and the Americas over the course of the past century. Freed by the example of the prose poem from the constraints of the autobiographical, free-verse dominant in contemporary poetry, the reconfiguration and reframing of possibilities for poetry in the prose poem novels of the last decade of Bolaño's career made possible an increasingly more capacious coming-to-terms and working through, a style and system for reimagining how truly contemporary poetry might more effectively respond to the aesthetic and political, historical and literary-historical changes of a post-Pinochet, post-*Nazi Literature*, post-1989 era.

Their invented mini-biographies resembling imaginary entries to a kind of anti-Wikipedia, the prose-poetic biographical sketches of *Nazi Literature* recall the cult of personality that led Pound, one of the most radically innovative figures of modern poetry, to become a supporter of Mussolini and Italian fascism. As Pound's and Breton's counter-examples show, and as Bolaño understands very well, an avant-garde poetry and poetics might lend itself just as easily to the right as to the left. Yet if all styles, including those of the various, heterogeneous avant-gardes, are a fraud, an autobiographical approach to poetry, especially poetry in and as verse, of the kind that remains hegemonic in *The Unknown University*, risks presenting the, or an, authorial self as disingenuously unmediated and unframed. Rather than presenting a self-consciously performative self, or selves—an "I" aware of itself not as singular and self-contained but as multiple, mutable, and interpellated by genre—the autobiographical (non-)style of the first-person lyric suggests that what counts and what doesn't, in poetry, depends on the programmatic "Direct treatment" imperative of Pound's Imagist manifesto that became, over the course of the twentieth century, in both Europe and the Americas, one of the limiting directives and hegemonic dogmas of modern and contemporary poetry.[37]

While most of the poems Bolaño assembled between 1991 and 1993 for *The Unknown University* adhere to this dominant—all but a very few of which, in Parts I and III, are entirely and unambiguously in verse—the collection's strikingly more innovative Part II explicitly challenges and vehemently contests it. As if placed at the heart of the collection like a detonation device designed to explode poetry as verse, including Bolaño's own, Part II does so most importantly and consequentially through its calculated recycling and pivotal placement, at the collected poems' literal center, of Bolaño's two most experimental prose-poetic works, *People Walking Away / Antwerp* and "Prosa del otoño en Gerona" ("Prose from Autumn in Gerona"). Most pointedly and succinctly, Part II's challenge to the dominant in poetry in and as verse, a three-pronged attack in effect on what Charles Bernstein has called "official verse culture," takes the form of the three verse poems "La poesía chilena es un gas" ("Chilean Poetry is a Gas"), "Horda" ("Horde"), and "La poesía latinoamericana" ("Latin American Poetry"). Concluding with the programmatic, erotic "Manifiestos y Posiciones" ("Manifestos and Positions"), which stretches prose-poem length to a single paragraph of thirteen pages, Part II answers its own questions about what poetry might open onto at the end of enjambment, what Agamben has called poetry's *sine qua non*, a poetry at the ends of its lines.[38]

In his career-long attention to the increasingly accelerated and unavoidable interdiscursive, interdisciplinary, above all intermedial reconfiguration and reframing of the question of genre and its implications both for poetry and the novel, as for all of literature, over the course of his last decade, Bolaño is a synecdochic figure precisely in his understanding of the extent to which the shaping parameters of his generation's imaginary were undergoing irreversible changes, its literary and extra-literary worlds becoming themselves no longer avant-garde, but historical. Seeking to retain and expand poetry's audience through a poetics at once freeing, from the constraints of both traditional verse poetry and the novel's interminable superfluous plot, and convenient and commodifiable (Baudelaire's "commode"), *Antwerp / People Walking Away* anticipates the trafficking, monetizing, and non-monetizing equipoise and disequilibrium of everyday life on the Web.[39] Encouraging not the traditional impulses to linearity and closure, the fill-in-the-blanks and tie-up-the-loose-ends orientation of the novel as traditionally conceived, but a modularity and interactivity more akin to the Internet's endless varieties of instantaneous coming and going, appearance and impermanence, *Antwerp* realizes *avant la lettre*, far more than the verse poems of *The Unknown University*, the ambitions of what it would be like to be a contemporary poet, to write a contemporary poetry now, not just in 1980, or 1993, but still in 2019 and beyond. Having already succeeded as a poet in the strongest sense, in *Antwerp*, before the collected verse poems of *The Unknown University* "failed," Bolaño laid the groundwork *in nuce* at the very beginning of his career for both the more minimalist prose poem novellas and more maximalist prose poem novels of his final decade.

While the brief autobiographical information Bolaño provides for the writing of *Antwerp / People Walking Away* should not surprise anyone who has read the text closely, what is most remarkable about the text's positioning at the heart of the collected poems in Part II of *The Unknown University* is still the relative opacity and illegibility of its context, its deliberate elision and strategic avoidance of autobiographical transparency, compared to the predominantly autobiographical verse poems of Parts I and III, poems like those dedicated to Bolaño's son, Lautaro, in the closing section called "A Happy Ending."[40] In its final turn from the poignantly straightforward, intimately autobiographical description of his two poems for Lautaro as "very simple" to his decidedly more oblique and complex metaphor for the act of reading he is encouraging as a form of "*Mutual protection*. Like the motto of a gang of undefeated mobsters," Bolaño's representation of his hoped-for legacy not only for his son but for his readers more generally raises again the importance of genre, and of the detective genre in particular, which figures significantly not only in the consecutive "Detective" poems of Part III but in the third, title poem of the first section of Part I, "La novella-nieve" ("The Snow-Novel")—"My literary work April 1980. Obsessed / with ... / ... gumshoes"[41]—and that section's equally tone-setting sixth poem, "El trabajo" ("Work"). Positioned squarely at the intersection of poetry, the detective genre, and autobiography conceived both professionally and personally, "Work" figures the collected poems' sustained inquiry into what he calls in the untitled fifth poem his "Strange gratuitous occupation," an occupation whose "ancient ways of being educated" include the "Odd complacency" of "the poet" for whom writing is "not about wealth or fame or even just /poetry," but maybe "the only way / to avoid fear."[42] Speculatively conceding that, whatever poetry's affective, autobiographical motivations, "In a thousand years nothing will be left / of all that's been written this century," only "loose sentences, traces of lost women, / fragments of motionless children," Bolaño encourages, in the first section's brief untitled eighth poem, with its echoes of Brecht's "Questions from a Worker Who Reads," an inclusive poetry that would remember those most likely to be forgotten, a poetry aligned with what Nietzsche calls in *Untimely Meditations* neither a monumental nor antiquarian, but a critical history.[43]

Consistently questioning the value of his own poetry, as of poetry more generally, in an expansively intermedial context, through the remaining sections of Part I, as well as Parts II and III—"(Poetry just doesn't do it for me anymore) . . .My poetry / (Garbage)"—while affirming as well what Auxilio Lacouture calls in *Amulet* the "non-power" of poetry ("su no-poder") as a discourse of the defeated and forgotten—"Poets of Troy / Nothing that could have been yours / Exists anymore / Not temples not gardens / Not poetry / You are free / Admirable poets of Troy," in *The Unknown University* Bolaño continually returns to poetry as an arena of struggle from which, as he nears the conclusion of Part III, he begins to articulate his withdrawal.[44] Establishing his distance from some figures ("*Once and for fucking all stop reading fucking / Raúl Zurita!*") and affirming his affinity with others ("There's no / Greater poet than Juan Ramón Jiménez"; "Visiting the monument / To Rubén Darío. / Goodbye, Rubén, we said"), aligning himself with "Pure inspiration / And no method at all" (recalling Amalfitano's rejection of both style and system in *True Policeman*), and remembering reading among others, in the fifteen-page free-verse narrative of his Latin American travels in "Los neochilenos" ("The Neochileans"), "Peruvian poets: / Vallejo, Martín Adán and Jorge Pimentel. / And Pancho Misterio," Bolaño circles back nostalgically, wistfully, in the concluding verse poems of *The Unknown University*, to a counter-factual imagining, at once personal and collective, of "a non-existent Chile / that's happy."[45] While the meta-poetic, meta-literary, interdiscursive, intermedial curriculum of *The Unknown University* is capacious, at the heart of its long journey remains the simultaneously privileged and marginal, indispensable yet disposable, unforgettable yet increasingly forgotten, enduring yet defeated genre of its own medium, poetry, in both verse and prose. Accordingly, even as he arcs toward abandoning poetry in and as verse in the final, verse poem, "Musa" ("Muse"), Bolaño remains as haunted as ever, as the novels of the remaining decade of his life will continue to be haunted, by poetry's shaping, informing influence and impact, as by its unrealized promise of being representative.[46]

The concluding poems of *The Unknown University* thus offer no closure at all, opening instead onto an endless coming-to-terms that circles back in the end—as in the first of the final section's last three poems, "Retrato en mayo, 1994" ("Portrait in May, 1994")—to Baudelaire, the poet who is the source of the opening epigraphs for both *The Unknown University* and *2666*, the poet from whom Bolaño learned more than from any other, absorbing as well, like Borges, the lessons of "Poe's Library," the freedom and promise of passing from poetry in verse to poetry in prose. Seeing himself as having been, like his son, "abandoned by the muse," despite his aspiration to become a representative poet of his generation, Bolaño remains haunted by "all we could have been, strong and unchanging" but didn't become, whether because he, and his generation, "didn't have faith," or because they "had it in so many things finally destroyed by reality / (the Revolution, for example, that prairie / of red flags, fields of fertile pasture) / . . . our roots . . . like Baudelaire's / clouds." Invoking again, at the pivotal turn of the poem in the fourteenth of its twenty-three lines, the closing line of the opening prose poem of *Le Spleen de Paris,* "L'Étranger"—"là-bas . . . là-bas . . . les merveilleux nuages!"—to which Bolaño returns repeatedly throughout his work, most notably in the open- ing and closing pages of *By Night in Chile*—Bolaño affirms the profound ambivalence toward "the Muse" that led him to turn away almost entirely over the final decade of his life (1993–2003), as Baudelaire did in his own final decade from the publication of *Les Fleurs du Mal* in 1857 to his death in 1867, not from poetry in its most capacious sense, but from poetry understood only as verse.[47] Published in its entirety, like *Le Spleen de Paris,* only posthumously, *The Unknown University* is both Bolaño's most ambi- tious attempt to establish himself as a poet, as the sixth and closing line of the untitled opening poem explicitly puts it—"Estoy poniéndolo todo de mi parte" ("I'm giving it my best shot")—and his farewell to that ambition as defined, and confined, to the aesthetic regimes of poetry in and as verse that dominate, almost exclusively, Parts I and III.[48] The calculated recy- cling and repurposing of *Antwerp* squarely at its center, in Part II, as the now unnumbered prose poem sequence *People Walking Away,* functions in this respect as a critical inflection point in Bolaño's career that clears the way for the explosion of prose poem novels to come and to which he would devote the final decade of his life and career.

Reprising, now in the context of "a Barcelona full of Latin Americans / with and without cash, legal / and illegal trying / to write," the decisive turns of Baudelaire and Rimbaud from poetry in and as verse to poetry in and as prose, Bolaño subsequently inflects that decision in the direction of both the novel, in the texture, architecture, and arch (in the double sense) ambitions of Bolaño's "bold" alter-ego in *2666,* the German novelist- protagonist, Benno von Archim*boldi* (nom de plume of Hans Reiter), and poetry, in the brief reappearance of the (there French) novelist Arcimboldi who shares his first name, Óscar, with another of Bolaño's alter-egos, the poetry (then philosophy) professor and central protagonist of *True Policeman,* Óscar Amalfitano (a first named shared as well, without the accent, by the African-American journalist in *2666*, Oscar Fate).[49] Positioning as "one of the wings / of the Unknown University!"—but only one—the verse poetry he had loved all his life but came to find, by the early to mid-1990s, as limiting as Poe, Baudelaire, and Rimbaud had found it to be a century-and-a-half earlier, the closing lines of the untitled, penultimate verse poem of Part I of *The Unknown University* set the stage for what would soon become one of the most productive, accomplished decades any writer has known.

CHAPTER 5

Post-Avant Histories
Distant Star (Estrella distante)

The central importance to Bolaño's fiction of structure, form, and scale manifests itself nowhere more clearly or elegantly than in the conceptual organization of the ten individually numbered chapters of his 1996 novel, *Estrella distante* (*Distant Star,* 2004), into four symmetrical parts, of three, two, two, and three chapters each. In the first of these four parts, which includes 1) the introduction of the novel's enigmatic central character, the aspiring young poet "Alberto Ruiz-Tagle," soon to be renamed "Carlos Wieder," and the poetry scenes in and around the University of Concepción in the two years from Salvador Allende's election (1971–1973) to Augusto Pinochet's September 11, 1973, coup; 2) Wieder's first poetic act, the skywriting of a poem in Latin, in the year Pinochet came to power, as seen from an internment center in La Peña; and 3) Wieder's further adventures as an aerial poet, including an expedition to the South Pole, and the introduction of the literary critic "Nicasio Ibacache"—prototype for the central figure "H. Ibacache" in Bolaño's *By Night in Chile*—who will help launch Wieder's literary reputation, Bolaño establishes Wieder as the representative, avant-garde, "revolutionary" poet of his generation, a figure through whom to explore the coup's traumatic legacy, its synecdochic importance and implications, not only for Chile and Latin America, and not only for Bolaño's generation, but for poetry, fiction, literary history, and politics more generally.[1]

When the reader first encounters Wieder, as Alberto Ruiz-Tagle, it is through the narrator's remembrance of his weekly interactions with him in 1971–1972 at the workshop in Concepción offered by Juan Stein, most of whose students, aged seventeen to twenty-three, "talked a lot, not just about poetry, but politics, travel . . . painting, architecture, photography, revolution and the armed struggle that would usher in a new life and a new era, so we thought, but which, for most of us, was like a dream . . . the only dreams worth living for."[2] Coming mostly from the Faculty of Literature, with the notable exception of the Garmendia sisters, Verónica and

86

Angélica, identical twins "who were studying sociology and psychology, and Alberto Ruiz-Tagle, who, as he said at some point, was an autodidact,"[3] Stein's workshop students share a marked political orientation: "We spoke a sort of slang or jargon, derived in equal parts from Marx and Mandrake the Magician (we were mostly members or sympathizers of the MIR or Trotskyite parties, although a few of us belonged to the Young Socialists or the Communist Party or one of the leftist Catholic parties), while Ruiz-Tagle spoke Spanish, the Spanish of certain parts of Chile (mental rather than physical regions)."[4] Held in a different part of the university, the Faculty of Medicine, the "rival workshop" run by Diego Soto "differed markedly from that of Stein in ethical as well as aesthetic matters, although the two were what used to be, and I suppose still are, called soul mates." Where for Stein what we might call a left poetics and a left politics are completely bound up with each other, the approach of Soto, later described "At the end of 1973, or the beginning of 1974" as "Juan Stein's best friend and rival" was decidedly apolitical. Where the prototypically northern European-looking Stein ("tall, fair-haired . . . strong and well-built") is "mainly interested in Latin American poetry," the more indigenous-looking Soto, "that ugly little Indian" ("short, dark" and with "a fine-boned body hinting at future plumpness") displays, by contrast, a marked orientation toward Europe, translating in particular "French poets who were at the time (and many of whom, I fear still are) unknown in Chile." While the two of them "were always together (except at their respective workshops) and always talking about poetry," Soto was "a socialist sympathizer, but that was all, he wasn't even a faithful socialist voter; I would have described him as a left-wing pessimist, as aesthetic in nature."[5] Forming together a pair of perfect oxymorons, an embrace of contraries with and against type, Stein and Soto figure a schematic binary of contrastive, complementary, perhaps (ir)reconcilable choices facing aspiring poets at the time of the coup.[6]

Afforded space within the university to meet, but not officially part of the university curriculum, the workshops offered by Stein and Soto draw different students, Stein's the Garmendia sisters and "the best poets or potential poets," and Soto's the poets Carmen Villagrán and "Marta Pasadas, known as Fat Marta" ("la Gorda"), the only medical student who attended the workshop in the Faculty of Medicine: "a very white, very fat, very sad girl who wrote prose poems and cherished the dream, back then at least, of becoming the Marta Harnecker of Chilean literary criticism"(11). Attending both workshops, like the narrator and the narrator's friend and alter-ego Bibiano O'Ryan, Wieder, known still before the coup as Alberto Ruiz-Tagle, is described by Fat Marta as the figure who "is going to revolutionize Chilean poetry" ("va a revolucionar la poesía chilena"), not through poetry he is going to write, but through poetry "he's going to *perform*" ("La que él va a *hacer*"), a speculation Bibiano and the narrator are quick to challenge (14–15).[7]

Anticipating the elaboration of poetic practices associated with Stein and Soto in chapters 4 and 5, the first three chapters track Wieder's emergence and rise to acclaim from among the cohort of poets associated with them—the narrator, his friend and alter-ego Bibiano O'Ryan, the Garmendia twins, Fat Marta—who taken together figure the range of paths available to poets of Bolaño's generation. As the only one among his peers not to attend university, a self-described autodidact and the only one besides the narrator and Bibiano to attend both workshops, Wieder pursues an apprenticeship into poetry that is marked by a detached eclecticism.[8] In the world of Concepción's two poetry scenes, which are broadly inclusive in their influences thanks to Stein's preference for poetry from North and South America, and Soto's for European, especially French poetry, Wieder figures a range of influences. In a pivotal passage describing the night shortly after the coup when Ruiz-Tagle/Wieder visits the Garmendia twins at their deceased parents' home on the outskirts of Concepción in Nacimiento, where, symbolically, the "New Chilean Poetry" is about to be born, Wieder's display of erudition references literary theory as well as a range of poets appearing retrospectively, in 2019, less eclectic than it may have been in 1973 or, certainly, as Bolaño was no doubt aware, by the time of the novel's publication in 1996.

On the night of the murder of the beautiful, talented Garmendia twins —in the view of the narrator as well as Stein the best poets of their generation—which ushers in the birth of the new Chilean poetry and the transformation of Alberto Ruiz-Tagle into Carlos Wieder, a Nietzschean figure of destructive repetition, the common denominator of an avant-garde poetics is its perceived unintelligibility and incomprehensibility. In the picture that emerges of the transition from the old to new Chilean poetry, Bolaño figures the future of a vanguard poetics as an advance into unknown territory involving, as Wieder's subsequent evolution into an aerial poet demonstrates, a militarized aesthetic aligning itself with the violence of Pinochet's fascist regime.[9] Or does it? While Wieder's murder of the Garmendia twins and his subsequent training as a pilot at the air force academy would seem to leave little doubt of his personal complicity with the regime, the status of his poetic acts as such, and as emblematic acts of an avant-garde aesthetic, raise complicated questions that are less easily answered. While innovative in its procedure, the inaugural poem of Wieder's aerial poetics (recalling Raúl Zurita's skywriting poetry) could scarcely be more conservative, reproducing in Latin, unintelligible to the masses, the creation myth on which the birth of Christianity relies, a conservative myth of origin underscoring the collusion between Chilean Catholicism, the Pinochet regime, and German fascism (through Wieder's German name as well as the Messerschmitt he pilots) subsequently explored in detail in *By Night in Chile*. Comparing "the symmetrical outline of the plane" ("su figura simétrica") to "a Rorschach blot," Bolaño suggests the extent to which the Old Testament verses Wieder inscribes in the sky over Concepción depend on their reception, on the uses readers and viewers make of them.[10] Adding, in Spanish, the language of the people, before the plane "vanished" ("desapareció"), Wieder concludes with an ambiguous imperative: "This time it [the plane] wrote only one word, in larger letters, over what must have been the center of the city: LEARN . . . the last word" ("Esta vez sólo escribió una palabra, más grande que las anteriores, en lo que calculé era el centro exacto de la ciudad: APRENDAN . . . la última palabra").[11] While Wieder's first poetic performance in the sky over Concepción "instantly won him admirers among the nation's enterprising minds," the effect of his marginally intelligible poetic gesture remains open to interpretation. Avant-garde in its formal conception and procedures, conservative in its language and execution, with a brief opening to the masses at its conclusion, Wieder's first poetic act is neither intrinsically "right" nor "left," but undecidably (un)intelligible. Its ethics, its politics, remain up in the air, as opaque in its intentionality as the subsequent "*lettriste*" poem alluding to the Garmendia sisters, which "went on to contradict itself," and the subsequent poem alluding to the poet Carmen Villagrán, "a working-class girl and a devout follower of Pablo Neruda".[12] Challenging the elitist assumption that his associates in the military "knew nothing about poetry," Wieder assures them that "they knew more about poetry than most people, more than a good many poets and professors . . . but his thugs didn't understand . . . For them what Wieder did in his plane was just a 'daring feat,' daring in more ways than one, but not poetry." Whether among right-wing officers under Pinochet, or in the eyes of "the people," both more traditional and more avant-garde practices of poetry are perceived as largely unintelligible and of little consequence.[13]

The contrast between mainstream and avant-garde poetic practices is figured early on in *Distant Star* through the first chapter's contrast between the beautiful Garmendia twins, stars of the more prestigious workshop run by Stein, and Marta Posadas. While the Garmendia twins' poetry is aligned with the North American mainstream success of "Anne Sexton and Elizabeth Bishop and Denise Levertov ... to the evident satisfaction of Juan Stein," if also less emphatically with the populist, aesthetically progressive works of Violeta and Nicanor Parra —the latter represented consistently by Bolaño as alternative to his generation's "Neruditis"—Marta Posadas suggests other possibilities. Attending Stein's friend and rival Soto's workshop at the Faculty of Medicine along with Carmen Villagrán, "a good poet, although not as good as the Garmendia sisters. (The best poets and potential poets went to Juan Stein's workshop)," Fat Marta figures, through her combined interest in prose poems and the Marxist literary criticism of her namesake, Marta Harnecker, an overtly prosaic, political orien- tation to poetry and poetics—avant-garde, alternative, experimental— in stark contrast to the elegant, belletristic approach of the well-heeled Garmendia twins, who "had no links with the so-called 'extremists'" and whose father's estate in Nacimiento included a "sizeable library."[14]

In keeping with the logic of the novel's contrast between the unattrac- tive, politicized, avant-garde alternative represented by Fat Marta and the beautiful, apolitical, mainstream poetics represented by the Garmendia twins, it is significantly not the latter, including Wieder's presumed lover, Verónica, but Fat Marta, the central protagonist's friend, who first represents him as the figure who "is going to revolutionize Chilean poetry," not through the poetry he has written or is going to write, but through the poetry "he's going to perform." While Fat Marta figures a potential synthesis of the poetic, the prosaic, and the political from a Marxist perspective, she is saddened with the recognition that Ruiz-Tagle does not share her Marxist orientation, agreeing with the narrator's assessment of his (a)political orientation, though not with their questioning of his revolutionary (aesthetic) potential, when the latter adds "I don't think he's even a socialist."[15] Concluding with the presumed (though not explicitly represented) murder of the Garmendia twins by Ruiz-Tagle, the first chapter stages the transition from a mainstream aesthetics of the beautiful in poetry to what may be called a poetics and aesthetics of the avant-garde sublime in what the narrator calls in the second chapter, as seen from the "transit center" at La Peña, figuring Bolaño's own brief internment, "Carlos Wieder's first poetic act,"[16] a "poem in the sky" written all in Latin with the exception of its final word ("IN PRINCIPIO ... CREAVIT DEUS ... CAELUM ET TERRAM ... / ... APRENDAN ['LEARN'"]) that is dispersed, distributed, disconnected, and interwoven within the novel's prose across several pages.[17]

If the form, means, medium, technology of Carlos Wieder's aerial poetry seem to make good on Fat Marta's claim that he will "revolutionize Chilean poetry," the content of that act could hardly be more traditional, less avant-garde. Parodying Zurita's skywriting experimentalism, Wieder's "first poetic act" displays not original lines of his own poetry, but the opening lines of Genesis. As if announcing the dawn of the Pinochet regime as an act of Divine Creation, the provocative gesture constitutes an ambiguous act of appropriation. The spectacle of the opening lines of the Latin Vulgate, made visible by smoke from a German Messerschmitt borrowed from Pinochet's air force, suggests, as the prisoner Mad Norberto at La Peña indicates, a displaced repetition of World War II and the war machine of German fascism—a recurrence signaled by the name Wieder (German "again"), the meaning, etymology, and resonances of which the text explains in great detail—as also the complicity between the Pinochet regime and the Catholic Church that will be the major focus of *By Night in Chile*. Made temporarily and almost illegibly visible in a form and language largely unavailable to the masses observing the performance, Wieder's skywriting recalls the association between poetry and incomprehensibility that emerges during Wieder's visit to the Garmendia twins' estate the night of their murder/disappearance: "In their innocence they *think* they understand ["*creen* comprender"], but they don't understand at all (the 'New Chilean Poetry' is about to be born) ..."[18] As an example of what such a revolutionary poetry might look like, it retains an indeterminate register.

Concluding the novel's first part, the third chapter of *Distant Star* tracks Wieder's poetic performances through a skywriting expedition to the South Pole that brings him to the height of his fame and what the sixth chapter will reveal to have been the apex of his career. It is in this chapter, where the novel offers its extended exegesis of the meaning of the name *Wieder*, that the reader first briefly encounters the character who will become the basis for the central protagonist of *By Night in Chile*, "one of Chile's most influential literary critics ... a certain Nicasio Ibacache ... a personal friend of Pablo Neruda (and Huidobro before that)" who "had also corresponded with Gabriela Mistral, been Pablo de Rokha's whipping boy, and (so he said) discovered Nicanor Parra." Voice of a mainstream literary establishment fully complicit with the Pinochet regime, Ibacache gives Wieder's career a boost through "an explication of Wieder's highly individual poetic style" in which he claims that, with Wieder, "we (Chile's

literate public) were witnessing the emergence of the new era's major poet."
In his warning to Wieder to avoid "the drawbacks of the literary avant-
garde" ("los inconvenientes de la vanguardia literaria"), Ibacache shows
himself to be both an apologist for the mainstream and the canonical and
an advocate for the synthesis of a conservative poetics and nationalist
politics. Mirroring Ibacache's right-wing aesthetics, poetics, and politics
at the height of his fame in 1974, Wieder is described as both a poet and
literary critic and historian: "He spoke of poetry (not Chilean or Latin
American poetry, but poetry full stop) with an authority that disarmed all
his interviewers . . . " Yet as a representative figure of the Pinochet regime,
and of poetry, poetics, and politics following the coup, condemning silence
as "like leprosy . . . like communism . . . like a blank screen that must be
filled," Wieder not only writes "verses in the sky," but records "on film and
in photographs" and appears "on television," mixing literary forms and
extra-literary media in precisely the avant-garde ways Ibacache warns
against.[19]

Resuming Wieder's narrative in the third section of the novel, comprised of chapters 9 and 7, the narrative pivots from the first three chapters'
tracking of his rise to fame through his exploits in aerial poetry in
Concepción, Nacimiento, southern Chile, and Antarctica, to his fall
from grace, through the disastrous photo exhibit in his apartment in
Santiago, that will lead to his disappearance and subsequent relocation—
a relocation that mirrors Bolaño's own—to Europe, Paris, and eventually
Spain, specifically Barcelona and Blanes. Interrupting this (dis)continuous
narrative with a digressive second section comprised of chapters 4 and 5,
Bolaño further develops the novel's development of a literary history by
other means through individual chapters devoted to the two poetry salon
leaders who come to represent a schematic history of modern poetry not
only in Chile but in western literature generally from the 1950s through the
1973 coup to the end of the Pinochet regime in 1990 through the publication of *Distant Star* in 1996: Stein and Soto. "Like the story of Chile itself in
those years," the fourth chapter begins, "the story of Juan Stein, who ran
our poetry workshop, is larger than life."[20] With these words beginning the
two-chapter interruption of the story of Wieder's rise and fall that is the
novel's primary focus, the narrative confirms Bolaño's abiding preoccupation with the novel as a form for exploring intersections of history and
literary history, in Chile, the Americas, and Europe, a lens through which
to explore historical, political developments and the history of modern
poetry in particular in mutual relation. As the history and politics of Chile
before and after the coup are inseparable from Stein's and Soto's stories, the

story of modern poetry is inseparable, for the generation of writers coming of age in Bolaño's generation, from the ur-trauma of historical, political developments surrounding the coup and the Pinochet regime's hold on power for close to two decades thereafter.

At once a national and transnational allegory of the intersection and mutual over-determination of history and literary history during that time, from Bolaño's and his generation's late teens through their early forties, *Distant Star* presents through the pivotal figures of Stein and Soto a schematic tale of two primary orientations toward the relation between poetry, poetics, and politics. While not necessarily mutually exclusive—the fifth chapter will go on to describe Soto as "Stein's best friend and rival," the two of them "always together (except at their respective workshops) and always talking about poetry. "If the sky over Chile had begun to crumble and fall, they would have gone on talking about poetry"[21]—the divergent orientations toward poetry represented by Stein and Soto, whether regarded as complementary or competing, serve to define the dominant, mainstream choices facing Bolaño's generation, both poetically and politically, choices rejected by Wieder—the only character, along with the narrator and his friend Bibiano, to attend both workshops—in favor of the more avant-garde, experimental poetic performances the sympathetically drawn Fat Marta, the only figure in the novel to write prose poems, suggests would revolutionize Chilean poetry.

What then, in the fourth and fifth chapters devoted to Stein and Soto, do these two mainstream choices look like? Haunted by Baudelaire's imagination of his "hypocritical" reader as "double" and "twin," the Stein/Soto dyad continues Bolaño's exploration of the trope of doubleness figured throughout the novel, from the Garmendia twins to the narrator's alter-egos, most notably Bibiano O'Ryan and, in the final three chapters set in Barcelona and environs, the detective Abel Romero, as well as, finally, the narrator and Wieder as figures for each other and for Bolaño himself, to which we shall return.[22] Said to have been born in 1945, eight years before Bolaño, which would make him twenty-eight at the time of the 1973 coup, or only a decade older than the students of his salon, Stein figures through the year of his birth the beginning of the post–World War II era and the poetic and political struggles that would come to prominence in the second half of the twentieth century in Europe and the Americas, a period so dominated in Latin America by the figure of Neruda—whose death along with that of Allende marked the end of a consensus convergence of a poetry and politics of the left—that Bolaño's narrator speaks of Stein as "having suffered from Neruditis since early childhood," so much so that he "could not so much as look at it without breaking out in hives." Against Neruda's mainstream dominance, Stein writes short poems influenced "Like most of the poets of his generation . . . by Nicanor Parra and Ernesto Cardenal, but also by Jorge Teillier's home-grown imagism, although Stein recommended we read Lihn rather than Teillier . . ." Rejecting Neruda's poetics in favor of those of Parra, Lihn, and Teillier, Stein nevertheless continues the Nerudian association of poetry with a left politics, writing a letter to "old Nicanor" reproaching him "in a tone somewhere between indignation and perplexity, reproaching him for some of the jokes he had seen fit to crack at that crucial moment in Latin America's revolutionary struggle." Underscoring the importance of these figures for Bolaño's characters and for Bolaño himself, the narrator tells us that "in the end they probably influenced us more than anyone else."[23]

While Stein's orientation toward a more overtly political poetics, and his influence on his students, is not so dogmatic as to exclude Diego's decidedly more apolitical approach—he was according to Stein "the best poet of his generation, and according to us was one of the *two* best, the other being Stein himself"—he figures above all, in contrast to Soto, the presumed interrelation and interpenetration of poetry and politics, in particular from a Marxist perspective, which came to distinguish to such an extent a consensus Latin American orientation toward poetry from that of a more depoliticized, or at least apolitical dominant in mainstream North American poetry, notwithstanding occasional convergences, in the second half of the twentieth century.[24] Figuring the nostalgic, lost potential of a left convergence between North American and Latin American politics and poetry, Stein's house includes "few books (Diego Soto's house, by contrast, was like a library)" and instead "a great many maps," as well as "an official portrait—of a Red Army general called Ian Chernyakhovsky," a cousin of Stein he considers "the greatest general of the Second World War" who died "in the front line" in the final year of the war which was also the year of Stein's birth.[25] Along with the photo of Chernyakhovsky, figurally speaking Stein's revolutionary Soviet twin, whose heroic exploits parallel his own in Nicaragua, Angola, and throughout Latin America, Stein possesses a photo of his poetic double, Mayakovsky, the "dream lover" of the Garmendia twins, and another imagined to be that of "William Carlos Williams doing his day job as a small-town doctor," a photo that led to a discussion with him about "Gramsci . . . And later still . . . poetry and the Paris Commune . . ."[26]

Overtly and emphatically political, but not dogmatically so—at one point in his participation in revolutionary struggles in Nicaragua he is said to have protested the exclusion of "poems by Nicanor Parra and Enrique Lihn for political reasons)"—Stein figures the tragic promise and failed indigenous struggles of attempts to articulate a convergence between a left poetics and a left politics with markedly different priorities than those Soto represents.[27] Where Stein continues his struggles on the left in the Americas following his disappearance from Chile after the coup, emerging as the type of poet who participates in revolutionary political struggle, Soto leaves Chile for Europe and the less eventful, more bourgeois fate of an apolitical poet in exile with a position "lecturing at a university" and "financial stability and time for writing and research" that allows him to be "happy, reasonably happy."[28] Ironically, in one of those crossings of expectations and binary oppositions so characteristic of Bolaño's dialectical imagination, while Stein, the narrator suggests, may not in the end have died a violent death as a guerrilla in Central America after all, as earlier supposed, but instead lived out a quiet life in southern Chile, it is the apolitical, yet profoundly ethical Soto who dies a tragic death, stabbed while attempting to rescue a "tramp" ("vagabunda") from "three young neo-Nazis" ("tres jóvenes neo-nazis") on his way home to Paris in Perpignan from "a conference on literature and criticism in Latin America, to be held in Alicante."[29] Continuing the trope of doubling in the chapter devoted to Soto's fate, the narrator tells the story within the story of "Petra," a boy "called Lorenzo who grew up in Chile without arms . . . in Pinochet's Chile" who "became an artist," who "is to Soto what Juan Stein's double is to the Juan Stein we knew," a figure the narrator goes on to say he considers, when he thinks of Stein and Soto, perhaps "the best poet of the three" in "the current socio-political climate," an "undercover poet" said to have gone on to enjoy success as a performer, following the close of the Pinochet regime, in the 1992 Summer Olympics in Barcelona.[30]

Concluding with this proleptic anticipation of a redemptive poetic, avant-garde performativity on the other side of the nightmare of the Pinochet regime ushered in almost two decades earlier, the fifth chapter returns the narrative from the second section's digressive yet pivotal schematic figuration of the poetic and political options represented by Stein and Soto to focus on Wieder's avant-garde, revolutionary poetics—apparently as aligned with the fascist right as Stein's with the socialist left—in "the year of grace 1974 . . . the height of his fame," which is also the moment of its impending implosion. Bookending the verses from Genesis in the Latin Vulgate that serve as the text of Wieder's inaugural poetic act, the shift in setting to Santiago in chapters 6 and 7, which make up the novel's third section, yields an original rather than appropriated poem by Wieder for what will prove to be his last aerial performance. In contrast to the inaugural skywriting performance's focus on birth and creation at the dawn of the Pinochet regime above the symbolically appropriate city of Concepción, the poem becoming visible in the skies over Santiago, figuring the growing number of *desaparecidos* in the capital and elsewhere across Chile a year after the coup, focuses relentlessly on death from the first line's "Death is friendship" ("*La meurte es amistad*") through its subsequent equations with "Chile," "responsibility" ("*respons-abilidad*"), "love" ("*amor*"), "growth" ("*crecimiento*"), "communion" ("*communion*"), "cleansing" ("*limpieza*"), the twice-repeated "my heart" ("Death is my heart / Take my heart" ["La muerte es mi corazón / Toma mi corazón"], followed by the name "Carlos Wieder," and the concluding "Death is resurrection" ("*La muerte es resurrección*").[31] More accessible by design, in Spanish rather than in Latin, their anaphoric structure, simple syntax, and oxymoronic, paradoxical logic is more familiarly "poetic," yet again dispersed, distributed, and interwoven across several pages of the chapter's prose like the lines from *Genesis* appropriated by Wieder for his first poetic act in Chapter 2.

Wieder's verses about death yet prove to those gathered below who can see them scarcely less illegible, incomprehensible: "Muy pocos descifraron sus palabras ... comprendieron lo escrito ... comprendieron o creyeron comprender la voluntad del piloto y supieron que aunque no entendieran nada estaban asistiendo a un acto único, a un evento importante para el arte del futuro" (89–92) ("Very few could decipher his words ... understand what had been written .... They understood or thought they understood the pilot's will, and they knew that although they couldn't make head or tail of it, they were witnessing a unique event, of great significance for the art of the future").[32]

Wieder's "art of the future" ("el arte del futuro"), which is at the same time Bolaño's parody of incomprehensible, ineffectual avant-garde strategies and intentions embedded in deadly serious, nonetheless humorous prose, comes to the reader in the narrator's self-conscious account of Wieder's final performance of aerial poetry as "may be reliable. Or not," possibly without official sanction of the regime: "It might be that Wieder wrote his poem in the sky over Santiago without asking permission or warning anyone, although it seems unlikely ... In 1974, hallucinations were not uncommon."[33] Recalling at this point in the novel the ambiguous potential effect of the imperative of Wieder's poetic act to "LEARN," the implicitly self-sacrificing self-identification with Christ in Wieder's ultimate aerial performance ("Death is my heart / Take my heart / Carlos Wieder / Death is resurrection") suggests the possibility that Wieder's final poem, which the text indicates may have been unauthorized, should be interpreted at once constatively, as a literal figuration of the reign of terror the Pinochet regime had unleashed on the country, and performatively, whether as a horrendous affirmation of the deaths and disappearances authorized by the regime, in which case Wieder must be read as a psychopath and sadist, or on the contrary, which seems equally plausible, as a protest against the reign of terror that might have some potential to awaken or encourage resistance to it, in which case Wieder could be read as having turned against the regime with a desire to expose it as the death machine it has become.

The sixth chapter's subsequent account of the disastrous photographic exhibition held by Wieder at his apartment in Santiago, which leads to the precipitous downfall of his reputation and counts among its attendees two representatives of the avant-garde left ("two surrealist (or super-realist) reporters") raises similar doubts about an unambiguous alignment between Wieder and the Pinochet regime. While "the surrealist reporters looked disapproving but maintained their composure," what they observed—the "hundreds of photos" revealing women who "looked like mannequins, broken, dismembered mannequins in some pictures"—constituted, the text tells us, "a progression, an argument, a story (literal and allegorical), a plan."[34] While the exhibit may be read as a morbid affirmation or display of sadistic indifference to the terrors of Pinochet's regime, it may also be read, like the "Death" poem of Wieder's final aerial performance, as a poetic act that is redemptively avant-garde precisely in its unstinting display of those same terrors for the purpose of generating resistance. However we are inclined to interpret it, Wieder's uncanny composure has the effect of putting on display for the Pinochet military unwanted attention, and thus implicitly calling into question, as does Bolaño's narrative, the crimes of the Pinochet regime and the troubling questions they raise concerning the articulation of a poetry, poetics, and aesthetics that might rise to the occasion of the historical, political demands of its time. What would such a poetry, poetics, and aesthetics look like?

Concerned with such questions to its core, the following chapter closes the novel's third section, and the arc of the first seven chapters altogether, all of which are set in Chile, with a summary of accounts of Wieder's fall from grace and subsequent legacy. Appearing briefly in "the shifting anthology of Chilean literature," associating "with various ephemeral literary magazines" and publishing under a variety of pseudonyms, his traces "becoming progressively fainter," he seems, like Rimbaud, namesake of Bolaño's doppelgänger narrator Arturo Belano, to have "turned his back on literature," his work nevertheless living on "precariously, desperately," read and reinvented by "A handful of young men." Disappearing from Chile and leaving behind "the passionate and contradictory readings to which his work gave rise," Wieder becomes "a mythic figure" who finds "a following," figuring prominently in the critic Ibacache's posthumously published *What the Writers Read*, a work that suggests a range of poetic choices in the years surrounding the critic's death and cremation in 1986.[35]

Underscoring his allegorical link to the Pinochet regime, Wieder's father is said to have died in 1990, the year Pinochet gave up power. Mentioned in subsequent years in "a judicial report on torture and the disappearance of prisoners" (1992), an "'independent operational group' responsible for the death of various students in and around Concepción and Santiago" (1993 and 1994), in Muñoz Cano's memoir, in "Exploring the Limits," a chapter of Bibiano O'Ryan's successful *The Warlocks Return* (a "highly readable study of fascist literary movements in South America from 1972 to 1989" that figures in Bolaño's *Nazi Literature in the Americas*), and in a "cyclical, epic poem" by the former maid at the Garmendia sisters' estate, "the Chilean citizen Amalia Maluenda," a work that is "partly the story of the Chilean nation" and defended only by three former military comrades, Wieder fades little by little into oblivion: "The country had too many problems to concern itself so long with the fading figure of a serial killer who had disappeared years ago. / Chile forgot him."[36]

Forgotten as well in Chile, the first paragraph of the following chapter tells us, are the narrator, who reappears there along with Bibiano O'Ryan, and a new Bolaño doppelgänger, the displaced Chilean detective Abel Romero. Shifting the novel's setting from Chile to Europe, and from the years surrounding the 1973 coup to a new time of narration in the early post-Pinochet era two decades later, 1993, the three chapters in Barcelona and Blanes that compose the novel's fourth and final section (with narrative displacements to Paris and Italy) announce an explicit focus on another of Bolaño's central literary-historical preoccupations, the relation between poetry and the detective genre that figures so centrally in his career, from *Antwerp* (set, like the final three chapters of *Distant Star*, in and around Barcelona) and *Monsieur Pain* to *The Savage Detectives, Woes of the True Policeman*, and *2666*. With the sudden appearance of Romero, a detective of some prior renown in his native Chile who has been hired by an unknown client to search for the mysterious Wieder, *Distant Star* reframes its history of modern poetry in the second half of the twentieth century in Chile and elsewhere through Wieder's legacy in a way that parallels the shift in Bolaño's own career from an emphasis on poetry to an investment, in every sense of the word, in prose, in particular in detective fiction as the genre of a specifically commercial fiction par excellence.

From his early years in Chile and Mexico into his twenties, as Bolaño remarks in an interview with Eliseo Álvarez first published two years after his death that he was writing, "in reality . . . only poetry."[37] Acknowledging that two decades later it had been "a long time since [he] knew anything about Mexican poetry," Bolaño concedes that what he did know "of those who do write it" was of "only those, like me, approaching their fifties."[38] Yet if he were "to win . . . the lottery," he had remarked previously in a 1999 interview with Óscar López, he "would write only poetry, four or five perfect poems . . . If a writer writes prose, which is the most boring kind of writing, it's for the money . . . Generally speaking I'm in the habit of combining short story and novel, because today, for me, writing poetry is a luxury."[39] Set a year after Bolaño began making a living from his writing —"I started to live from literature starting in 1992 and *Savage Detectives* was published in 1998. Starting in 1992, which coincides with a grave illness, my income has been exclusively gained from literature"—the first of the three Barcelona/Abel Romero chapters with which *Distant Star* concludes figures the transition in Bolaño's career from the life of a writer who aspired to live like a poet and write poetry in and as verse to that of a writer fully invested in prose fiction, and in the detective novel in particular, above all for its commercial potential.[40]

While at the height of his reputation "In certain literary circles, the legend of Carlos Wieder had spread like wildfire . . . 'in the art and politics of a distant southern land,'" Wieder's disappearance and fading reputation as the poet Marta Posadas had said would "revolutionize Chilean poetry" has set the stage, by the first of the novel's final three chapters, both for the emergence of the detective Abel Romero as the narrator's, and Bolaño's, new alter-ego, and for the corresponding shift in focus away from poetry to an investment in prose fiction generally, and in detective fiction in particular, that is motivated first and foremost by the desire to make money: "During the time of Allende, Romero had been something of a celebrity in the police force. Now he was in his fifties . . . Bibiano O'Ryan had given him my address in Barcelona . . . . There's money in it, said Romero, if you help me find him."[41] Left with "fifty thousand pesetas in an envelope and a suitcase full of literary magazines . . . all European . . . not the usual sort of right-wing literary magazines," and Romero's claim that "the two best police forces in the world, at least as far a homicide was concerned, were the

British and the Chilean," the narrator, who is in "pretty poor health" (like
Bolaño at the time), finds himself "gradually being drawn into the story of
Carlos Wieder" until one night he dreams of "writing a poem, or perhaps
writing in my diary," waking to realize that "... Wieder and I had been
travelling in the *same boat* ["en el *mismo* barco"]; he may have conspired to
sink it, but I had done little or nothing to stop it going down." The
narrator's, and Bolaño's, identification with Wieder at this point complete,
notwithstanding Wieder's earlier characterizations as "a serial killer" ("un
asesino múltiple") and "a criminal, not a poet" ("un criminal, no un
poeta"), the detective genre story of Romero's search for Wieder, which
is also that of the narrator and of Bolaño, becomes in effect an allegory of
the search for the "murder" of poetry of whatever kind, "revolutionary,"
"avant-garde" or not, at the hands of prose, the hands of the literary
marketplace itself.[42]

It is significant, in this respect, that the detective novel itself quickly
gives way, in the first of the Romero chapters, to visual media, including
television and film: "I don't watch television, I said. Well you should, you
don't know what you're missing ... I saw a film with Paul Newman once,
he said. He was a writer and they gave him the Nobel Prize and then he
confessed that for years he'd been writing detective novels under
a pseudonym to earn his living. I respect that sort of writer ... Wieder
on film? ... They were low-budget pornographic films." Referring in
passing, ironically, in a prescient foreshadowing, to the novelist Bolaño
has arguably since come to displace as the Latin American writer du jour,
Gabriel García Márquez, whose novel Romero brings him as a gift, and
which the narrator had "already read," the narrator's mention of a "second
cameraman" at the close of the eighth chapter, "A certain R.P. English . . . .
Were Wieder and English one and the same? Romero thought so," figures
a link between a certain violence to and in literature, the detective genre's
commercial selling-out of "serious" literary fiction, and the ascendancy in
the 1990s marketplace of pornographic film subsequently superseded, since
the time of writing of *Distant Star*, by the rise of the Internet.[43]

Anticipating a certain death not only of poetry but of literature generally—
a death that will coincide with Romero's implied (but, like the deaths of the
Garmendia twins earlier in the novel, never explicitly depicted) murder of
Wieder in the novel's final pages in chapter 10 —the narrator begins the ninth
chapter with a farewell to literature that recalls the reported rumors of
Wieder's own: "This is my last communiqué from the planet of the monsters.
Never again will I immerse myself in literature's bottomless cesspools. I will
go back to writing my poems, such as they are, find a job to keep body and

soul together, and make no attempt to be published." Emerging in this context in its familiar role as the quintessential genre of literature as anti-commodity, to the extent that what is called "literature" may be said to pursue and retain, as in the detective genre, commercial ambitions, poetry makes its final appearance in *Distant Star*, in a chapter devoted to the narrator's discovery of "Raoul Delorme and the sect known as 'the barbaric writers.'" Radically democratic in its conception, the movement attracted disciples who, like Delorme himself, "were uneducated and came from humble backgrounds." Against the earlier claims of the Pinochet era, concerning Wieder's purportedly revolutionary right-wing avant-garde practices, that "the future of art is not for herds," the movement of the "'barbaric writers,'" aligned with the left avant-garde aspirations of Paris in May 1968, is said to have promised "the advent" of a "new literature . . . that could in principle belong to everyone . . . Naturally, most of 'the barbaric writers' were poets, although some wrote stories and others experimented with short plays." Referencing Salvador Dalí and the desecration of books as a way "to improve one's spoken and written French," in an essay published by one Jules Defoe arguing that "literature should be written by non-literary people, just as politics should be and indeed was being taken over by non-politicians," Defoe is said to have claimed that the "corresponding revolution in writing . . . would, in a sense abolish literature itself," resulting in a time when "poetry is written by non-poets and read by non-readers." Suspecting "this parti-cular champion of barbaric writing" (Defoe) was Wieder himself, the narrator continues: "As to the poem (a narrative poem, which, to my eternal shame, reminded me of John Cage's poetic diary . . . It was one of Carlos Wieder's ultimate jokes. And it was deadly serious.")[44]

Revealing in his final assessment of Wieder a sympathy that runs against the grain of the novel's previous invitations to judge and condemn him, the narrator reframes the question of the avant-garde as a question of witness, as much as of invention or intention, a question of poetry's, of the novel's, of art's capacity generally (the acronym of Wieder's original name, Alberto Ruiz-Tagle, is A.R.T.) to engage with the urgency of its historical and literary-historical moment. Wieder's fate, which figures that of aesthetic and political movements left, right, and center, remains an open-ended question of reading, as well as of writing, in a time such as ours when reading and writing themselves, and not merely of poetry and fiction, seem increasingly threatened. The threat of violence that haunts the novel's narrative, from the opening chapter's evocation of the rise of the Pinochet regime and its subsequent disappearances to Romero's suggestive, ultimately unknowable final gesture, gives rise in the end to a quiet yet telling resistance, or is it resignation: "It's not worth it, I persisted. It's over now. No one needs to get hurt now. Romero slapped me on the shoulder. Better you stay out of this, he said . . . "

Evoking, at that precise instant, the "increasingly distant stars," the text suggests the complex role reading and writing may play in encouraging and discouraging potentially reductive, totalizing (dis)identifications of every aesthetic and political orientation. As Romero emerges "a half-hour later . . . the spitting image of Edward G. Robinson"—the classic protagonist and antagonist of so many films noirs, foreshadowing, anticipating, inscribing the novel's own cinematic adaptation—the narrative moves quickly to its literal payoff, the handing over by Romero to the narrator of "an envelope" containing "three hundred thousand pesetas": "I don't need this much money, I said after counting it. It's yours, said Romero . . . You've earned it. I haven't earned anything, I said." In this final accounting, in every sense, of the term, *Distant Star* figures all the ambivalence, yet also the irresistible pull, of Bolaño's attraction to detective prose fiction at the expense of a more exclusive orientation toward poetry, an expenditure and an investment that drew him successfully into the rarefied sphere he has come to occupy, himself a "distant star" of the highest magnitude, shining brightly in the literary stratosphere into which the commercialization of his fiction has propelled him. Appearing in the end, by contrast, "small and tired," Romero, the detective genre's synecdochic figure par excellence, leaves the narrator twenty years his junior, lover of poetry at the expense of all literature, alter-ego of the young Bolaño, as the narrator leaves off his synecdochically personal and impersonal, individual and collective, historical and literary-historical, aesthetic and political narrative, with a future that may or may not be for the herds.[45]

Part Three

CHAPTER 6

Dismantling Narrative Drive
The Savage Detectives (Los detectives salvajes)

Bolaño's 1998 novel *Los detectives salvajes* (*The Savage Detectives*, 2007) appears, at least initially, as a quick glance at the back cover of Picador's English translation tells us, to be an "ambitious novel" of monumental scope. Weighing in at a hefty 609 pages in the original, it was doubtless in no small measure the book's length, its sheer scale, compared to that of Bolaño's previous works, that contributed to securing "his international reputation" as "one of the greatest Latin American authors of our age." Praised as a "masterwork" (*Vogue*) which "alone should grant him immortality," as Ilan Stavans' *Washington Post Book World* review puts it, *The Savage Detectives* has led more than any other of Bolaño's works prior to the posthumous publication of *2666*, as the aptly titled collection *Bolaño salvaje* suggests, to Bolaño's canonization, comparable to that of Gabriel García Márquez among writers of the previous Latin American "Boom," as the synecdochic writer of his generation, the "expanding universe" of whose reception, in Chris Andrews' useful formulation," has come to include a growing sense of his pivotal importance, "After Bolaño" and *Beyond Bolaño*, in Sarah Pollack's and Héctor Hoyos', for what Hoyos calls *The Global Latin American Novel*, what Rebecca Walkowitz calls *The Contemporary Novel in an Age of World Literature*, and what the most recent collection of essays on his work calls simply *World Literature* more generally.[1]

While *The Savage Detectives* continues to play a central role in Bolaño's increasingly global reception, the stakes of his literary monumentality and "immortality" raised that much further by the even more monumental *2666*, the genre identity of *The Savage Detectives* as a singular "novel" (like that of 2666 as well) merits skepticism. Recalling Poe's dismantling of the idea that there is any such thing as a long poem, the fractured, fragmented, modular, prose-poetic structure of *The Savage Detectives*—divided into three parts of radically different lengths: "I. Mexicanos perdidos en México (1975)" ("I. Mexicans Lost in Mexico (1975)"); "II. Los detectives salvajes

(1976–1996)" ("II. The Savage Detectives (1976–1996)"); and "III. Los desiertos de Sonora (1976)" ("The Sonora Desert (1976)")—invites readers to challenge the analogous idea that there may be any such thing as a long novel. Characteristically poet- and poetry-centered, by far the longest of Bolaño's novels of poetic (though no longer, with the publication of *2666*, of novelistic) apprenticeship, arguably Bolaño's most consistent concern and signature contribution, *The Savage Detectives* is composed conceptually not of three parts, as it appears, but of two, the relatively condensed first and third parts of which—at 126 and 54 pages each a combined novella-length of 170 pages—are (chronologically, narratologically, conceptually, affectively, stylistically) continuous, yet separated from each other by the massively longer, in fundamental respects radically different 455-page, central Part II. Where the predominantly monological Parts I and III are unified by the framing narrative of the displaced autobiographical, seventeen-year-old aspiring "visceral realist" poet and diarist, Juan García Madero (whose surname suggests perhaps a "wooden" apprentice version of García Márquez), the wildly multiplying narratives of Part II, which bears the novel's plural title, are dispersed among the voices of over fifty character-narrators recurring with varying degrees of frequency and distributed across twenty-six numbered, prose-poetic testimonial sections ranging from one to nine named narrations, on average around four to six each. Encompassing throughout the obliquely narrated, ubiquitously present-absent, absent-present stories of García Madero's two mentors and co-protagonists, Arturo Belano and Ulises Lima, whom the reader comes to know only indirectly through the voices of others, the radically polyphonic, heteroglossic procedure of *The Savage Detectives* doesn't so much fulfill readers' preconceptions of more traditional, conventional novels, as question the novel as such as a coherent, unified form, including its association with "epic" ambitions.[2]

Through its aleatory, leisurely, at once literal and figurative unraveling, its seemingly endless deferrals of what we may call "narrative drive"—figured through the gathering, generative conceit of a drive through the Sonora Desert from which it continually departs and returns—*The Savage Detectives* both recycles and dismantles the trope of tropes of literature itself as odyssey, as journey, as "Voyage," as Bolaño puts it, echoing Baudelaire, so crucial to Bolaño as a synecdoche for poetry's full capacity, not for monological, self-expressive purity and condensation, but for heteroglossic amplification and hybridity.[3] Encompassing drives in both the Freudian and Nieztschean senses, at once libidinal and political ("Triebe" and "Wille zur Macht"), so interconnected throughout Bolaño's oeuvre, the trope of the main characters' drive north from Mexico City into the desert offers a formal, structural, narratological strategy that comes ultimately to resemble less a novel in the traditional sense—postponing as it does continually and relentlessly the melodramatic closure readers expect from a conventional detective novel until the very end—than an impossibly sustained assemblage of loosely linked prose poems on an "epic," "novelistic" scale.[4] Finding its diverse, alternative, at once prose-poetic and "novelizing" forms, in Bakhtin's sense, in the daily journal entries of García Madero that make up Parts I and II, and in the wildly dialogical, heteroglossic individual testimonies and remembrances of the fifty-plus individual narrators making up the novel's central, massively modular, deliberately unwieldly Part II, which bears the novel's title, *The Savage Detectives*, radically raises the stakes of Bolaño's lifelong commitment as a writer of fiction to the development of what he refers to in a pivotal passage as "poemas-novela" in prose, or prose poem novels.[5]

Through its continually stalled-out meta-narrative "voyage" into what his posthumously collected poems call *The Unknown University*, of which the Sonora Desert is in this case a synecdoche, *The Savage Detectives* radically embraces, expands, and extends to its readers the freeing invitation Bolaño understood the prose poems of Baudelaire and Rimbaud represented as a challenge and alternative to the traditional realist novel's singular, linear drive.[6] That Bolaño named his most autobiographically resonant protagonist "Arturo Belano," a punning condensation and displacement of his own name with those of the prose poem's two founding figures, suggests the central importance of the prose poem's anti-generic impulses both to Bolaño's sense of what has mattered most in the history of modern poetry and to his approach to the writing of fiction in general and the novel in particular.[7] As co-leader of the self-named visceral realists —"los real visceralistas o viscerrealistas e incluso vicerrealistas" ("visceral realists, or viscerealists or even vicerealists")[8]—Belano represents and reconfigures, within a novelistic frame, the prose poem's own marginality, its frequently suppressed status in the history of modern poetry and literature as the ur-modernist, utopian, genreless genre of the marginal *tout court*. Belano's visceral realist co-leader, friend, and doppelgänger, Ulises Lima—whose names conjoin allusions to Homer's *Odyssey*, Joyce's *Ulysses*, and the Cuban writer and poet José Lezama Lima—figures similarly, as does their brief companion in the final two months of 1975 and the first two months of 1976, the seventeen-year-old aspiring poet Juan García Madero, the narrator of Parts I and III. Through the fictive representations of its three central characters and fifty-plus narrators, *The Savage Detectives* is above all a prose-poetic literary history by other means and parody of the detective genre, an endlessly deferred, sustained unraveling and Quixotic quest with Cervantes and Borges as guides.

Lost, abandoned, stalled out in the middle of the Sonora Desert, the reader is set adrift, in Part II, on a vast ocean of testimonials from Mexico City, Santiago, Paris, New York, Los Angeles, Buenos Aires, London, Berlin, Barcelona. At the center of the novel's quest, its homage, is Cesárea Tinajero, founding figure of visceral realism, the slightness of whose oeuvre is surpassed, as the novel gradually reveals over the course of its six-hundred-plus pages, only by that of the self-identified poets Belano and Lima themselves, whose actual writing of poetry survives only as rumor. Tinajero, like Belano and Lima (and in contrast to García Madero), is central to the novel's unfolding, its unraveling and dismantling, yet does not narrate her own story. An absent presence, with Belano and Lima, is driving something close to a plotless plot to the end's resolutely anticlimactic, detective-story conclusion (car chase + double murder). Recalling Ariadne and Penelope, Tinajero figures a gender-coded alternative (to penelopize, delay), to the narrative drive of Odysseus (his namesake, Ulises Lima), that driven character, no less gender-coded, who has himself come to figure, through his seemingly ceaseless journeys, a narrative of endless deferrals, a plotless plot that seems never to want to arrive at an end, the weaving and unweaving, raveling and unraveling of its narrative threads resisting becoming whole cloth, "una teja," in Penelope's, Odysseus' case, a death-shroud. Carrying with it, along with her nickname "Tinaja" ("jar")—"una tal Cesárea Tinajero o Tinaja" ("somebody called Cesárea Tinajero or Tinaja")[9]—echoes of "tejer" and "tejido," "tejedor" and "tejo," Tinajero's last name suggests the shaping and fracturing, weaving and unweaving, raveling and unraveling of plots. Explicitly linked to Lautréamont,[10] Tinajero figures, more than all those who have become canonized, as Belano and Lima see it, the dogged pursuit of being searched for and remembered, recollected and recognized, the lost poet who most deserves to be found.

Configuring at its conclusion an alternative vision both of what "poetry (real poetry)"—"la poesía (la verdadera poesía)"[11]—and a more real world pedagogy might involve, Cesárea Tinajero offers an alternative, counter-Caesar to that figured in the novel's beginning by "Julio César Álamo," the poet and poetry professor García Madero first encounters in the opening pages, whose pedagogy contributes to his decision to drop out of the university. Much more closely aligned, as the rhyming of their first and last names suggests, with the poet whose name means "beloved Caesar,"

Aimé Césaire, who shows up as an admired figure in Bolaño's *Nazi Literature in the America* and *Woes of the True Policeman*, and whose own *Odyssey*-echoing *Cahier d'un retour au pays natal* (*Notebook of a Return to the Native Land*) provides the title for Bolaño's "Fragmentos de un regreso al país natal" ("Fragments of a Return to the Native Land"), Tinajero is the figure of a poet and poem, by extension of a novelist and novel, of a poet-novelist and prose poem novel lost at sea, in the desert—Homer's Mediterranean (as still the Caribbean of Derek Walcott's *Omeros*) in epic verses; the Caribbean and Paris of Césaire's *Cahier* (*Notebooks*) in alternating verse and prose; the Dublin of Joyce's *Ulysses*, the Mexico City and Sonora of *The Savage Detectives* (but for a few quoted verses, diagrams and drawings) all in the novel's prose—of an impossible, oxymoronic, plotless plot told in an impossible, oxymoronic genreless genre.[12] In its seemingly endless, often undeniably, even unrelentingly tedious deferral of anything remotely resembling an "event" or "action," *The Savage Detectives* offers a conspicuous "case" in the end of misplaced genre fulfillment, a book with all the appearance of a detective novel (its length, its ambition, in prose) that includes by way of real (simulated) violence only the two murders ritualistically, stereotypically, in the end predictably offered up, at last, at the book's conclusion.

What counts as action, as event, as plot, emerges as a question inextricable from that of the relation between poetry and prose. How can the reader know the difference? What is central? What is marginal? What matters in the end, as in the beginning, as form, as content, as the content of the form and the form of the content? In posing and responding to these questions, readers of *The Savage Detectives* find themselves in the novella-length Part I, "Mexicans Lost in Mexico" (126 pages in the original, 139 pages in the English translation), as in Part I's chronological sequel and culmination, Part III, "The Sonora Desert" (54 and 59 pages, respectively), in the hands of seventeen-year-old would-be visceral realist poet, García Madero, whose first-person narration is sustained and developed through daily journal entries, the form of which is in keeping with the prose poem's average length of a half-page to three pages. Part II, the novel's narrative middle, pursues a similar formal strategy, expanding its reliance on the formal device of journal entries as prose poems, or prose poems as journal entries, through its proliferation of trial-like testimonies. A radical parody in effect of Bakhtinian polyphony and heteroglossia, it has the form and function, sandwiched between García Madero's opening and closing first-person narrations, monological yet in their way no less fragmented, of a constant interruption.[13]

In the first-person voice of García Madero, the autobiographical opening and closing sections of *The Savage Detectives* develop the narrative of an aspiring young poet precociously knowledgeable, as his daily journal entries repeatedly demonstrate, about the history of poetry and poetics. Recalling perhaps more than any other text Poe's "The Rationale of Verse," with its encyclopedic, tediously pedantic rehearsal of ancient verse techniques, the opening pages of García Madero's journal entries in Part I, like those in Part III, establish him as a representative figure of Bolaño's own lifelong obsession with poetry, poetics, and literary history, an obsession Bolaño continues to work through not only in his own poetry, but, even more consequentially, in the role poetry plays in his fiction. Announcing, in his first entry, November 2, 1975, his proud acceptance of an invitation to "join the visceral realists," García Madero figures the pervasive preoccupation of Bolaño's fiction with questions of poetic apprenticeship, poetic belonging, and the complex, ever-changing dynamics of literary-historical remembering and forgetting. The second entry, from November 3, 1975, poses such questions acutely in terms of the kinds of career and life decisions every aspiring young poet at some point must address. In this ur-scene of traumatic entry into the deeply disciplinary, hierarchical community of poets, Bolaño positions poetry as a career and life choice at once discursively and existentially, through the figure of García Madero, against the more "realistic," practical option of a career, and life, in the law. Clashing almost immediately with his potential mentor, the Emperor-like "Julius Caesar" of the poetry workshop, poetry's guardian and gate-keeper but also its potential last defense and defeat, García Madero quickly realizes that the "scenes" of poetry are, above all, not scenes of cordiality or hospitality, but of competition, not only between mentor and apprentice but among peers. The workshop format becomes in this sense, in García Madero's words, "an ideal method for ensuring that no one was friends with anyone, or else that our friendships were unhealthy and based on resentment."[14]

Rescued from his rude awakening to poetry as a scene of intense rivalry and competition, in the workshop's fifth session, by the appearance of Belano and Lima, whom Álamo (parodying the academy as site of poetry's last-stand) berates as "cut-rate surrealists and fake Marxists" in response to their questioning of his "critical system," García Madero gains a sense of belonging in being embraced by Belano, Lima, and the visceral realists as "one of their own."[15] In the aftermath of Belano's and Lima's appearance at the workshop, which García Madero describes as "clearly a hostile visit, hostile but somehow propagandistic and proselytizing too," García

Madero finds himself configured among three options: 1) the formalist leanings he initially brought to the workshop, which succeeded in enraging the workshop's professor and prompted García Madero's peers to reject him as "pedantic" and "academicist" ("me acusaron de pedante (uno dijo que yo era un academicista");[16] 2) the work of Octavio Paz, the "only Mexican poet," according to Lima, who shares the kind of formal, technical knowledge García Madero prizes, who is yet visceral realism's "great enemy," and 3) Belano's and Lima's favored visceral realists, "a Mexican avant-garde group ... active in the twenties or maybe the thirties" represented by Tinajero. Mentioned along with Lautréamont in the context of Lima's "mysterious claim" that "the present-day visceral realists walked backward," Tinajero emerges in the opening pages of Part I of *The Savage Detectives* as a synecdochic figure for what Marjorie Perloff has called a new "arrière-garde" invested in reclaiming the historical avant-gardes as vital models for contemporary poetic practice.[17]

The development of a poetics, as García Madero comes quickly to understand through the medium of the workshop, has to do not so much with "individual" choice but with the overdetermining role of available group formations, whether implicit or explicit, whether named by others, like the impressionists and cubists, or self-named, like the surrealists and visceral realists. In being asked to join the latter, García Madero writes, "they asked me to join the gang. They didn't say 'group' or 'movement,' they said 'gang.' ["No dijeron «grupo» o «movimiento», dijeron pandilla y eso me gustó"] ... I said yes, of course." As Belano's, Lima's, and García Madero's embrace of the term "gang" over the more genteel terms "group" or "movement" suggests, what characterizes their aesthetic and poetics as visceral realist at its core is their recognition that literary history is, in García Madero's words, like history and politics more generally, a "battle," not the polite community of writers, poets, scholars he had imagined but a complex of competing positions.[18]

The distance between the verse poems García Madero mentions and the prose-poetic journal entries of his fragmented narrative is the distance between the naïve aspiring apprentice and the mature, visceral realist, prose-poetic, still poetry-obsessed Bolaño. Discovering "an amazing poem" by the poet and lawyer "Efrén Rebolledo (1877–1929)," about whom he says, "They never said anything ... in any of our literature classes," García Madero copies out Rebolledo's sonnet "El vampiro" ("The Vampire") in its entirety.[19] Unsurprisingly, for a seventeen-year-old poet about to embark on his first sexual adventures, "El vampiro" exemplifies, in Bolaño's deployment of it as exhibit, the appeal of a more conventional poetics associated with love and traditional verse forms. Recalling Poe's constrained investments in such forms, García Madero's literal reproduction of Rebolledo's appropriation and variation of Baudelaire's identically titled, six-quatrain poem, "Le Vampire," echoing Poe's "The Raven" and other gothic-erotic poems, figures poetry itself as "Vampire" verse, as fetishized object, pure product, pure genre, pure kitsch.[20] In stark contrast to Poe's radical dismantling of the poetry/prose binary in "The Poetic Principle" and "The Philosophy of Composition" and experimental, genre-defining, genre-expanding range as a writer of prose fiction, with all its proto-visceral realist qualities, García Madero's enthusiasm for "The Vampire" suggests his identification with poetry as an adolescent genre, as the genre of adolescence as such.

Recalling the ostentatious, precocious-yet-naïve references to traditional verse forms and ancient sources García Madero's workshop peers found "pedantic," García Madero's enthusiasm for Rebolledo's gothic conventionality suggests the gap between the visceral realist ambitions of Bolaño's doppelgänger and namesake, Belano, to "change Latin American poetry," and García Madero's adolescent incapacity to access the transformative power, at once poetic and political, of what Rimbaud called almost a century earlier "secrets pour changer la vie."[21] Written at seventeen, the same age as Rimbaud when he wrote the bawdy, romantic-erotic verse poem, "Le Coeur volé" ("The Stolen Heart")—the only other poem quoted in its entirety in *The Savage Detectives* and one of the last verse poems Rimbaud would write before his revolutionary "Alchimie du verbe" ("Alchemy of the Verb," 1871)—García Madero's prose-poetic journal entries recall the final stage of Rimbaud's apprenticeship in poetry as verse and his subsequent, Paris-Commune-inspired turn, almost exactly a century earlier, from verse to the prose poem.[22]

Extending from November 2 to December 31, 1975, and from January 1 to February 14, 1976, respectively, the fourteen-week period of García Madero's fragmented first-person entries in Parts I and III closely approximate the fifteen-week duration of the Paris Commune from March 8 to May 28, 1871. Divided into two parts of asymmetrical lengths (126 and 54 pages) separated by the massively fragmented, polyphonic Part II (415 pages), Parts I and III together make up a continuous narrative (from November 2 to December 31, 1975, and from January 1 to February 15, 1976) with a single narrator (García Madero), in effect a single novella of their own. At roughly two hundred pages, the total length of Parts I and III of *The Savage Detectives* thus demonstrates a formal affinity with each of the novellas from the same astonishingly prolific, five-year period in

Bolaño's work (1995–2000)—*Distant Star, Amulet,* and *By Night in Chile*—which together make up an intricate tetralogy of novels of poetic apprenticeship, a sustained literary-historical investigation of modern and contemporary poetry and poetics from the mid-nineteenth through the final two decades of the twentieth century, encompassing both Europe and the Americas.

While the continuous narrative of Parts I and III of *The Savage Detectives* might easily have been published as a single, entirely cohesive, self-contained novel, at a novella-length approximating those of Bolaño's three integrally interrelated yet self-contained novels of poetic apprenticeship, the singular drive, at once literal and figurative, of García Madero's first-person narrative is instead interrupted, complicated, and seemingly endlessly deferred by the explosively exhaustive polyphony, and frequently exhausting cacophony, of the novel's central, title section. Slightly more than twice the length of Parts I ("Mexicans Lost in Mexico") and III ("The Sonora Desert") combined, Part II ("The Savage Detectives") distributes its trial-like testimonials even more asymmetrically, from a temporal, historical perspective, across the twenty-year period following the events of García Madero's fourteen-week narrative—the last eight weeks of 1975, the first six weeks of 1976—from 1976 to 1996. At the heart of García Madero's prose-poetic, continuous yet fractured first-person narration of Parts I and III, and of what gets recounted about the events of that fourteen-week period retrospectively, in the post-facto interruption and polyphonic gathering of narrative accounts in Part II, is the search of Arturo Belano and Ulises Lima for the mysterious, all-but-forgotten founding figure of the all-but-forgotten visceral realist movement, the poet, Cesárea Tinajero, of whom the reader eventually learns only a single poem remains. As the MacGuffin who, as absent center, drives the novel's plot in what amounts to a continuous play on meta-narratological tropes—as on "conducir" and "manejar," "impulsos" and "impulsiones," "trama," and "trauma"—Tinajero occupies a central role in what emerges from the beginning as the novel's central concern. At once present, as one of the novel's central characters, and absent, in not being one of its many narrators, Tinajero figures Belano's and Lima's search for what is and is not poetry. Or perhaps, more importantly, for an understanding of what happens to those who invest in "whatever has . . . been called poetry," as Friedrich Schlegel put it, "at any time and at any place."[23]

As a founding figure of "visceral realism," whose legacy of a sole poem outnumbers what remains from García Madero, Belano, and Lima combined, Tinajero figures what is perhaps the most conspicuous aspect of

Bolaño's fiction, the pervasive fascination with poetry and poetics coupled with a near total absence of citations from actual poems. As the first of Bolaño's two exceptions to this conspicuous absence, Rebolledo's "The Vampire" figures the extent to which García Madero's poetic apprenticeship remains in thrall to the traditional forms and themes of late Romantic verse, even as his newfound alliance with the visceral realists, recounted in the prose-poetic form of his journal entries, points in a more modernist direction. The only other exception to this otherwise systematic rule, the quotation of Rimbaud's "Le Coeur volé" near the beginning of Part II, figures a similar watershed moment, paralleling that of García Madero's poetics and by implication of the adolescent Bolaño, in the history of modern poetry. As we learn in the crucial fifth dated entry of Part II in which "Le Coeur volé" appears ("Luis Sebastián Rosado, La Rama Dorada coffee shop, Colonia Coyoacán Mexico City DF, April 1976"), Rimbaud, modernist poetics, "visceral realism," "stridentism," and "the future of Mexican poetry" are all bound up with each other.[24] For Lima, as the follow-up testimony by one "Alberto Moore" tells us, the story of Rimbaud's writing of "Le Coeur volé" is the story of a forgotten history linking Rimbaud, the French invasion of Mexico, and the Paris Commune, and thus, by extension, the history of modern French and Mexican poetry. Reenacting and reconfiguring the quintessentially Rimbaldian story of a coming-of-age into poetry that is simultaneously a farewell to poetry as such (or at least as verse), the apprentice poet García Madero's first-person narrative in Parts I and III figures the shift in Bolaño's own priorities from adolescence to adulthood, from his early, failed aspiration to be recognized primarily as a writer of poetry as verse, to his eventually successful career and expansively acclaimed accomplishments as a writer of prose fiction, haunted by poets and poetry.

Buried in this plot, interrupting and subsequently resuming García Madero's narrative, is Lima and Belano's quest for Tinajero. Of the novel's fifty-plus narrators, thirty-nine of whom have only one entry, fourteen more than one, the most prominent in the sprawling central section that gives the novel its title is the venerable Mexican writer/critic, Amadeo Salvatierra, whose thirteen entries easily outnumber those of its other narrators. Beginning and ending with two of those entries, Part II establishes him as its framing figure, the character whose recollections open most crucially onto the search for Tinajero and her writings. Arcing back to 1976, the year following the events of Parts I and III that marks the beginning of the twenty-year period it encompasses, Part II elaborates the full context and stakes of Belano and Lima's literary-historical detective work.[25] In its movement from 1976 to 1996 and back again, including the thrice-repeated question of Salvatierra's final entry— "is it worth it? is it worth it? is it really worth it?" (anticipating the dying priest and poet-critic Urrutia Lacroix/H. Ibacache's six-times repeated "Is there a solution?" in the closing pages of *By Night in Chile*)—it prepares the way for the resumption of García Madero's narrative in Part III. Picking up where his closing entry in in Part I leaves off (December 31, 1975), following Part II's more than four hundred page, extravagantly polyphonic interruption, his first entry in Part III (January 1, 1976) establishes a continuous narrative between the novel's opening and closing sections.

Framing and reframing the end of Part I and the beginning of Part III as a liminal moment that drives the novel's third, concluding section from Mexico City to the Sonora Desert, both literally and figuratively, is the movement from verse to prose, from García Madero's abandoned apprenticeship into poetry as verse to a fiction concerned, as figured in Belano and Lima's search for Tinajero, with poets and poetry. In the company of the adolescent García Madero and the aging Salvatierra, Belano and Lima emerge first and foremost as companion researchers, without official sanction, of a forgotten literary history they take to be of great urgency for the present. *Amateurs* in the full sense, unauthorized outsiders, literary detectives and lovers of literature, they are quintessential representatives of the Unknown University. Mentors of García Madero—who aspires to nothing more, at the same age Rimbaud was when writing the prose poems of *Une Saison en Enfer* and *Illuminations*, than to emulate and impress Lima and Rimbaud's namesake, Belano—and interviewers of the jaded Salvatierra, Belano and Lima figure the reassessment and turn in Bolaño's identity as a writer at roughly the same age, twenty-three, and in the same year, 1976, following his move from Mexico to Barcelona, from a primary emphasis on the writing of poetry in and as verse to the writing of prose fiction about poets and poetry, a project that would allow him to combine poetry, fiction, and literary history over the course of his career.

Published in 1998, when Bolaño was forty-five, *The Savage Detectives* offers the mature perspective of a writer in his prime, neither naïve, like García Madero, nor in transition, like Belano and Lima, nor jaded yet still hopeful, like Salvatierra, who has never fallen out of love with poetry but has sought to move, like Poe, like Baudelaire, like Rimbaud, beyond its limitations. Continuing and expanding the prose-poetic turn of these three pivotal figures, the prose-poem-like journal entries of Parts I and III and condensed polyphonic testimonies of Part II amplify and extend their legacy within a prose-poetic frame. Attesting to the centrality of poets and poetry to Bolaño's fictive imagination, as also to his understanding and construction of alternative literary histories, the novel's narrators testify, as in a murder trial, to a certain death of poetry, to its murder, as it were, by prose. As the inventor of the modern detective genre, the genre to which *The Savage Detectives* is most indebted, along with the prose poem, and to which it aspires to belong, as it both honors and dismantles its conventions, Poe was arguably the first to understand this death, this murder of poetry— of a certain kind of, or approach to, poetry such as that of "The Rationale of Verse," or García Madero's pedantic displays—as a necessity for the liberation, the enhanced range, of the more narrowly poetic, as well as more broadly literary, imagination. To survive, much less to thrive, as the prose poem understands from its inception programmatically, and as Bolaño understands with Poe, Baudelaire, and Rimbaud, the literary must encompass the prosaic, the visceral, the savage, the non-poetic, the extra-literary. In the case of the detective genre, Poe's most enduring contribution, Bolaño finds his other great preoccupation alongside poetry, poetry's other, a popular literary genre within which, in his hands, poetry's past may perhaps find its future.

The case of *The Savage Detectives* is in this sense about the death, or murder, of poetry, if also a case for poetry's survival, a case in which poetry has also, in and through the work of the novel itself, an afterlife, a place where it survives and thrives. Its detective story is in this sense poetry's own, a story of the search for true poetry—for what rings true in poetry and for a poetry that rings true—epitomized by the search for Tinajero, . . . the search for whom finally ends, García Madero tells us in his January 31 entry, in the northern Mexican town of Villaviciosa. Finding her "wasn't hard," yet there was "nothing poetic about her ["Cesárea no tenía nada de poética"]. She looked like a rock or an elephant. Her rear end was enormous and it moved to the rhythm set by her arms, two oak trunks."[26] Having "nothing poetic about her," Tinajero, the forgotten poet and founder of visceral realism, emerges as the most prosaic of figures. Recalling Baudelaire's famous reference, in the Preface to *Le Spleen de Paris,* to the dream of a "poetic prose, without rhythm and without rhyme," Tinajero's prosaic rhythms, shapes, and forms serve, by contrast, as a reminder that the most enduringly transformative legacy of Baudelaire's invention of the prose poem lay not in the new (anti-)genre's more conventionally "poetic" capacity to adapt to the "lyrical movements of the soul" and "undulations of dreaming," but in its prosaic capacity to be "supple enough and rugged enough"("assez souple et assez heurtée") to adapt to the "jolts of consciousness" ("soubresauts de la conscience"), a capacity born "above all" from "the exploration of huge cities" ("la fréquentation des villes énormes") and the "crossings of their innumerable relations" ("croisement de leurs innombrables rapports"),[27] figuring not the regular, metronomic rhythm of rhymed, metrical verse, as in Rebolledo's "El vampiro," Rimbaud's "Le Coeur volé," Poe's "The Raven" and "The Bells," but the mundane "rhythm" of a "rock," an "elephant," of a "rear end" that is "enormous," of arms like "two oak trunks." Finding Tinajero figures the possibility of finding not so much a *poetic* prose—or verse, which as we have seen is almost entirely absent— as an everyday visceral realist capacity for poetry, or what is called poetry, as such, in prose.[28]

Deferring, unfolding, unraveling, for over six hundred pages, its prose-poetic, "savage," visceral realist story, figured as a literal and figurative pursuit from Mexico City into the Sonora Desert, with three violent deaths waiting at the end, *The Savage Detectives* concludes where conventional detective stories often begin, with a case that needs to be solved. What counts, as story, as event, and what doesn't, is as much in question as the definition of poetry. What is at stake is nothing more and less than the story of poetry's demise, as verse, and rebirth in another form, the form of the prose poem novel. The novel ends, anticlimactically, with the conventionally expected detective-genre event of characters meeting a violent death—Alberto, spurned pimp of Lupe, the former prostitute who has become García Madero's girlfriend; the complicit policeman with whom Alberto has given chase to retrieve Lupe; and finally, Tinajero, figure of visceral realist poetry, as of poetry itself, whose crushing weight (figuring the weight of too much tradition, "rocking like a phantom battleship") saves both Lupe and Tianajero's contemporary visceral realist heirs, García Madero, Belano, and Lima, all of whom, but for the visceral fictive reality of *The Savage Detectives*, would be no less forgotten. Sacrificing herself, in the end, in their defense, Tinajero had given up poetry, as the three heirs only learned on the eve of finding her, for what today we would call a certain cognitive mapping and urban planning, a complex project aligned with radical critiques of education from Paulo Freire's class-based *Pedagogy of the Oppressed* to Rancière's *Le Maître ignorant*.[29]

The ensuing story of the development of Tinajero's relationship with her friend, Flora Castañeda, while working at a canning factory between 1936 and the factory's closing in 1945, situates the question of what matters in and about poetry in relation to questions of pedagogy, gender, sexual orientation, class conflict, and war. Writing, not poetry, in those days, in Castañeda's recollection, but rather about "a Greek woman . . . Hypatia . . .

an Alexandrian philosopher killed by Christians in 415" with whom, "the thought occurred to her . . . Cesárea identified," Tinajero is said to have "read a lot," but only as much as her long hours at the canning factory allow.[30] In the search for Tinajero that soon results in her death along with the deaths of the pimp Alberto and his complicit, corrupt policeman, what counts above all is not the deaths themselves, which fulfill, at a bare minimum, the demands of the plot of a conventional detective novel, but the definition of poetry. While the "savage" of *The Savage Detectives*, of the poetic "gang" called the "visceral realists," carries within it, parodically, the detective genre's melodramatic frisson, and the trial-like, dated entries of the novel's narrator-witnesses establish it as a kind of (anti-police) procedural, the novel's primary eventfulness does not lie in fulfilling, anticlimactically, the detective genre's conventional expectations of violent death, but in the literal and figurative drive to discover what poetry, specifically a visceral realist poetry, might be.

As much a matter of *aesthesis* as of *poiesis*, poetry's discursive identity hinges no less on acts of reading and interpretation than on acts of writing. Following García Madero's fraught first encounter with the writing and reading of poetry in an academically sanctioned environment, straying from "the law school's hallowed halls" to register "for Julio César Álamo's poetry workshop in the literature department," one of the pivotal moments in the novel's synecdochic representation of poetry from the perspective of aesthesis occurs in García Madero's lustily amateurish reading of Rebolledo's "The Vampire."[31] Exemplifying and parodying academic protocols of close reading, including its potential uses and abuses for poetry, García Madero's exegesis serves his own personal ends. Raising the stakes of the Baudelairean, Rimbaldian turn to the prosaic, the profane, the "visceral realist," his explicitly sexual interpretation subjects Rebolledo's associations of poetry as verse, and before him Poe's, with the Romantic Sublime, to a process of unabashed desublimation, far removed from his apprentice display of knowledge of poetic techniques in Álamo's poetry workshop.

But what kind of knowledge is the knowledge of poetry? And what then does poetry know? If Julio César Álamo's name suggests a combination of imperiousness and desperation, empire and defeat, his workshop "in the literature department" figures the precariousness of poetry's discursive, disciplinary situation on the margins of official knowledge, the margins of the known university. García Madero's dispiriting workshop experience, followed by his subsequent private, sexualized explication of "The Vampire," prefigures what is arguably the novel's climactic scene, some four hundred pages later, roughly two-thirds of the way through the novel's central section and the novel "as a whole." If the core of the novel's plot is the search of the literary detectives Belano and Lima for Tinajero, and if the search for Tinajero, founding figure of a visceral realist poetry, is a search for what counts as poetry, the novel's true climax may be said to reside not in the discovery of Tinajero the person and the depiction of her death, but in the discovery, and interpretation, of what reveals itself to be "the only poem by Cesárea Tinajero that existed in Mexico . . . the only poem in the world by Cesárea Tinajero," all that remains of her "Complete Works."[32] The revelation of Tinajero's sole surviving poem and its interpretation by Belano and Lima in conversation with Salvatierra, roughly two-thirds of the way through *The Savage Detectives,* mark in a fundamental sense both the height of the novel's action and the culmination of its leisurely unfolding.[33] Conspicuous by its almost total absence, in citation, throughout the novel, poetry as verse finds at last, in what a "real" poem by Tinajero turns out to look like, an object of study that calls poetry's character and value profoundly into question. Resumed some fifty pages later, the discussion of what makes Tinajero's poem a poem, and what it might mean to read, interpret, understand it, continues to challenge all received assumptions about what poetry might be taken to be.

Recalling the "academicist" approach of García Madero's conventional close reading of Rebolledo's conventional verse poem, "The Vampire," but extending its protocols and procedures to what might generally be considered a decidedly non-, anti-, or a-poetic visual object, one that is entirely non-verbal apart from its title, Belano and Lima take Tinajero's schematic, abstract visual "poem" as an occasion to challenge Salvatierra's more conventional view of what counts, and what doesn't, as poetry. The "desolation of poetry" notwithstanding, what is perhaps most striking is their affirmation of the shared pleasure of reading and writing, the happiness Belano and Lima find in both *aesthesis* and *poiesis*—in which Salvatierra participates as well—and the extent to which these are understood to be inseparable, mutually generative activities. Concluding some 150 pages later, in the last few pages of Salvatierra's entry with which Part II comes to an end, their discussion of "the only poem by Cesárea Tinajero that existed in Mexico . . . the only poem in the world by Cesárea Tinajero"—which they are last seen "still studying" in what Salvatierra calls "Cesárea Tinajero's wretched magazine"—finds the two undeterrable literary detectives committed to finding the poem's author "even if we have to look under every stone in the north." Telling Salvatierra they will find her and her "Complete Works" not for him but "for Mexico, for Latin America, for the Third World, for our girlfriends," because they "feel like doing it," Belano and Lima conclude Part II with a final, equivocal question: "¿No estaban de broma? ¿No estaban de broma?" ("Were they joking? Weren't they joking?").³⁴

What is most striking and consequential for the novel's revisioning of poetry's capacities is above all its serious playfulness, and playful serious-ness, in entertaining such questions. Recalling Lima's long poem *Muerte de Narciso* (1937) and novel *Paradiso* (1966),³⁵ the arc of the prose poem novel's drive into the Sonora Desert in search of Tinajero that structures Part III may be said to encompass a death drive (*una pulsión de muerte*; Freud's *Todestrieb*), a death plot (*una trama de muerte*), and a death trauma (*un trauma de muerte*) that figure, like Salvatierra's name, a certain death of poetry, or rather the death of a certain view or kind of poetry, on which poetry's salvation depends.³⁶ At the heart of this salvation is humor, the capacity for poetry not to take itself too seriously. For Belano and Lima, as for Bolaño throughout his career, such a capacity for poetry finds perhaps its strongest example in the work of Nicanor Parra, particularly as an alternative and counter to that of Neruda. Programmatically placed fol-lowing 1) the full citation and discussion of Rimbaud's "Le Coeur volé," 2) reference to Belano and Lima as "determined not to acknowledge that there could be anything good about Paz," and 3) their first exchange with Salvatierra about Tinajero, Bolaño writes in the narrative voice of one of Belano's friends from adolescence, the poet Perla Avilés, that a certain director with whom she was involved had said "that Neruda was shit and that Nicanor Parra was the greatest poet of the Spanish language." Recalling the dominant choices young aspiring poets faced in Mexico City and throughout Latin America in 1975–1976, the time of narration of Parts I and III, when Belano (and Lima) "couldn't have been more than twenty-three," Avilés "story of the 'fight … about Neruda and Parra'" marks a pivotal moment in Belano's poetic apprenticeship echoing both García Madero's workshop trauma at seventeen and Bolaño's own experi-ence at the same age in 1967–1968. As García Madero's response to his trauma suggests the later, mature Belano's (and Bolaño's) movement away from a more emotive, sentimental Nerudian poetics toward Parra's more cerebral, satirical, humorous "anti-poetics," so the treatment of García Madero's knowledge of poetic techniques and tropes undergoes a dramatic shift, from the beginning of Part I to the beginning of Part III, from the tediously pedantic to the productively playful.³⁷

While an investigation of the humor of poetry, as of humor generally, is pervasive throughout *The Savage Detectives*, the resumption of García Madero's narrative in Part III marks a dramatic shift in the representation of his position in relation to poetry and humor. Where the joke of that relation, in Part I, is on García Madero—"I remember Álamo laughing along with the four or five other members of the workshop. I think they may have been making fun of me"—Part III makes clear from the beginning that he is now in on the joke, is in fact the source, the author, whose playful, improvisational *poiesis* allows the journey into the desert to feel less a matter of desperation than a source of entertainment.[38] Where the pedantic display of his precocious knowledge of poetic techniques and tropes alienates him from the workshop's professor and his peers, a source of comedy for the novel's readers but not, within the fictional world of his own experience, for him, that knowledge resurfaces in the ebullient linguistic, poetic, literary-historical delirium that makes up the opening pages of Part II. Transformed from a source of tragi-comic humiliation (tragic for him, comic for the reader), in the context of their search for the forgotten poet Tinajero and her poetry, into a running gag, improvisational comedy routine, the inside joke of Garcia Madero's precocious poet-apprentice knowledge, as shared with the four protagonists in the car speeding through the Sonora Desert, is no longer at García Madero's or any other characters' expense, but a source of joy they share within the fictional frame, the literal/figurative "vehicle" of their experiences, which the novel shares as well with its readers. Insiders all, the novel's characters, and its readers, are liberated from the constraints of poetry as un-free verse to enjoy the linguistic burlesque of Bolaño's comedic prose, a kind of prose for which Rimbaud's bawdily comedic "Le Coeur volé," in contrast to Rebolledo's self-serious, self-consuming "Vampire," figures a jumping-off point both for Rimbaud's turn to the prose poem and for Bolaño's turn to a prose-poetic, detective-genre-inflected prose fiction.

From the beginning of his career, dating back to the bawdy comedy of his first prose poem detective novel, *Antwerp,* Bolaño's alignment of poetry with humor and the play of language, in prose, has been a defining aspect of his oeuvre. In the second of the first two entries of Part III of *The Savage Detectives,* dated January 1 and 2, 1976, respectively, as García-Madero, Belano, Lima, and Lupe begin their drive into the Sonora Desert that gives the concluding part its name, Bolaño turns Part I's parody of García Madero's pedantic display of poetic techniques and tropes in the manner of Poe's "The Rationale of Verse" to a source of pure linguistic, comedic,

prose-poetic pleasure in the form of a dialogue extending across roughly
ten pages:

> 2 de enero
> Salimos del DF. Para entretener a mis amigos les hice algunas preguntas
> delicadas, que también son problemas, enigmas (sobre todo en el México
> literario de hoy), incluso acertijos. Empecé con una fácil: ¿Qué es el verso
> libre?, dije . . .
> —El que no tiene un número fijo de sílabas —dijo Belano.
> —¿Y qué más?
> —El que no rima —dijo Lima.
> —¿El que no tiene una colocación precisa de los acentos —insistió Lima.
> —Bien. Ahora una más difícil. ¿Qué es un tetrástico?
> —¿Qué? —dijo Lupe a mi lado.
> —Un sistema métrico de cuatro versos —dijo Belano.
> —¿Y un síncopa?
> —Ah, jijos —dijo Lima.
> —No lo sé —dijo Belano—. ¿Algo sincopado?
> —Frío, frío. ¿Se rinden?
> —Un síncopa —dije—, es la supresión de uno o varios fonemas en el
> interior de una palabra. Ejemplo: Navidad por Natividad, Lar por Lugar . . . .
> Ahora una fácil. Qué es una sextina?
> —Una estrofa de seis versos —dijo Lima.
> —¿Y qué más? —dije yo . . .
> —Ponnos ahora una más fácil —dijo Belano.
> —Bien. ¿Qué es un zéjel?
> —Carajo, no lo sé, qué ignorante soy —dijo Belano.
> —¿Y tú, Ulises?
> —Me suena a árabe.
> —¿Y tú, Lupe?
> Lupe me miró y no dijo nada. A mí me dio un ataque de risa, supongo que de
> los nervios que tenía, pero igual les expliqué lo que era un zéjel. Y cuando acabé
> de reírme le dije a Lupe que no me reía de ella ni de su incultura (o rusticidad)
> sino de todos nosotros.

January 2
We were on our way out of Mexico City. To entertain my friends, I asked
them some tricky questions, questions that were problems too, and enigmas
(especially in the Mexican literary world of today), even riddles. I started
with an easy one: what is free verse? I said . . .
"Something with no fixed number of syllables," said Belano.
"And what else?"
"Something that doesn't rhyme," said Lima.
"And what else?"
"Something with no regular placement of stresses," said Lima.

'Good. Now a harder one. What is a tetrastich?'
'What?' said Lupe beside me.
'A metrical system of four verses,' said Belano.
'And a syncope?'
'Oh, Jesus,' said Lima.
'I don't know,' said Belano. 'Something syncopated?'
'Cold, cold. Do you give up?'
'A syncope,' I said 'is the omission of one or several phonemes within a word. For example: bosun for boatswain, o'er for over ...
    Now an easy one. What's a sestina?'
'Six six-line stanzas,' said Lima.
'And what else?' I said ...
'Ask us an easier one,' said Belano.
'All right. What's a zéjel?'
'Fuck, I don't know, I don't know anything,' said Belano.
'What about you, Ulises?'
'It sounds like Arabic to me.'
'And you, Lupe?'
Lupe looked at me and didn't say anything. I couldn't help laughing, probably because I was so nervous, but even so, I explained what a zéjel was. And when I had stopped laughing I told Lupe that I wasn't laughing at her or her ignorance (or lack of sophistication) but at all of us.[39]

Recalling fundamental aspects of Wittgenstein's language game as well as Bakhtin's provocative insight that "even the very language of the writer (the poet or novelist) can be taken as a professional jargon on a par with professional jargons," the poetry and poetics game played by García Madero, Belano, and Lima serves as a reminder that not even those possessing the most erudite command of a particular field's jargon, whether inside or outside the academy, possess anything like a universal, all-encompassing fluency in the virtually infinite number of speech and sub-speech genres making up a "single"—in reality always multiple, fractured, ever-changing—"natural" language.[40] What is most striking, and winning, about the way the three outsider visceral realist poets play their game is how playful, amiable, self-deprecating, and open they are to expanding their knowledge, not assuming mastery but enjoying playing, unconstrained by the stuff of higher education and the known university. Rather than the joke (of the jargon) being on them, they are enthusiastically, ebulliently part of the game. One game leading to another, the pleasure they take in their game of poetry and poetics—understood, as indeed a joke of its kind, as recondite subject matter—leads effortlessly to an extension of that game into an at first glance apparently diametrically opposed, in reality very similar *case*, that of street slang and dialect, the

language of Bolaño's "Unknown" university, in which Lupe demonstrates
the greatest fluency:

> —A ver, sabelotodo, ¿sabes tú qué es un prix?
> —Un toque de marihuana —dijo Belano sin volverse.
> —¿Y qué es muy carranza?
> —Alguien que es viejo —dijo Belano.
> —¿Y lurias?
> —Déjame que conteste yo —dije, pues todas las preguntas en realidad
> iban dirigidas a mí.
> —Bueno —dijo Belano.
> —No lo sé —dije tras pensar un rato.
> —¿Tú lo sabes? dijo Lima.
> —Pues no —dijo Belano.
> —Loco —dijo Lima.
> —Eso es loco. ¿Y jincho?
> Ninguno de los tres lo sabíamos.
> —Si es muy fácil. Jincho es indio —dijo Lupe ríendose— ¿Y qué es la
> grandiosa?
> —La cárcel —dijo Lima.
> —¿Y quién es Javier?
> . . .
> —¿Quién es Javier?
> —La policía —dijo Lupe—, ¿Y la macha chaca?
> —La marihuana —dijo Belano.
> 'All right,' Mr. Know-It-All, can you tell me what a *prix* is?'
> 'A toke of weed,' said Belano without turning around.
> 'And what is *muy carranza*?'
> 'Something very old,' said Belano.
> 'And *lurias*?'
> 'Let me answer,' I said, because all the questions were really for me.
> 'All right' said Belano.
> 'I don't know,' I said after thinking for a while . . .
> . . .
> 'Crazy,' said Lima.
> 'That's right, crazy. And *jincho*?'
> None of the three of us knew it.
> 'It's so easy. *Jincho* is Indian,' said Lupe, laughing. 'And what is *la
> grandiosa*?'
> 'Jail,' said Lima.
> 'And what is *Javier*?'
> . . .
> 'What's *Javier*?' said Belano.
> 'The police,' said Lupe. 'And *macha chacha*?'
> 'Marijuana,' said Belano.[41]

Based not on pedantry but on play, not on exclusion but on togetherness, the combined games of poetry and poetics, slang and dialect, dismantle the high-low distinction, combining diverse linguistic repertoires and fields of knowledge of poets and prostitutes, of academic and non-academic speech genres, of the known and the unknown university, learning equally from both.[42]

The joke of literary history, of the history of poetry, as also of the novel and of detective novels about poetry, as Bolaño indicates throughout his work, is first and foremost that, in the end, few survive. The "poem novel" in prose, or prose poem novel, Bolaño's late-twentieth-century oxymoron, is no joke. And yet is, infused to its core with humor, satire, comedy. It is a joke, above all, on genre, revenge and vindication of those unsuspecting literary apprentices to generic conventions and on the generic policing they experience, policing that threatens to do them in.[43] This ironic relationship to, this joke on, genre, arguably Bolaño's signature contribution—an inheritance not only from Baudelaire and Rimbaud, Breton, and Kafka, but also from Borges and Parra, Cortázar, and Perec, among others— makes poetry both subject and object, something like David Foster Wallace's idea of an *Infinite Jest*.[44] Bolaño exploits and ironizes the conventions of the detective novel, together with his and his characters' preoccupation with poetry and poetics, to dismantle, explode, and implode genre identities and generic frames into a thousand pieces. The real "plot" of the eventual violent deaths of the mother of visceral realist poetry, Tinajero, as of Alberto the pimp and the corrupt policeman, is in this sense the violent death of interpellations of and into genre, the fulfillment of genre conventions and expectations with which Bolaño understands himself to be fully complicit, however ambivalently, for the sake of a successful career in the literary marketplace.

Complicit as he knows himself to be with the detective genre as a marketable form, Bolaño understands the modern genre invented by Poe, as Baudelaire understood, as both a "savage" threat to poetry and, in his prose-poetic reworking of it, as a site for poetry's potential death, rebirth, and redemption, the latter figured by Part II's tenuously central, framing figure, Salvatierra. Representing the situation of Mexican, Chilean, and Latin American poetry generally as located, from a French perspective, in Bolaño's ventriloquized Michel Bulteau voice, at "the edge of civilization," *The Savage Detectives* emphasizes throughout the shaping role of modern poetry in French, especially since Baudelaire, on Latin American poetry. As García Madero's November 10 entry tells us, after a night at the "Encrucijada Veracruzana" bar, the "three books apiece" Lima and Belano were carrying were all French.[45] Agreeing that Mexican poetry must be transformed," that the situation of Mexican poets is "unsustainable, trapped ... between the reign of Octavio Paz, and the reign of Pablo Neruda," Lima, Belano, and the visceral realists prize above all bookstores the "Librería Francesa" and "Librería Baudelaire"—where there's "lots of *French* poetry, but not much *English* poetry."[46] Knowledge of modern French poetry thus emerges early on in *The Savage Detectives* as a measure of poetic value among the poets with whom Belano has aligned since moving from Chile to Mexico.

The story "Lima and Belano know well," linking themselves and Tinajero, the object of their search, back to Baudelaire and Rimbaud, back to Poe, is a source of black humor that "cracks us up" ("Nos morimos de risa"), which is meant to be found "Hilarious" ("Qué risa")—like the story of *The Savage Detectives* itself—of and on the literary violence of the detective genre as a genre, or game, of absurd, even violent conventions and connections.[47] As the violence, the savagery, contained in the name Villaviciosa suggests (anticipating the detective-story's sequel in *2666*), *The Savage Detectives* moves towards a violent farewell to poetry—the death of the forgotten poet Tinajero in the Sonora Desert, recalling the myth of Rimbaud's silence and death in Africa—that is in effect never-ending, a farewell reminding us there is always more to learn from the search for the unknown, for the unknown university, that is poetry, not least in its dark humor, in which everyone is invited to participate, without prescriptions and proscriptions about what counts as a poem, and what doesn't.

The novel's radical questioning of what is and is not poetry reaches its conclusion in a reprise and further elaboration of the dismantling of the verse/prose binary that defined poetry before Poe first put forward in the passage explored above focusing on Belano's and Lima's interpretation of Tinajero's sole surviving poem with Salvatierra, the poem and interpretation that leads Salvatierra to ask, despairingly, if it is all (poetry, the interpretation of poetry) "a joke": "Are you going to deny yourself the privilege of higher education?" twenty-four-year old Perla Avilés recalls asking Belano in the second of her two 1976 entries.[48] Reaching back six years earlier to 1970, when she was an eighteen-year old aspiring writer, "reading Lautréamont," Belano was seventeen, and both had "quit school for awhile," she remembers Belano laughing in reply, saying "that in college he was sure he'd learn exactly what he'd learned in high school: nothing."[49] A college dropout at seventeen, like García Madero five years later, Belano had given up the "known" for the "unknown" university.

Committed like Rimbaud, like Bolaño at the same age, to a life dedicated to poetry, he finds himself years later, as reported in the testimony of his former lover, Susana Puig, a divorced father, like Bolaño, living in the coastal town of Blanes, near Barcelona, contemplating not "suicide, at least for now," but leaving Europe, as once Rimbaud did in abandoning poetry, for Africa.[50]

Its radically suspended, fractured, prose-poetic narrative drive proceeding, in terms of generic narrative conventions, in reverse, making the reader wait, anticlimactically, for the murder that is to be solved to surface only at the end of the story, rather than at the beginning, putting the drive of the narrative on hold for four hundred pages to hear trial-like testimonies before the reader can know what violent event the testimonies concern, *The Savage Detectives* turns the detective novel's generic expectations inside out, its "case" literally making itself up as it comes along. At the end of the road which Bolaño understands never really ends, following the violent deaths of Tinajero, Alberto the pimp, and the policeman, *The Savage Detectives* returns in its conclusion to the uneventfulness that preceded for over six hundred pages its anticlimactic fulfillment of conventional generic expectations. Against the emplotment of violent death that is the detective genre's sine qua non and raison d'être, which yet emerges, at the end of *The Savage Detectives*, as little more than an afterthought—"I hope they buried them [the three bodies] with their guns," García Madero writes, "Whatever they did, I hope they got rid of the guns!"—the novel returns in its conclusion to the uneventfully playful investigation of poetry and interpretation, the pleasures of aesthesis and poiesis, that are fundamentally its real plot.

"I've read Cesárea's notebooks," García Madero's February 8 entry tells us. Recalling Belano, Lima, and Salvatierra's playful interpretation of Tinajero's "poem" and their complementary games with Lupe concerning poetic techniques and tropes, street slang and dialect, the game García Madero initiates on February 9 "to make the trip go faster" on the road to the town of El Cuatro, shortly before finding Tinajero, composed of lines and circles, "pictures, puzzles" he was taught to draw in high school—beginning "'An elegiac verse?' said Lima," 'A Mexican smoking a pipe,' said Lupe'" and ending with "eight Mexicans watching an invisible cockfight," concluding with "Four Mexicans keeping vigil over a body"[51]—what follows García Madero's reading of the notebooks, without commentary, dated February 10, 11, and 12, is a series of proper names "Cucurpe, Tuape, Meresichci, Ododepe" / "Carbó, El Oasis, Félix

Gómez, El Cuatro … " followed by three drawings, the first a solid square with a small triangle inside center-left, the second a solid, empty square, the third a perforated square the same size as the first two with evenly distributed gaps or breaks (eight left and right, nine top and bottom) opening up all four sides. Dated respectively February 13, 14, and 15, the three final days of the novel, and preceded by the thrice-repeated question, "What's outside the window?" ("¿Qué hay detrás de la ventana?"), each of the drawings takes the sole surviving poem-drawing of Tinajero a step further. Immediately followed by the words "A star" ("Una Estrella"), "A sheet" ("Una sábana extendida"), and no word at all, respectively, the three drawings figure transcendence, death, writing, nothingness, certainly, but also a literal opening up of the frames of poetry—the legacy of Tinajero, as of Belano, Lima, García Madero, and Lupe—to unlimited possibilities, the full range of potentialities the prose poem novel that is *The Savage Detectives* itself has come to represent. While the triadic structure of the three drawings suggests the dialectical progression that led Baudelaire and Rimbaud, by way of Poe, from the binary of prose and poetry (as verse) to the *Petits poèmes en prose,* the open frame of the final drawing suggests, like the novel itself, a movement beyond such dialectic structures, as also of the tragedy/comedy binary, toward a more inclusive, open-ended historical and literary-historical, at once aesthetic and political imaginary, toward literary worlds that make room for jokes and games, for ceaseless play, including the interplay of the verbal, the visual, and the performative.[52]

Less concerned with elaborating poetic taxonomies, including those based on identity and affiliation, than with the development of an inclusive, collaborative, interactive aesthesis and poiesis without borders, such a "barbaric" (read "radically democratic") project would raise the stakes of Baudelaire's invitation in the Preface to *Le Spleen de Paris*, to cut, to unravel, dismantle, however we please, our dreaming, all writers, our writing, all readers, our reading. Offering a radical realization of the anti-generic, anti-poetic, anti-literary impulses of the modern prose poem at its beginnings with Baudelaire and Rimbaud, against what Rancière has called *The Hatred of Democracy* and what Ben Lerner has called *The Hatred of Poetry,* such a project and its "corresponding revolution" would "in a sense abolish literature itself," resulting in a poetry "written by non-poets and read by non-readers," a "politics taken over by non-politicians," the "advent of the new literature," a literature "written by non-literary people" that "*could* in principle belong to everyone."[53] The prose-poetic structures of *The Savage Detectives* conclude with an emphasis on a poetics of openness and inclusiveness, a poetics of play challenging the emphasis of the detective novel, and of the novel generally, on a certain violence of narrative emplotment, the monetized violence of narrative drive, the violence of traditional, linear narrative as plot itself.

CHAPTER 7

Making Visible the "Non-Power" of Poetry
Amulet (Amuleto)

In "Positions Are Positions and Sex Is Sex," Bolaño's interview with Eliseo Álvarez first published two years after his death, Bolaño spoke of the differing impacts of his time in Mexico and Spain, the latter the setting for the three concluding chapters of *Distant Star*, the first of the several novels that would firmly establish his reputation, as well as for the posthumously published *The Third Reich*, his first full-length (arguably most conventional) novel; and the first of his prose poem novels, *Antwerp*. Responding to Álvarez's question about Mexico and Spain after a quarter of a century of living and writing in Blanes, Bolaño remarked: "More than anything I owe Mexico my intellectual education. My sentimental education? I owe that more to Spain, I think. When I came to Spain I was twenty-three or twenty-four years old . . . for me a sentimental education is almost synonymous with a sexual education" (245).[1]

As strongly identified as Bolaño has tended to be, as a Chilean, Mexican, Latin American writer, the first decade of his novels, all widely available only posthumously, all written in Blanes, from *Antwerp* and *Monsieur Pain* through *Consejos de un discípulo de Morrison y un fanático de Joyce* and *The Third Reich*, reflect in their settings, plots, concerns, and literary influences the aspirations of a writer intent on establishing himself as a novelist of both Europe and the Americas. While Bolaño's most recent posthumously released novel, *El espíritu de la ciencia-ficción* (2018, *The Spirit of Science Fiction*, 2019),[2] provides something of an exception to this rule (set in the Mexico City of 1970, completed in Blanes in 1984) and exiled, displaced-autobiographical Latin American figures play an important, at times integral role in the early novels' Europeans settings (most memorably the dying, absent-but-present Vallejo in the Paris of *Monsieur Pain*, with its two Latin American detectives), it was not until the mid-1990s, when the Pinochet era finally came to an end, that Bolaño returned to Latin America in his novels for what amounted to a long-delayed reckoning.[3] It was not until his final decade, after assembling between 1991 and 1993 the collected

130

poems that would appear, again only posthumously, as *The Unknown University*, that he would finally turn, in 1996, in the two pivotal books he would publish that year, *Nazi Literature in America* and *Distant Star,* to a sustained focus on the Americas generally, and on Chile in particular. While he would return to a focus on Chile one last time four years later in *By Night in Chile*, it would not be until 1998, mid-way between the two Chilean novels of 1996 and 2000, with the publication of *The Savage Detectives*, and a year later in his vastly more condensed, novella-length, in its scale no less innovative and powerful *Amuleto (Amulet)*, that he would finally turn his full attention as a novelist back to Mexico.

As vital, ambitious, and concise an exploration as *Distant Star* represents of the intersection of poetry, poetics, ideology, literary history, history, and politics from the years surrounding the September 11, 1973, coup to the official end of the Pinochet regime in 1990 and the first half of the decade thereafter (Pinochet's detainment in London in 1996 coinciding with the year of *Distant Star*'s publication), its movement from Chile to Europe, and to Spain in particular, leaves largely unexplored the country and capital city Bolaño lived in from ages fifteen to twenty-four, before his departure in 1977 for Europe and permanent residence in Spain. While *The Savage Detectives* (published when Bolaño was forty-five, five years before his death in 2003) explores that territory and experience in the most expansive way possible, and while it too is at its core a novel, like *Amulet*, of poetic apprenticeship in Mexico, *Amulet* offers between the two the far more concise coming-to-terms with the state of poetry, history, and politics in Mexico, in the years leading up to and following the 1973 coup in Chile, focusing on the traumatic events in and around Mexico City between July 26 and October 2, 1968.[4]

Narrated entirely from the point of view of Auxilio Lacouture, said to have immigrated from Uruguay to Mexico City in 1968, the same year Bolaño moved there with his family from Chile, *Amulet* provides a complementary narrative to *Distant Star*'s mapping of Chilean poetry and politics, in the years before and during the Pinochet regime, in its corollary mapping of the state of Mexican poetry and politics in the years surrounding the student uprisings at the National Autonomous University of Mexico (UNAM) and the Tlatleco massacre.[5] At the core of the novel's characterization of its narrator and central protagonist is the familiar, often idealized, romanticized relation between poetry and marginality, poetry and poverty: "I had enough money to get by and the poets educated me in Mexican literature by lending me books, their own books of poems for a start (you know what poets are like), then the essentials and the classics, so my expenses were minimal. / ... The Mexican poets were generous and I was happy ... I became a fixture in their group." As a regular and "the only woman, except, occasionally, for the ghost of Lilian Serpas," attending the Mexican poets' literary gatherings," Lacouture is a friend of Bolaño's namesake, Belano ("Arturito," she affectionately calls him), whom she claims early on, in the book's opening paragraphs, to have met in 1970 "when he was a shy seventeen-year-old who wrote plays and poems and couldn't hold his liquor."[6]

Where in *Distant Star* the poetry salons of Juan Stein and Diego Soto play a pivotal role in figuring the two dominant, at once competing and complementary orientations available for aspiring young poets in Chile in the years leading up to the coup—the former focused on poetry of the Americas, North and South, in English and Spanish, the latter on European, especially French poetry—*Amulet* offers a pair of corollary figures in the aging poets León Felipe and Pedro Garfias, with whom Lacouture, the self-described "mother of Mexican poetry," "mother of all the poets" ("la madre de la poesía Mexicana," "la madre de todos los poetas"), moves in after arriving in Mexico City from her native Montevideo.[7] Suggesting a by then residual, traditional, old-guard poetics in stark contrast to the at the time still emerging dominant of the early 1970s—figured in the opening chapter of *Distant Star* by Violeta and Nicanor Parra, William Carlos Williams, Anne Sexton, Elizabeth Bishop, and Denise Levertov, among others, all by the time Bolaño wrote *Distant Star* and *Amulet* two decades later squarely canonical—Felipe and Garfias are said never to have lost their "distinctive Spanish accent ... their prickly little music, as if they were circling the zs and the ss, which made the ss seem lonelier and more sensuous," a residual indication, in Raymond Williams' terms, prompting Lacouture's assertion that "dust and literature have always gone together."[8]

As figures of a growing obsolescence of poetry, of literature, or at least of certain kinds of poetry and literature at specific literary-historical, historical moments, that much more pointedly in the condensed version of Lacouture's story in *The Savage Detectives*—"And then the bubble of Pedro Garfias's poetry went pop and I closed the book ["Y entonces la burbuja de la poesía de Pedro Garfias hizo blip y cerré el libro"] and got up, pulled the chain, opened the door, said something out loud. *Che*, I said, what's going on outside? But no one answered me"—Felipe and Garfias raise questions within the Mexican context resonating with those focused on Chile in *Distant Star* through the figures of Stein, Soto, and their coup-aligned avant-garde student, Carlos Wieder, concerning poetry, literary history, history, and politics. While Lacouture falters in remembering the exact date of her arrival in Mexico, her recollection situates the poetry of the two Spanish poets she admires on the cusp of what she subsequently calls "the birth of History" ("el parto de la Historia"), the epochal events of 1968.[9]

As the allegorical resonances of her name suggest, Auxilio Lacouture's "boundless devotion" to "those two great Spaniards, those universal minds" figures a still traditional, gendered, subservient, handmaiden's role for female readers of poetry at the moment of feminism's renewal and ascendancy in Europe and North America, if less so at the time in Mexico, a role that places her aesthetically and politically behind the assertive positions occupied under the Allende regime before the coup, as depicted in *Distant Star*, by such emerging poets as the Garmendia twins, Carmen Villagrán, and Fat Marta.[10] Where the twins emerge early on as "the best poets" of their generation in *Distant Star*, which also takes the poetry of Villagrán and Fat Marta seriously, Lacouture reports that when she moved in with Garfias and Felipe, reported to have died in 1967 and 1968, respectfully, she "didn't expect them to read my poems or take an interest in my personal problems." Seeking at the same time to lead a life "apart from . . . those luminaries of Hispanic letters," she proceeds to "hang around the university, specifically the Faculty of Philosophy and Literature . . . Sometimes, not often" finding "paid work; a professor . . . or the department heads or the faculty," in short leading "a bohemian life with the poets of Mexico City."[11]

Disrupting what she describes as her "happy" life among the "generous" Mexican poets, and moving her into the historical moment that gives rise to the first chapter's claim, in its opening sentence, that the text that follows belongs to the genre of "a horror story. A story of murder, detection and horror" ("una historia de terror . . . una historia policiaca, un relato de serie negra y de terror"), the second chapter takes the reader to the novel's literary-historical center: "And so I came to the year 1968. Or 1968 came to me . . . the first (and last) piñata of that innocently festive January was smashed open." In the urgency of that historical moment, Lacouture questions the value of Garfias' poetry and the extent to which any poetry might effectively engage the exigencies of particular historical, political situations: "and the book of poems by Pedro Garfias again on my lap, and although I didn't feel like reading I began to read . . . but then my reading . . . sped out of control . . . the poetry of Pedro Garfias could not withstand that free-fall reading (some poets and poems can withstand any kind of reading, but they are rare exceptions; most can't)."[12]

Figuring in the context of Mexico City in 1968 a set of questions similar to those posed by *Distant Star* in the context of the 1973 Chilean coup, *Amulet* tracks through the figure of Lacouture, as does *Distant Star* through the figure of Wieder, the resonances and implications for poetry and poetics of traumatic historical events that reframe both the production and reception of poetry. Where *Distant Star* focuses on the former, on the writing of poetry, on *poiesis* and poetic performativity through Wieder's "revolutionary" avant-garde practices (including sky-writing, photography, and film), *Amulet* situates itself, through Lacouture, on the side of the reader, in the process staging a pronounced gendering—more one-sided in *Amulet* than in the condensed kernel of her story as it first appears a year earlier in Part II of *The Savage Detectives,* in both texts in the mode of a feminist critique—of the relation between writing and reading, *poiesis* and *aesthesis*. In keeping with its emphasis on her as reader rather than writer—"you get on with your work, you keep writing, don't mind me, just pretend I'm the invisible woman"[13] —especially on her act of reading and its disruption in the bathroom of the Faculty of Philosophy and Literature, an act coded as maternal and passive—even as, as the novel's narrator and central protagonist, she narrates the story to which the novel returns again and again with the compulsiveness of both a Nietzschean eternal return and a Freudian working through of trauma at once personal and collective—*Amulet* establishes her as a synecdochic, representative female figure of her generation, the heterosexual yet childless "mother of Mexican poetry," "mother of all the poets," whose paternal counterpart will emerge a year later in *By Night in Chile*, in the dual or split identities of the homosexual or asexual, equally childless and unmarried "father" figure, the Catholic priest and poet Sebastián Urrutia Lacroix, also known as the critic H. Ibacache, who combines *poiesis* and *aesthesis* in the same tortured figure.[14]

Where *Distant Star*, in keeping with its focus on *poiesis*, offers two exhibits of Carlos Wieder's poetry, *Amulet* does not include a single line of verse from any source, including from the pivotal book of Garfias' poetry the narrator is reading in the bathroom at the moment the army and the riot police arrive. Although the kind of poetry she is reading remains a mystery, the novel provides in the opening chapter a Borgesian clue recalling *El Aleph*: "Then I thought: Does Pedrito Garfias know what's hidden in his vase? Do poets have any idea what lurks in the bottomless maws of their vases? And if they know, why don't they take it upon themselves to destroy them? . . . Why did the poet sit there looking at the vase instead of . . . picking up the vase with both hands, and smashing it on the floor. But then my anger subsided . . . I came to realize that, over the years, Pedrito Garfias had already smashed his fair share of vases . . . on two continents! So who was I to find fault with him?"[15] Having passed through his own aesthetic battles, Garfias has left Lacouture with a book of poetry that recedes with him, in the traumatic context of the year following his death, into questionable relevance, its personal, literary-historical, and political resonances reframed, transformed, perhaps permanently eclipsed, by events he and his work did not envision.[16]

Recalling from her childhood in Montevideo, now in reference to Garfias, at the time of narration, her "father's desk, Doctor Lacouture's old house, my father the doctor, who died so long ago," the narrator's cultured, literate past recalls that of the Garmendia twins in *Distant Star,* anticipating as well the Baudelairean-named estate "Là-bas," of the literary critic, Farewell, where the narrator and central protagonist poet-critic of *By Night in Chile,* Lacroix/Ibacache, receives his baptism into the world of letters.[17] While all three novels figure poetry's inextricable connections with cultural and economic privilege, the bohemian setting of *Amulet*—set like *Distant Star* in and around the academy, the University of Concepción in the former, UNAM in the latter—projects poetry on a distinctive trajectory, within its particular Mexican context, that ultimately places poetry, poetics, literary history, history, and politics within a trans-historical, mythological frame. What September 11, 1973, is to *Distant Star* and *By Night in Chile,* September 18, 1968, is to *Amulet,* a traumatic event that triggers a sustained narrative inquiry into the poetry and poetics of Bolaño's generation, in Chile and Mexico, as well as its literary-historical, historical, and political implications and resonances within a more broadly American and European context. Yet where both *Distant Star* and *By Night in Chile* maintain an insistently historicizing orientation toward their central characters, embedding them deeper and deeper over the course of each narrative, albeit with very different narratological strategies, into their overlapping histories, *Amulet* moves quite literally, as we shall see, from history to mythology, a narratological strategy that historicizes myth and mythologizes history in ways that cast doubt on our ability to distinguish one from the other. With its first-person narration in the voice of the mother not only of Mexican poetry but of all poets, *Amulet* recalls the emphasis on repetition and recurrence evoked by the name of the central protagonist of *Distant Star,* Carlos Wieder.

Returning again and again to the central scene of Lacouture's act of reading (and no longer being able to read) Garfias's book of poems in the bathroom of the Faculty of Philosophy and Letters on September 18, 1968, the date the army and riot police came to occupy UNAM, *Amulet* figures the unreliability of memory circling back to the primal scene of a trauma at once personal and historical (25).[18] Staging a profound tension between a historiographic memory, or should we say imagination, understood along the lines of a Marxist, linear narrative of historical progress, and a more mythological, Nietzschean model of eternal return, Lacouture's recollections loop unpredictably and insistently forward and backward, confounding teleological projections of whatever political orientation, as well as any narrative of progress, tending instead toward an etiological evacuation and evaporation of the so-called reality of history into myth. Where *Distant Star* (like *By Night in Chile*) moves forward in a frame of temporal reference understood to be thoroughly historical, in its case from the time surrounding the 1973 coup to the immediate post-Pinochet regime some two decades later in the early to mid-1990s, *Amulet* arcs toward the in the end no less historical, yet nonetheless deeply mythological time-sense of ancient Greece.[19]

For all its recursive, etiological movement, including its hallucinatory mix of "present, future, and past all mixed together," the structure of *Amulet* resembles that of *Distant Star,* divided into numbered chapters.[20] Where the ten chapters of *Distant Star* may be grouped into four principal parts of three, two, two, and three chapters each, the fourteen chapters of *Amulet* may be configured into six, each varying, similarly, between two and three chapters: 1) chapters 1–3, introducing Lacouture, Belano, and the poetry scene surrounding UNAM's Faculty of Philosophy and Literature (recalling the poetry scene associated with the Stein and Soto poetry salons around the University of Concepción), and the trauma of the occupation on September 18, 1968 (recalling the trauma of September 11, 1973, in Chile); 2) chapters 4–6, exploring scenes and influences within Mexican poetry, and Auxilio's and Belano's to them, in and around 1970–72 (the same years explored through the salons in *Distant Star* before the coup), leading up to the time of Belano's (figuring Bolaño's) brief return to Chile; 3) chapters 7 and 8, exploring through its focus on the so-called "Rent Boys" ("los putos") and homosexual poet San Epifanio poetry, fiction, marginality, and sexual violence; 4) chapters 9 and 10, devoted to Lacouture's alter-egos, Remedios Varo (former lover of French surrealist Benjamin Péret, from whom she is said to have parted in 1942), looping back to 1962–1963, and the artist and self-proclaimed "real mother of

Mexican poetry" sixty-year old Lilian Serpas, the story of whose son, the painter, Carlos Coffeen Serpas, opens onto 5) chapters 11–12, retelling the myths of Erigone, Cronus, and Orestes; and finally 6) chapters 13–14, the narrator's return to a tragic, now thoroughly mythologized, mythologizing account of the fate of poets and poetry in Mexico, Latin America, and beyond in the aftermath of the events at UNAM and Tlatelolco in 1968.

At the core of *Amulet*'s investigation of history, mythology, and narration are questions of causality and randomness, of the (auto)biographical and historical, that figure early on in Lacouture's willing subservience to Felipe and Garfias, two aging Spanish poets in exile in Mexico, as well as in her affinity to Belano, Bolaño's doppelgänger, whom she calls in chapter 6 her "favorite young poet, although he wasn't Mexican."[21] Like Wieder, Stein, Soto, the Garmendia twins, Fat Marta, Bibiano O'Ryan, in *Distant Star*; like the father/priest, poet-critic Urrutia Lacroix / H. Ibacache in *By Night in Chile*, Lacouture provides a lens through which to explore the history of modern poetry. In *Amulet*, that history yields a vision of poets and of poetry as, above all, orphaned, with an uncertain future. Against a narrative of historical progress, and corresponding progress of poetry, that might have been made possible, in Chile, through the successful "paternity" of the democratically elected Allende, a Nietzschean counternarrative of repetition and recurrence takes hold, in Bolaño's trilogy of novellas of poetic apprenticeship, on September 11, 1973, in Chile and on September 18, 1968, in Mexico in ways that lead, in *Amulet*'s staging of that date's significance, to a thoroughgoing dissolution of stability and predictability, a tragic if wistful vision of the "songs" of poets, and of poetry as, in the end, a mere amulet, as sign and token, the potential power of which remains beyond telling.

In *Amulet*'s self-reflexive, Poe-inflected opening narration by Lacouture, which defines the book's generic identity from the outset as a "horror story," Bolaño figures a view of history as "another recurring and terribly Latin American nightmare" ("otro terror recurrente y mortalmente latinoamericano"), not one from which the narrator is trying to awake (pace Stephen Daedalus), but one that leaves her sleepless. Her problem, she says, "isn't how to wake up, but how to fall asleep again."[22] Thus, following the end of the third chapter, which concludes the first part of the novel with an emphasis on the value of a resistance approaching "the edges of companionship and love" ("los bordes de la socialbilidad y el amor"), the novel's fourth, fifth, and sixth chapters map the choices facing poets in the first two years of Lacouture's acquaintance with Belano, from "the poetry of Ezra Pound and William Carlos Williams and T.S. Eliot," to Belano's preference in theater, which was "not Latin American at all but that of Beckett and Jean Genet," to Rubén Darío, W.B. Yeats, Vicente Huidobro, Pound, and José Emilio Pacheco.[23] Against the "horror story" of Mexico City in 1968, the novel figures poetry in 1970, the year Allende was elected president in "faraway Chile," as a "utopia of words" ("utopía de la palabra") filled with the promise of the "'young poets' and "new generation.'"[24] Remembered in the "afternoon of 1971 or 1972 . . . prospectively from 1968 . . . From the fourth floor of the Faculty of Philosophy and Literature, amid talk of Cuba and resistance," poetry's promise involves the possibility of living "in a lonely world of love and slang" ("en la soledad del amor y en la soledad del argot") that is also the promise of "modernism and the avant-garde . . . an island of words that never were" ("el modernismo y la vanguardia . . . una isla . . . inexistente, palabras que jamás fueron"), including the "imaginary encounter between Darío and Huidobro" that "would have been able to found a more vigorous avant-garde, what we might name the non-existent avant-garde, which had it existed, would have transformed us and changed our lives" ("el hipotético encuentro entre Darío y Huidobro . . . hubiera sido capaz de fundar una vanguardia más vigorosa aún, una vanguardia que ahora llamamos la vanguardia inexistente y que de haber existido nos hubiera hecho distintos, nos hubiera cambiado la vida").[25]

This utopian potential notwithstanding, having mapped, like the establishing-shot opening chapter of *Distant Star* on the salons led by Stein and Soto and the individual chapters devoted to each, the situation of poetry at the crux of a moment of historical, political urgency, the chapter closes with a discussion about "poetry, new poetry" ("hablando de poesía, de nueva poesía") "turned into an argument" ("el diálogo se trocó en discusión y la discusión en gritos e insultos").[26] The two chapters that follow at the heart of the novel, making up its third section (chapters 7 and 8), are set in Mexico City (in the memory of Lacouture) following Belano's return from the brief internment in Chile in January 1974 that both distanced him from the next generation of "desperate Latin American kids" and young(er) poets and associated him in their eyes with the "palette of epic poetry" as a "revolutionary veteran," an association that opens onto the novel's reference to a "cemetery in the year 2666."[27] Pivoting from the promise of the "imaginary encounter between Darío and Huidobro" that might have yielded "a more vigorous . . . nonexistent avant-garde," that could have changed everything, to two chapters that align the avant-garde with those on the margin (as does the end of the Soto chapter in *Distant Star* with its story of Petra/Lorenzo, the armless poet-painter-performer), chapters 8 and 9 flash back to the younger poet San Epifanio, a "Mexican homosexual poet" whom Belano frees from sexual slavery at the hands of the "King of the Rent Boys," an act that figures as its "hidden purpose," the imagination's power to "stop him from being killed."[28] Affirming the "adventures of poetry" as an alternative to the violence of history—"I don't think I'm cut out for horror stories," says Lacouture—the novel's fourth section, chapters 9 and 10, chronicles stories of two of the narrator's alter-egos, "Remedios Varo" and "Lilian Serpas," that reach back to the historical avant-gardes ("the French surrealists and the Catalan surrealists") while flowing "freely through time . . . [backward and forward] from September 1968."[29]

Like Stein and Soto in *Distant Star*, like Felipe and Garfias earlier in *Amulet*, Varo and Serpas figure paired possibilities for poetry and poetics superseded, in the history of modern poetry, by the impact of historical events. On the other side of these options, the two subsequent chapters that make up the novel's fifth part, chapters 11 and 12, figure the hope of an escape from the Faculty of Philosophy and Letters in 1968, "that decrepit time-warp" within history ("aquella casa que se estaba desvencijando en el túnel del tiempo"), through recourse to Greek mythology and the story of Serpas's painter son, Carlos Coffeen Serpa—whose father is of uncertain origin ("North American . . . English, or Mexican")—and the legend of Erigone, a legend which, in Lacouture's retelling, opens history and myth into mutual relation: " . . . in the Faculty of Philosophy and Literature . . . I was heading for the operating room . . . for the birth of History . . . It's over now; the riot police have left the university, the students have died at Tlatelolco . . . History announced its birth with raucous cries . . . Then day broke once again over the capital of Mexico."[30]

Bringing to a conclusion the novel's historicizing of myth and mythologizing of history, in the wake of the story of Carlos Cofeen Serpa as Orestes and Lacouture as Erigone, the two chapters that make up the novel's sixth and final section, chapters 13 and 14, figure the history of modern poetry, and of literature generally, as a kind of Möbius strip, a historical, temporal, spatial (dis)continuum that allows the literature of one era to re-emerge in another time, space, and history that are not really other, yet not quite the same, after all, a space-time of disappearance and reappearance, neither quite linear nor circular, that yields unpredictable literary-historical displacements and a continual rewriting and revisioning of literary history: " . . . puedo ver el futuro de los libros del siglo XX . . . / Vladímir Maiakovski volverá a estar de moda allá por el año 2150. James Joyce se reencarnará en un niño chino en el año 2124. Thomas Mann se convertirá en un farmacéutico ecuatoriano en el año 2101" ("I can see what the future holds for the books of the twentieth century ... / Vladimir Mayakovksy shall come back into fashion around the year 2150. James Joyce shall be reincarnated as a Chinese boy in the year 2124. Thomas Mann shall become a Ecuadorean pharmacist in the year 2101").[31]

Against a historicist model that would recount history, including literary history, as Benjamin famously describes it, as if it were a "string of rosary beads" (*Rosenkranz*), Bolaño offers in this pivotal passage, as he does throughout *Amulet* through the figure of Auxilio Lacouture, a radically disjunctive, prose-poetic, fictive history and literary history by other means, in another form, one fully aligned with the counter-model of the historical materialist who "grasps the constellation into which [her] era has entered, along with a very specific earlier one" and a "conception of the present," of the "now-time" (*Jetztzeit*) of history and literary history, as "shot through with splinters of messianic time": "... mis profecías son éstas ... / Marcel Proust entrará en un desesperado y prolongado olvido a partir del año 2033. Ezra Pound desparecerá de algunas bibliotecas en el año 2089. Vachel Lindsay será un poeta de masas en el año 2101" ("These are my prophecies ... / For Marcel Proust, a desperate and prolonged period of oblivion shall begin in the year 2033. Ezra Pound shall disappear from certain libraries in the year 2089. Vachel Lindsay shall appeal to the masses in the year 2101").[32]

In keeping with this conception, as Lacouture tries but fails to keep reading the poetry of Pedro Garfias in the bathroom of the Faculty of Philosophy and Literature, an eclectic mix of more and less canonical figures of twentieth-century literature floods in and out of her memory. Remembering the poetry of Robert Frost in a hallucinatory, mythic environment of snowy mountains—precisely at that moment, in that constellation of past, present, and future as she is waiting for the birth of an alternative history—she is unable, she says, to "forget anything"—"That's my problem, or so I've been told ... the mother of Mexico's poets ... the only one who held out in the university in 1968." Thinking of "all those modernist poets prepared to give their lives for poetry," of the "vanity of writing ... of destruction," of all "the young people ... singing and heading for the abyss," she concludes, finally, offering a glimmer of hope at the end of the novel's dark parable, with "the love ... the heroic deeds of a whole generation of young Latin Americans led to sacrifice ... courage and mirrors, desire and pleasure," affirming that generation's "song" ("ese canto") will be, in the novel's final words, "our amulet" ("nuestro amuleto").[33]

"Auxilio." A helping figure. A call for help. A figure of poetry as timely and untimely, enduring and ephemeral, in fashion and out. "Lacouture." As sobering and harrowing a vision of poetic apprenticeship, of interpellations into poetry, into fiction, into literature, as *Amulet* presents for poets, for all writers, of Bolaño's generation and beyond, its vision of poetry in the most capacious sense, not as mere *Gedicht* (as poem or song only) but as *Dichtung*, as hope and charm, is ultimately inseparable from and fully recuperable within history, unable to escape its consequences. Yet despite the impasses, injustices, and unpredictability of history and literary history, that double, conjoined "horror story" written by the victors, despite "the slaughterhouse of literature," despite what may well seem to resemble less Lacouture's missing, wished-for utopia of words than "a vast minefield," *Amulet* offers through Lacouture's prophecies a vision oriented not finally, or not only, toward the Benjaminian angel of history, but toward the alternative, open-ended futures of a Blochian "Noch-Nicht", "César Vallejo será leído en los túneles en el año 2045. Jorge Luis Borges será leído en los túneles en el año 2045. Vicente Huidobro será un poeta de masas en el año 2045" ("César Vallejo shall be read underground in the year 2045. Jorge Luis Borges shall be read underground in the year 2045. Vicente Huidobro shall appeal to the masses in the year 2101"). Such unforeseeable revisionings, reimagings, such acts of making visible, for poetry, for fiction, for literary history, for politics, make up what Bolaño calls "The Unknown University," the as-yet-unimagined where, the as-yet-unimaginable when, as Lacouture puts it at *Amulet*'s most decisively utopian moment, "La poesía no desaparecerá. Su no-poder se hará visible de otra manera ("Poetry shall not disappear. Its non-power shall make itself visible by other means, in another form").[34]

CHAPTER 8

Poetry, Politics, Critique
By Night in Chile (Nocturno de Chile)

Returning a year after the publication of *Amulet* to the site of the historical trauma of his generation twenty-seven years earlier, Bolaño's 2000 novella *Nocturno de Chile* (*By Night in Chile*, 2003) takes up again the challenges of a coming-to-terms with the 1973 coup's legacy which he had made the sustained focus of his fiction for the first time, four years earlier, in *Distant Star*. Combining *Distant Star*'s focus on *poiesis*, through the coup-aligned avant-garde poet Carlos Wieder, with that of *Amulet* on *aesthesis*, through the "mother of Mexican poets," "mother of all poets," Auxilio Lacouture, *By Night in Chile* completes Bolaño's trilogy of short novels of poetic apprenticeship by exploring the conjunction of *poiesis* and *aesthesis* in a single character who is, like Lacouture, both the novella's narrator and its central character, yet who in this case figures synecdochically as both a writer and a reader, the Catholic father/priest and poet-critic Sebastián Urrutia Lacroix/H. Ibacache.[1]

Composed of a single paragraph, without chapter divisions or breaks of any kind until its one-line concluding sentence, the novella unfolds its at once historical and literary-historical, aesthetic and political investigation, in the specific context of the coup and more generally, through the uninterrupted narration of its dual, split, (dis)integrated figure, across a taut, densely packed 130 pages. What may strike the reader at first glance as a daunting, rambling, disorganized, potentially ungraspable, stream-of-consciousness narration, the genre interpellations, conventions, protocols, and expectations of which it plays both with and against, is in fact an intricately conceived, carefully organized, meticulously structured and executed literary performance. Resistant as the experience of *By Night in Chile* is, from the side of *poiesis*, to a segmented reading, from the side of *aesthesis*, by contrast, such a reading is not only possible but necessary for a close analysis and thorough understanding of the text. Mirroring the central protagonist's dual identities as poet (Urrutia Lacroix) and critic (Ibacache), the text inscribes, through its uninterrupted monological structure, a maximal tension between acts of writing and reading, production and reception.

Recalling, on a similar novella-length scale, the death-bed narration of Leo Tolstoy's *The Death of Ivan Ilyich* (1886), *By Night in Chile* combines into the single guilt-ridden, tormented character of Urrutia Lacroix/ Ibacache the tensions between *poiesis* and *aesthesis* so unforgettably and amusingly on display in Borges's "The Aleph" between the Nerudaesque but mediocre poet, Carlos Argentino Daneri (eventual second-place winner of the Argentine National Prize for Literature), and Borges' fictionalized, author-identified narrator, a figure who recalls as well, as a critical reader of Daneri's poetry, Poe's equally parodic short story, "How to Write a Blackwood Article."[2] Recollecting his past from his death bed—"I am dying now," the opening sentence reads, "but I still have many things to say"—("Ahora me muero, pero tengo muchas cosas que decir todavía"),[3] Urrutia Lacroix immerses the reader in a stream of narration that demands for its comprehension a sense of structure the text itself conspicuously refuses to provide.

Where *Distant Star* offers itself to the reader in ten clearly organized, transparently structured chapters, from which as we have seen we may constellate four principal parts, and *Amulet* fourteen chapters that may be grouped into six, the continuous narrative stream of *By Night in Chile*, set in Santiago in 1993, two decades after the Pinochet coup, may be organized into eleven principal scenes comprising, like *Distant Star*, four principal parts: 1) scenes 1–3, including introductions to Urrutia/Ibacache, fifty-three to fifty-four at the time of narration, 1993, looking back on himself at thirteen and fourteen, circa 1953, the year of Bolaño's birth and also the year Urrutia/Ibacache is ordained as a priest and receives his baptism into the world of letters through his encounter with "Chile's greatest literary critic," who will become the narrator's mentor, "Mr. González Lamarca," known simply as "Farewell" (in English throughout in the original), and Farewell's counterpart and friend, Chile's consensus greatest poet, Pablo Neruda, at the country estate of Farewell with the Baudelaireian, Huysmanian name "Là-bas"—in French throughout, English "Over there"[4]—along with Farewell's story of the Chilean novelist Don Salvador Reyes' encounter, during World War II in Paris, with the German novelist Ernst Jünger; and similarly allegorical story of the efforts of a Viennese shoemaker to persuade an Austro-Hungarian Emperor to build a monument to fallen war heroes; 2) scenes 4–6, detailing the rise of Urrutia Lacroix/Ibacache's "brilliant career," his meeting with the two thinly encrypted, allegorically named Opus Dei representatives "Odeim" and "Oido" (reversed spellings of "Miedo" and "Odio"; in English "Reaf" and "Etah," "Fear" and "Hate"), and his Opus Dei-sponsored mission to Europe; 3) scenes 7–9, from Urrutia Lacroix/Ibacache's return from Europe to Santiago in 1973, on the eve of the coup and the deaths of Allende and Neruda, when Urrutia Lacroix would have been thirty-three, the age of Christ in the year of his crucifixion (the same age as Bibiano in *Distant Star*), through Urrutia Lacroix/Ibacache's classes in Marxism following the coup for Pinochet and the ruling Junta, and the rumors of his instruction at the height of his successful career as poet and critic, through his eventual boredom; and, finally, 4) Urrutia Lacroix/Ibacache's attendance at the soirées held on the outskirts of Santiago at the home of the writer María Canales and her husband, the American DINA agent Jimmy Thompson, Farewell's death, and the repeated references to the "Judas Tree" that figure the unresolved complicity, mutual betrayal, and residual bad conscience of Chile and its writers in the aftermath of the Pincochet regime, for which Urrutia Lacroix/Ibacache offers himself up as a sacrificial, representative spokesman.[5]

Echoing in its opening pages, in a parodic, contrapuntal mode recalling the famous agricultural fair scene of *Madame Bovary*, the limitations for poetry of what the narrator of *Distant Star* calls "Neruditis," *By Night in Chile* calls into question from the outset Neruda's hegemonic legacy and the limitations of a Nerudian poetics, the intractable disease of his outsized influence, for now several generations of younger poets in Chile in particular as in Latin America more generally and beyond. However tone-setting a role Neruda's poetry may once have played for an avant-garde, surrealist, Latin American left, Bolaño's representation of him through the eyes of Urrutia Lacroix leaves no doubt that, by the time the narrator first encounters him at the estate of the renowned, comically named Farewell—an allegorical staging of an aspiring young Chilean poet's fantasy "literary baptism" at the hands of the country's greatest poet and critic in a single setting—Neruda had become a monument and exhibit, already some twenty years before receiving the Nobel Prize (a signal moment later in the novella), an establishment figure of the highest order.[6] As Farewell's featured guest at "Là-bas," with its parodic echoes of J.K. Huysman's identically titled novel and the final line of Baudelaire's "L'Étranger" ("The Stranger"), the opening prose poem of *Le Spleen de Paris*—"J'aime les nuages ... les nuages qui passent ... là-bas ... là-bas ... les merveilleux nuages!" ("I love the clouds ... the clouds that pass ... over there... over there ... the marvelous clouds!")—Neruda figures a poetics of the Romantic Sublime, poetry's most conventionally popular image. Sharing that evening an "exquisite" meal with wine "from the estate," Urrutia Lacroix remembers "Farewell and the young poet. Myself" and another young poet who "Naturally . . . turns out to be a Nerudian."[7]

Aligning his aspirations as a poet, and later as a critic, with the economical and cultural privilege enjoyed by Neruda and Farewell, Father Urrutia Lacroix sets off on his career path at Là-bas in a context that allows Bolaño to parody as well Pound's Italian-fascist-leaning avant-gardism intertwining repeated, wryly mocking lyrical allusions to *Hugh Selwyn Mauberley* and *The Cantos,* over the course of several pages, with innuendoes of homosexual seduction involving the poet-critic apprentice and both the Great Poet and the Great Critic of his generation.[8] Following the young priest's callous interaction thereafter, in getting lost while wandering Farewell's estate, with a group of peasants he finds "ugly . . . their words incoherent," consoled, on finding his way back, by the "Baudelairean clouds" ("las nubes baudelairianas"), Urrutia Lacroix immerses himself, in subsequent conversations with Farewell on his return to Santiago, predictably speculating about "literary immortality," taking the first steps toward a career that would lead him to prominence, as a critic under a new name (in *Distant Star* Nicanor—as in Nicanor Parra—Ibacache) as one of Chile's influential literary arbiters.[9]

Bringing the first part of *By Night in Chile* to a close, Urrutia Lacroix/Ibacache's articulation of his double identity as poet and critic opens onto a pair of parables, in the second part of the novella that follows, both narrated by the jaded, cynical Farewell, for the very impure possible consequences of an unchecked desire for literary celebrity and immortality. In the first, which recalls in Urrutia Lacroix/Ibacache's memory the "black bile that is eating away at me now, sapping my strength, bringing me to the brink of tears when I hear the wizened youth's words," Farewell recounts Don Salvador Reyes's obsession with the recognition and approval of the German right-wing writer Ernst Jünger, a recognition ultimately, yet pathetically granted, in his appearance as the only Chilean mentioned in Jünger's memoirs.[10] In the second, Farewell tells the story of a Viennese shoemaker, once a prosperous, accomplished artisan/artist who "made a fortune" manufacturing and selling shoes of the highest use and quality, whose obsession with immortality, in the form of the monument he calls "Heldenberg or Heroes' Hill . . . dedicated to the heroes of the [Austro-Hungarian] Empire," leads him to ruin and utter oblivion.[11] Situated in both cases within a World War II frame, the first with its focus on recognition from one of the most celebrated writers of Nazi Germany and the period of the Third Reich, Ernst Jünger, the second with its closing perspective on the ruins of Heroes' Hill at the end of the war, from the point of view of the liberating Soviet army, the two parables taken together prepare the way for Urrutia Lacroix/Ibacache's tour of Europe, on a fellowship and mission sponsored by Opus Dei, in the year leading up to the Pinochet coup.

Concluding both parables of the novella's second section with the question he asks Urrutia Lacroix/Ibacache four times, "Do you understand?," Farewell succumbs to his own envy, setting up the third section's prophecy of changes to come: "And then . . . he said: Pablo's going to win the Nobel Prize . . . . Chile is going to change . . . . but, no . . . There is no comfort in books . . . Everything falls apart, time devours everything, beginning with Chileans."[12] Urrutia Lacroix/Ibacache adds, reflecting on Farewell's sobering observations years later in the present time of the novella's narration: "the swarm of Chilean poets whose works implacable time was demolishing even then . . . my reputation resembling a sunset . . . the writers . . . whose work I criticized, the moribund of Chile and America whose voices called out my name . . . think of us as you walk away from Farewell's house . . . like a castellated shadow of Sordello . . . not even the sun can obliterate . . . . My destiny. My Sordello . . . . I wrote articles. I wrote poems. I discovered poets. I praised them. They would have sunk without a trace if not for me."[13] On the heels of this bleak view of the futile pursuit of literary fame, a view Urrutia Lacroix/Ibacache has come to share by the end of his life with his mentor, Farewell, the novella's second section moves to his encounter with the allegorical Mr. Raef and Mr. Etah, whose invitation to travel to Europe on a mission for Opus Dei—of which the narrator says he was "probably the most liberal member"—prepares the way for Urrutia Lacroix/Ibacache's ascent to the height of his career. Protesting that he would like to have told the figure of the "wizened youth—whose critical, at times insulting voice ("Opus Dei queer, did he say?") haunts the dying narrator's reflections throughout—that "even the poets of the Chilean Communist Party were dying for a kind word from me, a word of praise for their poetry. And I did praise their poetry. Let's be civilized, I whisper," Father Urrutia recounts the onset of boredom in the years leading up to the coup, the years of Allende during which his "poetic activity . . . underwent a dangerous mutation," his poems becoming so "full of insults and blasphemy and worse" that he "had the good sense to destroy them . . . without showing them to anyone."[14]

During this period, at the extreme point of the narrator's boredom with both reading and writing, with aesthesis and poiesis of any kind ("Y entonces dejé de dar clases. Dejé de decir misa. Dejé de leer el periódico . . . Dejé de escribir con claridad mis reseñas literarias . . . . El aburrimiento no disminuía"

["And then I stopped giving classes. I stopped saying mass ... reading the newspaper ... My book reviews became muddled .... The boredom did not abate"]), the novella's figures of "fear" and "hate" come to call, inviting him on the "delicate mission" that will prove to be another parable, a mission that begins with the restoration of *aesthesis* in the privileged space of the ship's reading room on the transatlantic voyage to Europe. While the personified figures of fear and hate, who worked for the Archiepiscopal College, "knew nothing about literature, except for a couple of Neruda's early poems," their invitation provides the tonic voyage the narrator needs to rediscover his love for literature: "I ... embarked on the *Donizetti* ... so many happy hours, absorbed in the works of the classic Greek authors and the classic Latin authors and my Chilean contemporaries ... regained my passion for reading, my literary instincts ... set off on the roads of Europe, determined to do a good job, light-hearted, full of confidence, resolution and faith."[15]

Continuing with renewed vigor his work "as literary critic, poet and teacher," Urrutia Lacroix/Ibacache travels throughout Europe from parish to parish—in Italy (Pistoia, Turin, Rome), France (Avignon, Provence, Paris), Spain (Pamplona, Burgos, Madrid), Belgium, Germany (Bavaria), Austria, and Switzerland—charged with the task of evaluating efforts to eliminate the "deterioration of churches" caused by "pigeon shit," a problem for which "A radical solution ... had been found."[16] Figuring the Catholic Church's historical complicity with the "radical [read "final"] solution" of European fascism in its German, Italian, and Spanish forms during World War II, Urrutia Lacroix/Ibacache's European journey prefigures the rebirth in Chile of a European-styled fascism under Pinochet (the figure of recurrence, of *Wieder* [German "again"], in *Distant Star*). Relocating the narrator from Europe to Santiago in 1973, the novella's third section chronicles the turbulent days leading up to the coup, which send the troubled narrator "straight to my Greek classics," the restoration of diplomatic relations with Cuba, the awarding of the Nobel Prize to Neruda, the expropriation of Farewell's estate in the Land Reform, and a million-person march in support of Allende, followed by "the coup d'état, the putsch, the military uprising, the bombing of La Moneda," Allende's "suicide," and then what the narrator describes as "Peace and quiet," an end to the troubles that restores Farewell's estate and has him "dancing a jig," despite learning that Neruda had "died of cancer."[17]

Returning in that context from "reading all those Greeks" to "the literature of Chile," Urrutia Lacroix/Ibacache tries "to write a few poems ... in iambic metre" at first then veering, without knowing, he says, what came over him, "from the angelic to the demonic." Writing "about women, hatefully, cruelly . . . about homosexuals and children lost in derelict railway stations," he describes his poetry as having undergone a shift from the "Apollonian" to a "Dionysiac mode" that is in fact not Dionysiac at all, but "just raving mad."[18] Pivoting from an explicit focus on poetics to an explicit focus on ideology, the novella challenges its readers to consider the relation between the two. Extending to Urrutia Lacroix/ Ibacache an invitation he can't refuse, the figures of "fear" and "hate" call on him to give lessons in "the fundamentals of Marxism" to Pinochet and the members of the military Junta, a charge he accepts and completes in "Nine classes. Nine lessons" that leave him questioning his conscience: "Did they learn anything? Did I teach them anything? Did I do what I had to do? Did I do what I ought to have done? Is Marxism a kind of humanism? Or a diabolical theory? If I told my literary friends what I had done, would they approve? Would some condemn my actions out of hand? Would some understand and forgive me?"[19]

Defending himself to Urrutia Lacroix/Ibacache, at the conclusion of his instruction, as a true intellectual, Pinochet contrasts himself as a reader and a writer invested, like the narrator, in both aesthesis and poiesis, with Allende, whom he describes as someone who read only "magazines. Summaries of books. Articles his followers used to cut out for him ("Sólo leía revistas. Resúmenes de libros. Artículos que sus secuaces le recortaban"). Proud to have written three books and "countless articles in journals" ("innumerables artículos"), he makes clear that his motivations for reading, whether "books about history and political theory" or "even novels" ("Para que sepa usted que yo me intereso por la lectura, yo leo libros de historia, leo libros de teoría política, leo incluso novelas . . ."), are at their core political: "¿Por qué cree usted que quiero aprender los rudimentos básicos del marxismo? preguntó. Para prestar un mejor servicio a la patria, mi general. Exactamente, para comprender a los enemigos de Chile, para saber cómo piensan, para imaginar hasta dónde están dispuestos a llegar" ("Why do you think I want to learn about the fundamentals of Marxism? he asked. The better to serve our country, sir. Exactly, in order to understand Chile's enemies, to find out how they think, to get an idea of how far they are prepared to go").[20]

Where in 1973, in the aftermath of the coup, the narrator's betrayal figures an inseparable intertwining, amid "rumors that had spread through Santiago's literary and artistic circles," the perspective two decades later, in the present time of the novella's narrative in 1993, amplifies the narrator's sense that "nobody gave a damn" ("a nadie le importaba un pepino") and that all political options, left and right, come to the same: "Ningún Sordello ... a nadie le importaran mis clases de introducción al marxismo .... Derecha, centro, izquierda, todos de la misma familia .... Hoy gobierna un socialista y vivimos exactamente igual ... (No Sordello .... nobody cared about my introductory course on Marxism .... The right, the centre and the left, one big happy family ... Now we have a socialist president and life is exactly the same"). Recalling the praise he received as both a critic and poet ("muchos alabaron mi obstinación en seguir publicando reseñas y críticas. ¡Muchos alabaron mi poesía! ...), his generosity in giving recommendations while publishing a book of poems and another book in Spain ("¡Y yo fui pródigo en recomendaciones .... publiqué un libro de poemas ... y publiqué otro libro en España"), his resumption of teaching and contributing to conferences ("y luego volví a mis clases y a mis conferencias"), of writing reviews and critical articles ("mis reseñas en el periódico ... mis críticas ..."), in short the professional recognition and full range of activities as poet, critic, teacher, and scholar he enjoyed during what he calls (anticipating the four European literary critics of Part I of *2666*), his time "to frequent the airports of the world" ("mi hora de pasear por los aeropuertos del mundo"), Urrutia Lacroix/Ibacache figures an eclectic mix of classical and avant-garde texts, all by the time of the novella's narration solidly canonical, the sense as well of a certain equivalence and indifference concerning both poetic and political choices: "la lectura de los griegos y de los latinos ... de los clásicos de España y Francia e Inglaterra, más cultura!, ¡más cultura!, la lectura de Whitman y de Pound y de Eliot ... de Neruda y Borges y Vallejo ... de Victor Hugo ... y la de Tolstói ... y la vida seguía ... Nos aburríamos" ("a return to the Greek and Latin greats ... the classics of Spain, France and England, more culture! more culture! read Whitman and Pound and Eliot, read Neruda and Borges and Vallejo, read Victor Hugo ... and Tolstoy ... and life went on ... We were bored").[21] As the articulation of a narrator racked by guilt, however, for his complicity with the Pinochet regime, his indifference to both aesthetic and political regimes challenges the novella's readers to articulate stances of their own, stances that might more effectively negotiate the challenges of their own circumstances, whether in *aesthesis* (as readers), *poiesis* (as writers), or both. While the narrator's own stance suggests an open-ended acceptance of a wide range of options, in which judgments of value may appear to recede, his explicit recommendation of a limited number of works he considers important, and exclusion of others, involves him (and by extension Bolaño) in an act of advocacy that can lay claim neither to indifference nor neutrality as such.[22]

Reframing this complex problematic in the novella's final section through his attention to the soirées of the politically compromised fiction writer María Canales, the narrator considers her "not without talent," yet says of her prize-winning story to a "left-leaning literary magazine" that, had he been asked to judge the competition, which invitation he would have accepted ("Literature is literature ... "), she perhaps "wouldn't have won first prize."[23] Adding that it was not "a positively bad story, but it certainly wasn't good," he confirms in his carefully parsed, dismissive assessment the questions of value, at once aesthetic, ideological, and political, that ultimately inform decisions of readers and writers alike—"We all have weaknesses, but we have to focus on our strengths. We're all writers."[24] Recounting interactions at María Canales' soirées with a "desperate poet, the novelist and the avant-garde painter," as well as with the "theorist of the avant-garde theatre" who discovered, in the basement of the Canales home where María Canales' husband, Jimmy Thompson, interrogated, and tortured, "subversives ... extracting all the information he could" before sending them "to other detention centres," the narrator asks, on returning to her house after the fall of the Pinochet regime: "Why go stirring up things that have gradually settled down over the years? . . . As if the Chilean generals were mafia bosses!"[25] Told in response to his question about what Jimmy was doing that she had in fact known and repented, "Like everyone else, Father," María Canales prompts Urrutia Lacroix to remember again the tree of betrayal, "the Judas Tree," an association that leads to the stoic conclusion, driving back into Santiago, that "That is how literature is made in Chile, but not just in Chile, in Argentina and Mexico too, in Guatemala and Uruguay, in Spain and France and Germany, in green England and carefree Italy . . . Or at least what we call literature, to keep ourselves from falling into the rubbish dump . . . The Judas Tree, the Judas Tree . . . And I remembered the day Farewell died. His funeral was discreet and orderly . . . alone in his house, looking around the library . . ."[26]

Figuring another of Bolaño's characteristic, yet never final good-byes to poetry, and to literature, the narrator's response to the death of his mentor, Farewell, signals a profound skepticism about literature's capacity to offer "imaginary solutions to real problems." [27] Referring as the novella draws to its close to the critical voice of the "wizened youth" that has haunted the narrator intermittently from its opening page to the end, the text concludes with an explicit thematization of "how literature is made," not only in Chile, or in Mexico, or in Latin America, or in Spain, but in Bolaño's own broadly encompassing literary-historical concern throughout his oeuvre, "the great works of Western literature" ("Así se hace la literatura en Chile, así se hace la gran literatura de Occidente").[28] Arcing toward the six-times repeated question "¿Tiene esto solución?" ("Is there a solution?")—a question the narrator says he posed to "a young left-wing novelist" ("a un joven novelista de izquierda") after mentioning his return, following Farewell's death, "to his old estate, Là-bas" ("Un día, tras la muerte de Farewell, fui a su fundo, el viejo *Là-bas*")—and leveling implicit answer, "Y después se desata la tormenta de mierda" ("And then the storm of shit begins"), the only sentence to claim a paragraph all its own apart from the preceding paragraph that otherwise makes up the book as a whole, the final pages of *By Night in Chile* suggest the extent to which relations between readers and writers, history and literary history, ideology and critique remain to be determined through a dynamic interplay of aesthesis and poiesis. Dismantling the (in) difference between the two terms, as has become increasingly clear in the nineteen years since Bolaño completed the last of his three late short novels of poetic apprenticeship, in this case of critical apprenticeship as well, has become an increasingly accelerated process in the digital era, a process recalling Urrutia Lacroix/Ibacache's closing vision of faces passing before his eyes "at a vertiginous speed," faces "admired . . . loved, hated, envied and despised . . . protected . . . attacked . . . hardened . . . against . . . sought in vain" ("Y entonces pasan a una velocidad de vértigo los rostros que admiré . . . amé, odié, envidié, desprecié . . .. protegí . . . ataqué, los rostros de los que me defendí, los que busqué vanamente").[29] That process carries within it the potential, though as recent convergences of "populist" movements and social media continue to demonstrate far from a guarantee, of more democratic configurations to come.

Part Four

CHAPTER 9

Literary Taxonomies after the Wall
Woes of the True Policeman (Los sinsabores del verdadero policía)

Appearing seven years after *2666*, a year after *The Third Reich*, Bolaño's third posthumously published novel, *Los sinsabores del verdadero policía* (*Woes of the True Policeman*, 2012), offers a striking inversion of the ratios and scales of *2666*'s second and fifth parts, a much expanded, more fully realized version of the former, "La parte de Amalfitano" ("The Part about Amalfitano"), which becomes along with its title character *True Policeman*'s primary, sustained concern, and a much abbreviated distillation of the latter, "La parte de Archimboldi" ("The Part about Archimboldi"), which *True Policeman* reduces, along with the figure of Arcimboldi (minus the "h"), to a comparatively minor role. In another sense, alternatively, since Bolaño began *True Policeman* a decade earlier, in the late 1980s, continuing to work on it along with *2666* in the last four years of his life until his death in 2003, *2666*'s second part could be considered a radical condensation (82 pages in the original) of *True Policeman*'s much more central focus on Amalfitano, its fifth part by contrast, on Archimboldi, a full novel-length amplification (326 pages) of *True Policeman*'s much shorter, much more cursory Part IV (38 pages), in a work now expanded to a monumental 1125 pages, roughly four times *True Policeman*'s total average-novel length of 320 pages.[1]

While both works share a five-part structure, *2666*'s is unnumbered in the contents page in the original edition, but numbered in the English translation; *True Policeman*'s numbered in both. Where the latter's contents page in the original lists each of its five titled parts in sequence—"I. La caída del muro de Berlín" ("The Fall of the Berlin Wall"); "II. Amalfitano y Padilla"; "III: Rosa Amalfitano"; "IV. J.M.G. Arcimboldi"; and "V. Asesinos de Sonora" ("Killers of Sonora")—followed by Carolina López's "Nota editorial" ("Editorial Note"), the English edition does not provide a contents page at all, presenting each numbered title only before its corresponding part begins. What is suggestive about these subtle but significant differences in structure and presentation, with respect to the recycling and re-presentation of material between *True Policeman* in *2666*, is the extent to which they call into question in fundamental ways the two works' presumed unity and integrity, both in themselves and in relation to each other. While it is clear enough from the original's contents page that the second and third numbered "parts" of *True Policeman*, "Amalfitano y Padilla" and "Rosa Amalfitano," bear an integral relation to each other, the titles of its fourth and fifth parts, "J.M.G. Archimboldi" and "Killers of Sonora," suggest by comparison and in reverse order, depending on how one frames the dates of composition, either amplified precursor texts or after-the-fact distillations of the fifth and fourth parts, respectively, of *2666*, "1. The Part about Archimboldi" and "La parte de los crímenes" ("4. The Part About the Crimes"). Where "The Infamous Ramírez Hoffman," the long short story, or short novella, that concludes Bolaño's *Nazi Literature in the Americas*, seems clearly an earlier draft of the more fully realized, full-length novel *Distant Star*, published the same year, the extensive recycling and duplication between *2666* and *True Policeman* allows no such clear differentiation. Given the integral relation between the two works, all the ways they resemble, differ, and appropriate from each other, the publication of *True Policeman* seven years after *2666* cannot help but reopen the question of any work's integrity and unity, in this case of each "novel" (in the singular) and "novels" as such, which the opening and closing "Note" of *2666* seeks to foreclose both preemptively and retrospectively.[2]

Recalling the early experimentation of *Antwerp*, the predominant form of utterance in *True Policeman* is again that of the prose poem. Where the average length of each text in the former generally falls within the genre's minimal length from a third of a page to two pages, that of each text in the latter tends to be somewhat longer, stretching to the genre's outer limits of two to several pages. Divided across its five parts into seventy-eight numbered sections—a scale roughly a third larger than that of the fifty-six sections in *Antwerp*— the 320 pages of the original *True Policeman* offer a numbered sequence of texts, part constellation, part progression, ranging in length somewhere between that of the prose poems of *Le Spleen de Paris*, at a minimum, and, at their outer limit, the short stories of Poe of which Baudelaire's prose poems offered a distillation. As "The Part about Amalfitano," at only 82 pages in the original, is by far the shortest of the five "parts" of *2666*, so "The Part about Archimboldi," at only 38 pages, is the shortest of the five parts of *True Policeman*. As Amalfitano is a relatively minor figure in *2666*, so, in *True Policeman*, is Arcimboldi. Where the narrative of the former may be read as a distilled, or at least shorter, version of the latter, the latter may likewise be read as an amplification, or elaboration, of the former. While Amalfitano and Archimboldi both figure in *2666* and *True Policeman*, their prominence between the two is thus reversed. Cast in a relatively minor role, in *2666*, as a professor of philosophy, Amalfitano reemerges as the central protagonist, in *True Policeman*, as a professor of poetry, his character's dual identity suggesting the extent to which, since Socrates, poetry and philosophy have always been understood in relation to each other, a binary relation of exclusion and inclusion that endures.[3]

As Amalfitano's discursive, professional identity, between *2666* and *True Policeman*, is at once unified and divided, a professor in both, yet of philosophy in one and of poetry in the other, so too that of Arc(h)imboldi, a novelist in both whose nationality is German in *2666* and French in *True Policeman*. As is pervasively the case in Bolaño, the discourses of poetry, criticism, and the novel, as of history and literary history, in both *True Policeman* and *2666*, are inextricably intertwined. Where *2666* begins, in "La parte de los críticos" ("1. The Part about the Critics"), with the intertwined narratives of four European literature professors devoted to the fiction of Archimboldi, circling back to the narrative of Archimboldi's life and career as a novelist in the fifth and concluding "The Part about Archimboldi," *True Policeman* begins with the literary-critical, literary-historical trope of an elaborate queer poetic taxonomy, especially of modern and contemporary poetry. Recounted as remembered by Amalfitano, professor of poetry at the University of Santa Teresa in northern Mexico— as crucial a site in *True Policeman* and *2666* as in *The Savage Detectives*— where he has been exiled after being forced to resign from the University of Barcelona following sex with a young male poet, the taxonomy is presented as having been developed by Amalfitano's former lover, Juan Padilla, the Barcelona poet turned novelist, author of a novel-in-process called *The God of Homosexuals,* whom we later learn—in the fifth and concluding "Killers of Sonora," the longest of the five parts at a novella length of 91 pages, recalling the much longer, and longest of the five parts of 2666, "The Part about the Crimes"—is in an acute stage of AIDS.[4]

As the proportion of attention given to Arc(h)imboldi and Amalfitano is reversed between *2666* and *True Policeman*, so is the attention devoted to fiction and poetry. Where the novel, literary criticism, and literary history focused on the novel, rather than on poets and poetry, are at the heart of *2666* for the first time in one of Bolaño's novels since *The Third Reich*, *True Policeman* devotes far greater attention, through Padilla's queer poetic taxonomy, to Bolaño's characteristic concern with poets and poetry.[5] As

True Policeman gives us to understand, the policing of genre is in the end
a question of identity, of what counts and what doesn't as synecdochic,
representative, exemplary, of what, and who, makes a "true novel," a "true
poetry," of what, and who, gets included and excluded and by what
criteria, and of who decides.[6]

From Ideology to Identity—The Fall of the Berlin Wall

Characterizing novels as, in Padilla's view, "in general, heterosexual,"
and, poetry as "on the other hand . . . completely homosexual," the
opening pages of "The Fall of the Berlin Wall," the first of *True
Policeman*'s five parts, focus exclusively on a taxonomy of poetry based
not on the technical terms deployed by the apprentice poet García
Madero in the opening pages of *The Savage Detectives* but on a set of
terms having apparently little to do, at least initially, with poetry as
a specific language game or kind of discourse, much less with the
historical frame announced by its title, and everything to do with questions of identity and above all sexual orientation. It is a taxonomy, in
other words, that has less to do with kinds or genres or styles of poetry
than with ways of categorizing poets in terms that would no doubt strike
sympathetic listeners and readers, if taken seriously, and even if taken
humorously, as offensive and derogatory, as a kind of hate speech,
coming from a heterosexual speaker or writer, yet might register on the
contrary, as elaborated by a self-identified queer such as Padilla, as a kind
of affirmative reclamation and reappropriation.[7]

   A tone-setting, relatively autonomous, self-contained prose poem in its
own right, the first numbered section, which consists in its entirety of
a three-page opening paragraph followed by a closing two-sentence
exchange between Amalfitano and Padilla, moves from the above passage's
queer taxonomy of individual poets to a queer taxonomy of poetic traditions within a more broadly nationalist, geopolitical frame. Describing
"Recent Spanish poetry" as generally lacking "in faggot poets until the
arrival of the Great Faggot of All Sorrows, Padilla's favorite poet, Leopoldo
María Panero," and the "poetry scene" as "essentially an (underground)
battle, the result of the struggle between faggot poets and queer poets to
seize control of the *word*" ("El panorama poético, después de todo, era
básicamente la lucha (subterránea), el resultado de la pugna entre poetas
maricones y poetas maricas por hacerse con la Palabra"), Padilla's counter-
history of poetry as a queer discourse, in all its variations, suggests the
extent to which questions of history and literary history, of identity and

questions of language, in poetry as in other kinds of discourse, are inseparable and mutually constitutive.[8]

Genres as genders, genders as genres. Sexuality as discursive position,
discourse as sexual orientation. Is the self-identity, self-identification,
self-determination of genres, as fixed and immutable, as fluid and
malleable, as that of genders, and vice-versa? Does a genre have
a DNA? To what extent, in what ways, is it ("merely") socially constructed? To what extent, in what ways, do we choose our languages,
our discourses, our disciplines, our genders, our genres, our positions,
our orientations?[9] To what extent, in what ways, do they choose us? In
respect to these questions, the irresolution of Amalfitano's identity,
whether as a professor of poetry or of philosophy, between *True
Policeman* and *2666*, may be seen not as a mere editorial oversight, but
as exactly appropriate in calling attention to the discursive instability of
the terms poetry and philosophy in relation to each other, both episte-
mologically and historically. Are they not only inherently or intrinsically, or essentially different, but opposed to each other, *an sich*? Or are
they or could they be one and the same? Is the choice between them that
of an optional either/or and/or of a necessary both/and? Is it a choice
between or within (a) particular discourse(s)? Is it a (discursive, non-
discursive) choice, at all? A binary choice or a choice among hybrids, or
multiples? A "black and white" choice and/or a choice along a spectrum
—or both—of genres and discourses as of sexual orientations, as in
Padilla's taxonomy? However we regard the ethics and politics of their
discursive identities, or split identity, singular, does poetry corrupt
philosophy? Or does philosophy corrupt poetry? However we read,
and write, them in relation to each other, in what sense do they corrupt,
and how, to what purpose(s), end(s)? What does it mean that it is the
youth, the poet, later poet-novelist, Padilla, who reaches out to take
Amalfitano's hand, rather than the reverse? And is Amalfitano corrupt-
ing or corrupted in accepting, not refusing, embracing, responding in
kind? Does the ethics, the politics, the scandal of their ensuing relation
that results in Amalfitano's forced resignation and exile have more to do
with the same-sex nature of their sexual relationship or with the yawn-
ing gap in their ages and their institutional positions as professor and
(former) student? Is the problem that their relation is corrupt—"I
disgust myself, he [Amalfitano] thought, though the truth is he didn't
disgust himself at all"—or is it rather, as the careerist Carrera puts it
"without conviction," in conveying to Amalfitano that he has little
choice but to resign, that it is "'the university'" that is "'rotten'"?[10]

Presenting the other side of the critique of personal self-absorption at the expense of political awareness and engagement that is at the heart of *Monsieur Pain*—against the backdrop of the Spanish Civil War and run-up to World War II, at the other end of the Cold War period—*True Policeman* probes the extent to which, after 1989, long-suppressed issues of identity and sexual orientation may emerge precisely because the frame-locked ideological battles of communism, fascism, and capitalism that governed the twentieth century through the end of the Cold War period have evaporated. Thus Almafitano, looking back with sadness and disappointment, if not utter disillusionment, in the wake of "The Fall of the Berlin Wall," on the entire synecdochic history of his failed political commitments and engagements, consistently aligned, like the dominant in Latin American poetry, with the radical left, remembers his love for his deceased wife, Edith Lieberman, and close relationship with their daughter, Rosa, even as he also discovers his homosexuality.[11]

In the wake of Bolaño's comparatively belated explicit coming-to-terms with the novel in Part V of *2666*, with its echoes of the earlier *The Third Reich*, arguably Bolaño's most conventional novel despite its focus on board games and electronic media, it is fitting that *True Policeman* should return to the intensely sustained focus on poetry that proved over the course of Bolaño's career to be the ironic, career-long, signature obsession of his fiction, and of his novels in particular. As the final seven numbered sections of "The Fall of the Berlin Wall" move toward its conclusion, poetry remains as central to the arc of the narrative as it does in Padilla's opening taxonomy. Posing the dual questions of how the departure of Amalfitano, the "wandering queer" ("peregrino maricón") from Barcelona to Mexico has affected both Padilla and "the Poet Pere Girau," the subtitled, prose-poetic paragraphs of section nine make it clear, in language that consistently figures poetry and sexuality in relation to each other, that the two are so absorbed in themselves and in each other that Amalfitano is, for the time being at least, barely missed. Comparing his own omnivorous homosexual orientation to that of "the Apollonian poets of nineteenth-century France who sated themselves with the stub-dicked boys from the Maghreb, youths who in no way fit the strict definition of classical beauty," Padilla differentiates himself from Girau by saying to him: "I love people and my insides are bursting, and all you love is poetry" ("yo amo a la gente y estoy reventando por dentro, y tú solo amas la poesía").[12]

Part I concludes, as it begins, with the relationship between Padilla and Amalfitano, in this case figured through an exchange of letters between them once Amalfitano has begun to settle in in Santa Teresa. "The Fall of the Berlin Wall" is thus framed in its opening and closing texts by the relationship between the fallen, exiled professional poetry professor and critic, Amalfitano, and Padilla, the former student turned amateur poet, working on his first novel, with whom Amalfitano discovers his homosexuality. Prompted by Padilla's description to remember "The wages of Chile," Amalfitano figures once again the integral relation between not merely poetry and the novel, but more specifically between the prose poem and the novel, that lies at the heart of Bolaño's fiction, thinking "fuck, he's describing the god of poets, the god of the poor, the god of the Comte de Lautréamont and Rimbaud," which is also a relation between literature and the general economy. As a professor and professional poetry critic, as the poet Girau rightly says, Amalfitano is at least "protected financially." Underscoring the asymmetrical financial situations of Amalfitano, the professional critic, and Padilla, the amateur poet-novelist, the closing exchange between them suggests a shift in the general economy of literature and criticism from the novel, as a "heterosexual," economically viable form, and poetry, as a "homosexual" form characteristically depicted as economically impoverished and impoverishing, to an economy in which the novel and poetry actually have more in common with each other, as economically suspect forms, than either does in relation to professional literary criticism within the academy as "protected financially." The more contemporary tension, then, is not so much between poetry and the novel, or between poetry and prose, as between literature and literary criticism, between amateur writers and professional literary critics like Amalfitano and the four European literary critics with whom, in Part I, "The Part about the Critics," the literary history by other means that is *2666* begins.

Suggesting Amalfitano's bisexual imaginary, where the lines between homosexual and heterosexual, as between poetry and the novel, become blurred, overlap, or intersect, Padilla's "The God of Homosexuals" figures a thoroughly sexualized class relation, a relation of classification and of hierarchies of genders as well as of genres, not just of poetry's relation to prose, but of all of literature, of the novel no less than poetry, to literary criticism, literary history, and literary theory. If the latter are coded as dominant, as heterosexual, as they tend to be in the academy in relation to all literature (not just poetry but also the novel), which by comparison tends to be coded as homosexual, subjected to critiques, schemes of classification, theoretical conceptualizations, distillations, and elaborations, then the dynamic may be said to have shifted in the general economy of literature from prose and poetry, or the novel and poetry, in the age of Baudelaire and Rimbaud, to literary criticism and literature, the corresponding frames of the first and fifth, opening and closing parts of *2666*, "The Part about the Critics" and "The Part about Archimboldi."

Interpellating Poetries—Amalfitano and Padilla

Part II of *True Policeman*, "Amalfitano and Padilla," as the name suggests, is not a departure from the previous part, but rather a continuation under the more explicit naming of the terms, or figures, of the central relationship at the heart of the more obliquely named "The Fall of the Berlin Wall." Where "The Part about Amalfitano," the second and by far the shortest of the five parts of *2666*, focuses primarily on Amalfitano as a recently arrived professor already settled in at the University of Santa Teresa, and on his growing concerns for his daughter, Rosa, in the context of the unsolved serial murders of women in the city and surrounding area, the further elaboration of his story in "Amalfitano and Padilla" continues to place at the center of the novel's concerns Amalfitano's mid-life discovery of his homosexuality through his relationship with Padilla in Barcelona, Padilla's own story, and the correspondence between the two following Amalfitano's resignation and exile to Santa Teresa, stories mirrored in the further elaboration of Rosa's story in Part III, "Rosa Amalfitano," the shortest of the five parts of *True Policeman*, devoted to the teenage friendship, platonic heterosexual attraction, and subsequent correspondence as well between Rosa and Amalfitano's former Barcelona colleague Carrera's son, Jordi. Discursively, as in *2666*, "The Part about Amalfitano" focuses on the relation between philosophy and poetry, the former figured by Amalfitano as a professor of philosophy (rather than of poetry), the latter, figured there as well as homosexual, through Amalfitano's reference to "'Baudelaire's faggoty (I'm sorry) clouds'" ("las mariconas nubes de Baudelaire [perdón]"), as well as its association with Padilla's Mexican counterpart in *2666*, the Dean's gay son Marco Antonio Guerra, whose back story, including the violent early encounters that inform Padilla's "faggot" vs. "queer" poetic taxonomy, both anticipates and echoes Padilla's own.[13]

Developing as its central discursive focus, by contrast, not the relation between poetry and philosophy but a relation within, internal to, poetry, in this case between Amalfitano as a professor of poetry rather than philosophy (in the first four parts of the novel, until the unexplained, unreconciled shift back to philosophy in Part V) and the two poets, Padilla and the poet Pere Girau, with whom he had become involved in a lover's triangle in Barcelona. As Part II of *True Policeman* begins, it further transforms

Amalfitano from the comparatively minor figure he is in *2666*, as the subject of by far the shortest of its five "parts," to the major figure he becomes, most centrally through the development of his relationship with Padilla, as the central protagonist of a full-length novel. Transposing him as well in the process from the predominantly pan-European opening and closing frames, in *2666*, of Part I, "The Part about the Critics," and Part V, "The Part about Archimboldi," to a more exclusive focus on Mexico and Spain, Santa Teresa and Barcelona, and from a temporal arc encompassing the entirety of the twentieth century, including especially World War II, the Cold War, and the first decade of the post-Cold War period, to a more exclusive focus on the latter from "The Fall of the Berlin Wall" forward, *True Policeman* recycles, anticipates, the focus in 2666 on the literary-critical, literary-historical, and contemporary discursive contexts and situation of fiction, to Bolaño's more characteristic, signature preoccupation with poets and poetry. Pivoting decisively from the ideological conflicts that governed the twentieth century to a more exclusively post-1989, post-Cold War emphasis on questions of identity, freedom, and especially sexual orientation, *True Policeman* reframes Bolaño's investigation of what counts, and what doesn't, as poetry, including how one goes about classifying and categorizing its various kinds or genres, as an inquiry into the aesthetics and politics of its particular ways of making visible. Elaborating his sense of himself as aligned with those who "will always be on the outside," in what could serve as a synopsis of Bolaño's own commitments, Amalfitano says to himself, recalling the closing "song" of *Amulet*: " . . . it's with the pariahs, with those who have nothing at all to lose, that you'll find some justification, if not vindication, and if not justification, then the song, barely a murmur . . . but a murmur that cannot be silenced."[14] In a complex, ambivalent, single-page apologia for what is in effect a deeply Romantic, fundamentally leftist aesthetic and politics, section 16 of Part I figures Amalfitano's position in a way that clearly brings it in close proximity to Bolaño's own, yet with the fundamental difference that where Bolaño has actively pursued his ambitions as a writer, as both a poet and novelist, Amalfitano has settled for a certain diminished comfort and conformity. While Amalfitano's choice of a career—"all I became was a literature professor"—allows him only to take consolation in his role as a reader, the value Bolaño attributes to that role in and of itself, notwithstanding the pervasive scorn reserved for professional critics, is not to be underestimated.

Where the familiar canonical juxtaposition of Paz and Neruda emerges as central to the dream of reconciliation that opens onto a nightmare in Part I's fifteenth section, in the single-page section 18, an especially succinct, self-contained prose poem in its own right, Amalfitano offers his students two poems by Nicanor Parra and Ernesto Cardenal.[15] Immediately following the pairing of Parra and Cardenal as exemplary poets for the "birth of modern Latin American poetry," with a pronounced preference for the former that places Amalfitano in close proximity to Bolaño, section eighteen returns to the classificatory impulses of Padilla's opening queer poetic taxonomy in the form of Amalfitano's parodic, satirical "Notas de una clase de literatura contemporánea: El papel del poeta" ("*Notes from a Class in Contemporary Literature: The Role of the Poet*").[16] Broadly humorous, and far less rhetorically complicated than Padilla's potentially insulting and offensive scheme, drawing not on such terms as "faggot" and "queer," yet still on a range of similarly identity-based categories having to do with poets as persons rather than poems and poetics, Amalfitano's "Notes" offer a less edgy and provocative, yet equally parodic taxonomy that reads like an "Academy Awards for Poets" from Europe and the Americas. Comprised of forty-seven Spanish- and twenty-three English-language poets, including in addition four French, three German, three Italian, and one Japanese, his unabashedly personal list registers, like the opening salvo of Padilla's queer poetic taxonomy, as a tongue-in-cheek critique of systematic approaches to literary criticism generally and to poetry criticism in particular. Closest in spirit, among examples of recent academic criticism, to the at once playful and serious "affective turn" of a work such as Sianne Ngai's *Our Aesthetic Categories: Zany, Cute, Interesting*—published in 2012, a year after the first edition of *True Policeman* in the original and the same year of its publication in English —Amalfitano's approach provides a mix of assessments based predominantly on categories of temperament, appearance, and companionability.[17] Mostly modernist, including some contemporaries, and almost exclusively male—the exceptions being Gabriela Mistral, Alejandra Pizarnik, Elizabeth Bishop, Violeta Parra, Emily Dickinson, Diane Di Prima, and "the female author of *Rincones románticos* (1992), whose name no one could remember"—the list of representative poets, by category, arranged in fairly random order, ranges from "*Happiest*: García Lorca" to "*Most tormented*: Celan. Or Trakl … the Latin American poets killed in the insurrections of the '60s and '70s …"; from "*Most Fun*: Borges and Nicanor Parra … " and "*Most desirable as a literature professor for all eternity*: Borges" to "*Fattest*: Neruda and Lezama Lima …"; from "*Banker of the soul*: T.S. Eliot" and "*Whitest, the alabaster banker*: Wallace Stevens" to "*Best deathbed companion after Ernesto Cardenal*: William Carlos Williams."[18]

Turning from his panoramically a- if not anti-systematic map of modern and contemporary poetry to his meditations "on his relatively recent homosexuality" in search of "literary affirmation and examples as consolation," Amalfitano finds little worthwhile in modern fiction and the novel: "All that came to mind was Thomas Mann . . . Nor did he find consolation in those few Spanish novelists who, once past the age of thirty, suddenly discovered that they were queer."[19] Committed to an affectively oriented pedagogy that includes reciting aloud the whole of Rimbaud's verse poem, "Le Coeur volé," "Amalfitano and Padilla" recycles the account of the poem found earlier in *The Savage Detectives*. Teaching his students, in Borgesian fashion, that a book is "a labyrinth and a desert," that there is "nothing more important than ceaseless reading and traveling, perhaps one and the same thing," that "all writing systems are frauds" ("todo sistema de escritura es una traición"), that "true poetry resides between the abyss and misfortune," that "the main lesson of literature" is "courage," that reading isn't "more comfortable than writing," that "by reading" one learns "to question and remember," and "that memory" is "love," Amalfitano advocates seeing literature as "in the service of" people," to paraphrase Breton, rather than the reverse.[20] In keeping with the identity-based categories informing both Padilla's and his own literary taxonomies, he implicitly places persons over texts: "I love people," Padilla had said earlier to his lover, the poet Girau, "and my insides are bursting, and all you love is poetry."[21]

Poetry in a Minor Key—Rosa Amalfitano

Reversing the suggestion of a potential shift in emphasis from poetry to the novel in Amalfitano's abrupt turn at the end of Part II to the figure who will give Part IV its title, "J.M.G. Arcimboldi," the expanded story of Rosa and Jordi in Part III, "Rosa Amalfitano," returns *True Policeman* to poetry as its greater preoccupation. As a comparatively minor figure there, despite the relatively brief elaboration of her story, as is her father in *2666*, Rosa remains significant in the allegory of genres at the heart of the novel as a figure through whom Bolaño further explores the question of poetry's continuing vitality for adolescent readers. Depicting a strong sense of poetry's value inherited from both parents—from her father, the professor of poetry, but even more decisively from her mother, Edith Lieberman— Rosa's narrative focuses on her brief interactions in Barcelona with Jordi

Carrera, the teenage son of one of Amalfitano's colleagues, and their subsequent correspondence after she moves with her father to Mexico. Where Jordi experiences poetry, and literature generally, as an obstacle to articulating what he might really want to say, Rosa experiences it as the air she breathes. Instilled by her mother as a child in Rio with "a love of the French poets," she develops from an early age a strong connection to poetry. Processing thoughts of her mother's death eight years earlier, she recalls in the context of her father's newly discovered homosexuality "fragments of a poem" by Gilberte Dallas, only the second poem quoted, after Rimbaud's "Le Coeur volé," in the entire novel, that "still echoed in her head."[22] Later rejecting the value of poetry she received from her mother, as her father rejected heterosexuality for homosexuality "at the same time that the Russians discovered their passion for capitalism," Rosa figures a new generation's embrace of electronic and digital media, after "The Fall of the Berlin Wall," at the expense not only of poetry, but of all literature.

In her pivotal transformation from precocious, omnivorous reader to "video addict"—recalling her relationship with Charly Cruz, the "video king," in 2666—it is increasingly no longer so much a question, after "The Fall of the Wall," of poetry's subordination to the novel, as of the continuing value, currency, viability, integrity, and marketability of literature as such in an increasing visual, electronic, digital age.[23] If the choice is no longer between poetry and the novel, but between poetry and people, or between literature and media, the amplification of Rosa's narrative sets the stage for *True Policeman*'s turn, in Part IV, to the novels of "J.M.G. Arcimboldi," precisely in the story of her abandonment of poetry, the genre privileged by both of her parents, as the quintessence of the literary itself. Reversing the trajectory of *Monsieur Pain* toward an affirmation of political engagement over narcissistic self-absorption, Rosa's centrality in *True Policeman* figures, by contrast, a desirable, even necessary reorientation, at the other end of Bolaño's career and in the post-Cold War context of "The Fall of the Berlin Wall," reaffirming the value of freedom and identity, including sexual orientation, over the kinds of ideological struggles that dominated the previous century. Where *Monsieur Pain* suggests there may be times, especially at moments of political urgency, when the personal in a narrow sense may be and even should be considered less important than the political in the broader sense of that term, *True Policeman* reclaims the value not only of the person, as in Amalfitano's exchange with the poet Pere Girau, over poetry—as also over the novel, the focus of "J.M.G. Arcimboldi"—or over literature *tout court,* but of questions of identity as integral to the articulation of both a poetics and a politics in whatever form.

Novel(izing) Taxonomies—J.M.G. Arcimboldi

Where *True Policeman*'s Part III, "Rosa Amalfitano," offers a still comparatively brief, 34-page amplification of Rosa's story in Part II, "The Part about Amalitano," of *2666*, its anticipation (or recycling) of Benno von Archimboldi's s story from *2666* in Part IV, "J.M.G. Arcimboldi," moves in the opposite direction. From the narratives in *2666* of Archimboldi's reception, in "The Part about the Critics," and of his *Bildung* and career as a novelist, in "The Part about Archimboldi"— a combined length of 520 pages, approaching twice the length of *True Policeman*—"J.M.G. Arcimboldi" condenses his story to a mere 38 pages. Turning the full novel-length narrative(s) of Benno von Archimboldi in the direction of the prose poem novella, or long short story, even as it focuses on Arcimboldi as a writer of novels far more than of poetry, "J.M.G. Arcimboldi" offers another formal variation, like *True Policeman* as a whole, on what might be called either Bolaño's prose-poetic formal approach to the novel or his novelizing approach to the prose poem, Yet another iteration of Bolaño's variations on the "poem-novel" in prose, or prose poem novel, that adheres to Poe's emphasis on intensity and immediacy of both affect and effect, balancing disjunctiveness and continuity, modularity and development, "J. M.G. Arcimboldi" suspends the predominant focus on poetry that characterizes the other four parts of *True Policeman* to reflect, briefly, on the work of Arcimboldi, the writer best known as a novelist, as a figure above all of the question of narrative, and of poetry's relation or non-relation to narrative, that is at the heart of the prose poem's resistance to the novel's hegemony.

Organized from the outset by genre, J.M.G. Arcimboldi's oeuvre is said to include "Novels," "Essays," "Plays" "Poetry," and "Translations." Only after establishing this systematic overview of his levels of production grounded in categorical classifications by genre—an approach in keeping with both the poetic taxonomies of Padilla and Amalfitano and the classificatory constellations of *Nazi Literature in the Americas*—does "J. M.G. Arcimboldi" proceed to offer descriptions of individual works, even then with far less of an emphasis on their individual features than on gathering them together by type. Dispensing entirely with the elaborate *Bildungsroman* back story and historical, literary-historical narrative that contribute to making the concluding Part V of *2666*, "The Part about

Archimboldi," a relatively autonomous text of full novel length, *True Policeman*'s vastly shorter Part IV, "J.M.G. Arcimboldi," launches directly into descriptions of Arcimboldi's publications from the 1940s through the mid-1970s, skipping back and forth among all four decades of Arcimboldi's publishing career in no particular order. Born not in 1920 in Germany, like Benno von Archimboldi, aka Hans Reiter, in *2666*, but in 1925 in France (Carcassonne), the Arcimboldi of *True Policeman* has in common only one work with the Archimboldi of *2666*, the novel *The Endless Rose* (recalling Umberto Eco's *The Name of the Rose*).[24] While neither is exclusively a novelist, and the opening synopsis of J.M.G. Arcimboldi's establishes a greater generic range, it is with novels, eleven of which he is said to have published with Gallimard, that Arcimboldi, like Archimboldi, like Bolaño himself by the end of his life, is primarily identified. At 90 and 180 pages, 140 pages, 185 and 140 pages, and 230 and 206 pages, respectively, the seven novels of his brought together under four rubrics are all comparatively short, in keeping with Bolaño's interest in prose-poetic brevity and intensity of effect, even in his two magnus opus novels, *The Savage Detectives* and *2666*.

As *Antwerp* acquires a double identity both as the only one of his "novels" that Bolaño said didn't embarrass him, and as the centerpiece of the collected poems posthumously published as *The Unknown University*, "J.M.G. Arcimboldi" lists two similar titles, suggesting perhaps two different versions of the same work, under the two separate categories of "Novels" and "Poetry." Along with the first major meta-category's focus on each work's length and the time spent reading, the second major meta-category for presenting Arcimboldi's work, also in four iterations, focuses on his personal relationships, interests, and history. Numbered and (sub) titled by section under the eight rubrics of the two major meta-categories, each work-titled section or subsection an average length of a half-page to several pages, "J.M.G. Arcimboldi" presents Arcimboldi's novel-dominated oeuvre in a prose poem-like-sequence that recalls Bolaño's earliest experimentations with the form of the prose poem novel, now in a work left unfinished at the end of his own novel-dominated life, in *Antwerp, Monsieur Pain,* and especially *Nazi Literature in the Americas.* Beyond its formal and structural affinities with these earlier works, "J.M.G. Arcimboldi" resonates of course in the most sustained way, and most directly in its subject matter, with "The Part about Archimboldi" in *2666.* In addition to the shared name, Arc(h)imboldi, and one common publication, the novel *The Endless Rose,* its numbered, titled individual sections and work-titled subsections recycle numerous echoes of the

German Archimboldi's narrative, now transposed to fit the French Arcimboldi's context, career, and publications. In addition to changing Arc(h)imboldi's identity from German to French, *True Policeman* also reverses the order of the final two "Parts" of *2666*, moving not from "The Part about the Crimes" to "The Part about Amalfitano," but from "J.M.G. Arcimboldi" to "Killers of Sonora."

Crimes of Gender and Genre—Killers of Sonora

Continuing the strategy of inversion between *2666* and *True Policeman* that makes Arc(h)imboldi the novelist a major figure in the one and a comparatively minor figure in the other, just as it makes Amalfitano the professor a comparatively minor figure in the one and a major figure in the other, the restructuring of the sequence of the fourth and fifth parts of *2666* as, in the corresponding narratives of *True Policeman*, the fifth and fourth, respectively, completely reframes the trajectory of the two in relation to each other. In addition to inverting the arc of the narrative trajectory in each work's final two parts, from "killings to novelist" in *2666*, from "novelist to killings" in *True Policeman*, Bolaño all but dispenses, in the latter, with the predominantly pan-European, later especially German and Russian focus of "The Part about the Critics" and "The Part about Archimboldi," respectively, moving back and forth instead between Spain (Barcelona) and Mexico (in and around Santa Teresa), Latin America, and the Americas more generally.

Among the many consequences and implications of these realignments, the sustained attention Part V of *2666* devotes to traditions of the German and Russian novel falls away entirely in *True Policeman*.[25] In this markedly different version of how Amalfitano comes to be a professor, and of philosophy rather than poetry, at the University of Santa Teresa, Amalfitano's decision has nothing manifestly to do with homosexuality, but rather with a heterosexual relationship with his beloved, now deceased wife, as well as the heterosexual attraction for him of a younger woman interested in inviting him to Santa Teresa to be her colleague, an invitation he accepts for apparently very different reasons than those given in the earlier account of the scandal created by his homosexual affairs with Padilla and other former students at the University of Barcelona. Although these two versions are not necessarily contradictory, since his turn to homosexuality is earlier described as being "recent," that is, long after he had first come to know Isabel Aguilar, it is unclear whether her hopes for developing a relationship with him will prove misplaced or whether, if his own sexuality remains as "fluid," as he tells Rosa sexuality can be, he will reciprocate her attraction to him. At the core of the imaginary and inquiry of *True Policeman*, in the fifth part as in parts I–III, is the question of what a knowledge, or lack of knowledge, of sexual identity involves.[26]

Understanding questions of sexuality as bound up not only with questions of gender but with questions of genre, Padilla's opening queer poetic taxonomy establishes from the outset the novel's recognition that construc- tions and performances of sexual identity and discursive (and non- discursive) choices, both literary and extra-literary, are mutually constitutive and informing.[27] Having begun with the epochal turn, made possible by "The Fall of the Berlin Wall," from the dominant ideological struggles of the mid-nineteenth- to late-twentieth centuries, to the post-1989 focus on identity, in particular the politics of sexual identity and orientation, the novel's final section figures the tensions ushered in by the collapse of the liberal-utopian fantasy of a post-ideological end of history, with its dream of a harmoniously global multiculturalism, within a decidedly post-9/11 frame. Reprising its sustained inquiry into the relation between literary genres and sexual identities, between poetry and homosexuality in particular, including the question of their relative fixity and fluidity, the seventeenth of part V's nineteen sections reconfigures and reframes this inquiry within a context shaped more by the events of 9/11 than by the fall of the Berlin Wall through a powerful anecdote about the explosive exchange on a train between the gay "poet from Girona" (renamed from the earlier "poet Pere Girau"), as recounted to Padilla and forwarded in correspondence to Amalfitano, and a man identified only as "el magrebí" ("the Maghrebi," "the North African").[28] Figuring the tension between the values of a non-religious gay Western man whose name explicitly identifies him as a poet, and those of a devout Muslim, the episode offers a queer, post-9/11 update of the brutal beating of the Pakistani taxi driver in London by two of the three libidinous, heterosexual Archimboldians, the French and Spanish literary critics Jean-Claude Pellier and Manuel Espinoza—the shared object of their desire, the younger British Archimboldian Liz Norton, looking on both horrified and sexually aroused—in "The Part about the Critics" in *2666*.

The vehemently ambiguous, ambivalent deployment of queer discourse in Padilla's exchanges with the North African near the conclusion of *True Policeman* recall as well the complex registers of Padilla's opening queer poetic taxonomy. Complicating questions of sexual identity and orienta- tion in relation to questions of personal belief and ideology, Padilla's encounter with the North African suggests the extent to which homosexual poets like the poet from Girona, Padilla, and his "poet friends" may understand themselves as co-participants in and co-contributors to Western narratives of progress, just as the Muslim who thinks of himself as tolerant, merciful, and compassionate may find the limits of his tolerance in his capacity to empathize with a Western poet who is gay. Placing what is called poetry at the center of such questions in a single-sentence paragraph all its own, the passage concludes: "I would have liked, said Padilla in conclusion, to take him to a hotel, he was a North African open to the poetry of the world ["abierto a la poesía del mundo"], and I'm sure he'd never been buggered."[29]

Situating its inquiries into the politics of genre, gender, sexuality, and identity after "The Fall of the Berlin Wall," after 9/11, *True Policeman* arcs toward a profound questioning of what progress we may claim to have made in negotiating conceptual, epistemological, ideological binaries and the degree to which, in reimagining poetry, the novel, politics, ideology, history, literary history, we may find it possible to develop a poetics of multiplicities, of apposition rather than opposition. In Padilla's next letter, accordingly —"the first that Amalfitano didn't answer right away"—Padilla figures his relationship with his friend and companion Elisa, who is "in the hospital now," in terms of a poetry-centered pedagogy. Recalling other pivotal moments in Bolaño's work that highlight the importance of reading and interpretation, Padilla's "simple" approach to "understanding," the "method (or something resembling a method) of reading" he shares with Elisa that yields not (mere) "comprehension," but a "desperation and communion" of reading, culminates in the generosity of presenting her as an outright gift, when she is discharged from the hospital, "all the books he had loaned her." Suggesting the healing properties of poetry in particular as well as genuine feelings for Elisa that lead him to reconsider the parameters of his own sexuality, Padilla gets "back to work" thereafter, though unenthusiastically, on his novel, *The God of Homosexuals.* Although "Very late one night, coming home drunk and high," finding her "sitting outside his building, waiting for him," Padilla sees her as "death," the story does not end there. While Amalfitano's "five-page letter" in reply, "hastily written between classes," relates to Padilla "the giant steps that science" is taking "in its fight against AIDS," Padilla's final letter to Amalfitano suggests his life is moving in a direction Amalfitano could not have imagined. Written "on the back of an airmail postcard from Barcelona," it announces that his life has taken "a radical turn," that he is living with Elisa and with his father, who is "beside himself with joy."[30]

The "radical turn" Padilla says his life is taking, including the new genre of a heterosexual ménage he is trying out with Elisa, is a life open to possibilities yet not manifestly full of them, a life that resists the dead-endedness of "closure" yet remains bound up with her dealing "heroin in her old neighborhood." Addictions of all kinds, all genres, Bolaño suggests, are hard to break, including the novel, including literature, including, perhaps above all, poetry. "At least, thought Amalfitano"—who "deep down was still a Marxist" ("en el fondo seguía siendo marxista"), just as Padilla aspired to be "the Aimé Césaire of homosexuals"—reflecting earlier on having only become a literature professor: "I've read thousands of books. At least I've become acquainted with the Poets and read the Novels . . .. At least I've read. At least I can still read, he said to himself, at once dubious and hopeful."[31]

Fundamental to Amalfitano's awareness of the knowledge reading and writing provide is his understanding of the ways they open not just onto the unknown but the unknowable, the undefined and undefinable, in relation to which all taxonomies, including of poetry, fiction, literary history, and politics, remain provisional: "In Managua, he was paid a pittance to teach Hegel, Feuerbach, Marx, Engels, Lenin, but he also taught classes on Plato and Aristotle, Boethius and Abelard, and he realized something that in his heart he had always known: that the Whole is impossible ["el Todo es imposible"], that knowledge is the classification of fragments" ["el conocimiento es una forma de clasificar fragmentos"].[32] The fundamental partiality, illegibility, unavailability, ephemerality, the becoming historical of all ideas of Totality, including of "poems" and "novels" and "poem-novels" presumed to be singular, in literary history and politics, are at the heart of the indelible combination of attraction to and ambivalence for literature Bolaño shares with Amalfitano, professor, between *True Policeman* and *2666*, of both poetry and philosophy; with the German/French novelist, Arc(h)imboldi, with the poet Pere Girau; with that other poet turned novelist, Juan Padilla: "The Whole is Impossible"; "knowledge is the classification of fragments"; "All you love is poetry."

CHAPTER 10

"What a Relief to Give Up Literature"
2666

As the first of his prose poem novels, more modular than narrative, book-end minimalist counterpart to the maximalist ambitions of *The Savage Detectives* and the even longer *2666*, *Antwerp* provides the touchstone and frame of reference for every literary compromise Bolaño understood himself to have made thereafter for the sake of literary marketability. Begun in 1999, twenty years after the "Big Bang" of *Antwerp* and a year after *The Savage Detectives* consolidated Bolaño's reputation as heir apparent, among Latin American novelists, to García Márquez—wryly suggested through the prose-poetic journal entries of the novel's young poet apprentice protagonist, García Madero—written over the four years remaining before his death in 2003, and published the following year, *2666* gives the most sustained, explicit priority of any novel in Bolaño's career not to a poet (or poets) and poetry, but to a novelist and the novel. While poetry maintains a place of some importance in *2666*, especially in the second, which is also tellingly by far the shortest, of the novel's five parts, "La parte de Amalfitano" (82 pages; "2. The Part about Amalfitano," 67 pages), its subordination to the novel as a principal preoccupation and concern is clear from the opening part's focus on the four professional literary critics devoted to Archimboldi's work to the book-by-book elaboration of Archimboldi's almost exclusively novelistic literary production in the novel's fifth, second longest, concluding part, "La parte de Archimboldi" (316 pages; "5. The Part about Archimboldi," 258 pages).

Thus we see, in the first of *2666*'s five "parts" (significantly not numbered in the original, in contrast to the English translation), "La parte de los críticos" ("The Part about the Critics"), through the French Jean-Claude Pelletier (Paris) and his Spanish colleague, Manuel Espinoza (Madrid)—two of the four literary critics at the heart of the novella-length first section whose careers focus on the German novelist Benno von Archimboldi—a tension between, on the one hand, the professional demand for a certain aesthetic, discursive, disciplinary purity of literary criticism itself as genre and, on the other, the shared political aspiration for a liberation at once individual and collective. Moving from the realm of what we may call in the figurative terms of Bolaño's collected poems *The Unknown University*, in *The Savage Detectives*, to the more literal academic world of the known university in *2666*, the latter's opening "part," "The Part about the Critics," marks a shift in the arena of Bolaño's fictive investigation of literary history from poetry to the novel, from the Latin American context of an unauthorized search by the amateur Chilean and Mexican literary detectives Arturo Belano and Ulises Lima for the visceral realist poet Cesárea Tinajero, to the pan-European context of a professional literary-historical investigation by three established scholars—Pelletier, Espinoza, the Italian Piero Morini (Turin), all academic specialists in German literature—and the English doctoral student and fellow Germanist, Liz Norton (her surname recalling T.S. Eliot's "Burnt Norton"), object of their shared desires—into the work of the character who figures as *2666*'s counterpart to *The Savage Detectives'* Tinajero, the German novelist Benno von Archimboldi.[1]

Encountered briefly early on, in the second, central part of *The Savage Detectives* that bears the novel's name, as a French rather than German novelist, Archimboldi figures there (as does the [again French] Arc[h]imboldi in *True Policeman*), as a decidedly minor, synecdochic figure, in this respect, of *The Savage Detectives'* principal literary-historical concern (again like *True Policeman*'s), not with the novel, but with poetry. Like Tinajero, the poet at the heart of the amateur literary-critical, literary-historical investigation that is *The Savage Detectives*, Archimboldi, the novelist at the heart of the professional, scholarly investigation in the first part of *2666*, first emerges as a MacGuffin-like figure who allows the novel to develop the plot of what appear initially to be its real concerns, the amorous relationships among its central characters. Where the former's focus on the relationships among three marginal young Latin American poets, García Madero, Belano, and Lima, all figures of the unknown university, yields an unauthorized literary history focused primarily on modern poetry, in France and Latin America in particular, the latter's focus on the relationships among four professional European literary critics, all representatives of the known university, figures a fully authorized literary history by other means, in another form, focused more centrally on the modern novel, in Germany and Latin America in particular. In both novels, the MacGuffin-like status of the central figures of writing and genre—Tinajero the poet, Archimboldi the novelist—takes on increasing urgency as the two narratives arc toward the conclusions of their fictive literary-historical investigations, into poetry and the novel, respectively, in the former's concluding Part III, "Los desiertos de Sonora (1976)" ("The Sonora Desert" [1976])—and the latter's fifth and concluding part, "The Part about Archimboldi." In keeping with the parallel structures and complementary genre concerns of the two novels, while the former's search for the poetry of Tinajero uncovers and focuses on her sole remaining "poem," the latter explores the full range of Archimboldi's prolific career as a novelist and more complex, variable reception both inside and outside of the academy.

Novel(izing) Critiques—The Part about the Critics

Whether attributable to a certain anxiety of influence, not as a poet but as a novelist, where the stakes over the course of his writing career proved higher, or a reluctance born of a competitive awareness of the risks involved in naming names and choosing up sides, or as *The Savage Detectives* puts it, one's "gang," Bolaño devotes far less attention to an explicit configuring of his place in the history of the novel than he does to the history of modern poetry.[2] With the fictive literary-historical investigation in *2666* of the work of Benno von Archimboldi, a writer whose literary fame also owes itself, like Bolaño's, to his success above all as a prolific novelist, Bolaño takes up that challenge most explicitly and emphatically over the course of what would prove to be the last four years of his life. While earlier works had mentioned writers of prose fiction to whom Bolaño always understood himself indebted—Cervantes, Poe, Robert Louis Stevenson, Arthur Conan Doyle, Kafka, Borges, Cortázar, García Márquez, Joyce, Agatha Christie, Ursula LeGuin, Tolstoy, Breton, Aragon—it is in *2666*, through the figure of Archimboldi, that Bolaño finally devotes the sustained attention to the history of the novel reserved previously in his work for the history of modern poetry.

The first mention of Archimboldi's fiction, early on in "The Part about the Critics," involves a trilogy of novels, the implicitly French-themed *"D'Arsonval"* along with "the English-themed *The Garden* and the Polish-themed *The Leather Mask*," all of which are mentioned as having been read by Pelletier in 1980—when he was nineteen—the year Bolaño wrote *Antwerp*. Recalling the international frames of reference of the trilogy of novels focused on modern and contemporary poetry in the Americas and in Europe—*Distant Star, Amulet,* and *By Night in Chile*—which Bolaño published between 1996 and 2000, the three novels that represent Pelletier's, and the reader's, first exposure to Archimboldi position his work as a novelist within an international, pan-European frame. Taken together, the four critics offer a range of generational perspectives on Archimboldi's career. Born in 1920, he is a surrogate German figure for the Latin American-European novelist, Bolaño, to compare with Bolaño's perspective on the great modern European, especially German, novels of his parents' generation. As the true plot of *The Savage Detectives* may be said to concern less the characters' relationships "among themselves" than their representative status as synecdochic figures of genre, more specifically of the relationship between poetry and prose and the dialectical overcoming of their (in)difference to each other that opens onto what Belano and Lima call the "poem-novel," the constellation of four European critics in the opening part of *2666* establishes what will prove its dominant literary-historical stakes, its configuration of Bolaño's take on the past, present, and future of the novel itself, as form and concept, and of his own contributions to the novel's history.

The politics of forms and the forms of politics are in this sense at the heart of Bolaño's understanding of what matters most in and about what is called literature, whether in poetry, in the novel, or a poem-novel hybrid. Framed by the constellation Borges-Dickens-Stevenson, the attack Part I stages on a Pakistani taxi driver by two professional European literary critics specializing in German literature, one Spanish, the other French, both rivals for their female English colleague's affection, speaks to where the history of such questions had arrived, in reality as in the novel and contemporary fiction generally, at the turn of the millennium. With Norton as witness, in one of the novel's most troubling and important passages, unable to stop them yet also sexually aroused, Espinoza and Pelletier "delivered kick after kick, shove Islam up your ass, which is where it belongs, this one is for Salman Rushdie (an author neither of them happened to think was much good but whose mention seemed pertinent), this one is for the feminists of Paris (will you fucking stop, shouted Norton), this one is for the ghost of Valerie Solanas, you son of a bitch, and on and on, until he was unconscious and bleeding from every orifice in the head, except the eyes."[3] Recalling the beating the theoretically, philosophically aware speaker of Baudelaire's "Assommons les pauvres!" attempts to give the beggar in the climactic, penultimate prose poem of *Le Spleen de Paris*—except that the beggar fights back and beats the speaker to a pulp, rather than the other way around—the passage's sardonic, prescient act of misplaced violence and vengeance opens onto the sexual violence of the turn of the two critics "to whores" through other, more contemporary extra-literary—non-poetic, prosaic, visceral realist—forms of publication, Pelletier looking for them in Paris "on the Internet, with excellent results," Espinoza finding them in Madrid "by reading sex ads in *El País*."[4]

Attending Archimboldi conferences in Germany, Italy, and the United States, the four scholars play a central role in contributing to his rising reputation. As his work begins "to circulate widely," the organizers of a conference in 1995 in Amsterdam signal the hierarchies in place in European letters based on language and nationality, leaving out "contemporary Spanish and Polish and Swedish for lack of time or money" while providing "luxurious accommodations for the stars of English literature," including as well "three French novelists, an Italian poet, an Italian short story writer, and three German writers, the first two of them novelists from West and East Berlin, now reunited, both vaguely renowned."[5] Positioned by his publisher's widow Mrs. Bubis, who is also his former lover and confidante, his reputation among German novelists rising in the 1990s (paralleling Bolaño's own rise during the same decade among novelists from Latin America), Archimboldi becomes "a candidate for the Nobel," in the scholars' opinion not just "the best living writer in Germany, but the best living writer in Europe."[6] Comparing his work to that of other German writers and novelists they admire, including Günter Grass, Arno Schmidt, whom Amalfitano considers "just as good," Peter Handke, Thomas Bernhard, and Kafka, "the greatest German writer of the twentieth century," the critics argue that Archimboldi is "the greatest German writer," if not of the "twentieth century," then at least "the greatest postwar German writer or the greatest German writer of the second half of the twentieth century," an estimation that demonstrates, in effect, both the implied wisdom of Amalfitano, whom they attack and dismiss as their unworldly, parochial inferior, and their own territorial provincialism and overestimation of Archimboldi's place in the history of the German and European novel and the novel more generally.[7] Reported to have been in Argentina in 1974 "because of the coup in Chile, which had obliged him to choose the path of exile," Amalfitano elicits, in Pelletier's assessment of exile as "full of inconveniences, of skips, and breaks," an intimate connection between exile and the forms of Bolaño's "poem-novels," including the radically broken, segmented procedure of *2666* (323).[8]

Turning back in its conclusion from news of the serial murders of women in and around Santa Teresa (for Juárez), Mexico, that will prove to be at the heart of *2666* to the scholars' preoccupations with Archimboldi and one another, their lives as literary critics and the soap opera of their amorous entanglements—from the "horror in the desert" to an "oasis of boredom," as the novel's epigraph from Baudelaire has it—the first part of *2666* sets the stage, in Amalfitano's terms, for the story of Amalfitano himself, "a nonexistent professor at a nonexistent university … a melancholy literature professor put out to pasture in his own field," in permanent exile at the heart of the desert scene the three critics leave behind to return to Europe. At 82 pages in the original, roughly the same length as the conclusion of García Madero's narrative in Part III of *The Savage Detectives* and half the novella length of his narrative in Part I—comparable to the first and third parts of *2666* and a third of the length of its second and fifth parts—"The Part about Amalfitano" is by far the narrative's most condensed. A largely self-contained story, as in effect all five parts of the novel may be said to be, that is more fully elaborated with significant duplication in *True Policeman*, Amalfitano's narrative focuses on his marginal, peripheral status as an exiled Chilean philosophy professor in the Mexican desert, far removed from the European centers of cultural capital (London, Paris, Madrid, Turin) where the four literary critics ply their trade.

Philosophy in the Desert—The Part about Amalfitano

As the narrative of an alter-ego who is neither a poet turned novelist, nor a literary critic or literary historian, but a professor of philosophy, Amalfitano's story triangulates poetry's central importance to Bolaño's fiction with the state of Amalfitano's academic discipline, particularly since 1989 and "The Fall of the Berlin Wall" that gives the opening section of *True Policeman* its title, and the question of a choice between shorter, "minor" fiction and the novel as "epic" prose.[9] The most poetic of the novel's five parts, by virtue of its formal brevity and intensity, coupled with its explicit focus on poetry as well as philosophy, "The Part about Amalfitano" begins with its title character's recognition of his decidedly minor status. Philosophy professor though he is, in the recollections of his time in Barcelona before being forced into academic exile in Santa Teresa, poetry figures at the heart of Amalfitano's, his ex-wife Lola's, and their daughter Rosa's stories. Concluding a meta-philosophical commentary on six complementary geometrical maps of the field and history of philosophy with the assessment that "the intersection of the horizontal by two slanted lines … was something like a joke," Amalfitano offers an analogue in the domain of philosophy that recalls Salvatierra's similarly baffled assessment in the domain of poetry, at the conclusion of Part II of *The Savage*

Detectives, in response to Belano's and Lima's commentary on Tinajero's sole-surviving, three-part, geometric "poem." Complicating the associations of both poetry, in *The Savage Detectives*, and philosophy, in *2666*, with radical, minimalist forms of intellectual abstraction, as well as more social, political concerns, both discourses accrue intimate connections over the course of *2666*, as even more emphatically, in *True Policeman,* with the question of sexual orientation in all its implications at once personal and political (2).

Suggesting the prose-poetic, interruptive, disruptive poem-novel structure of *2666* itself, including as well its social, political implications, Amalfitano dreams one night of "signs and numbers and something Amalfitano didn't understand . . . 'history broken down' or 'history taken apart and put back together' . . . a scribble in the margin, a clever footnote" ("de signos y de números y de algo que Amalfitano no entendía . . . ≪historia descompuesta≫ o ≪historia desarmada y vuelta a armar≫ . . . un comentario al margen").[10] Preparing for his next day's class, Amalfitano produces on a "blank piece of paper" the following list of names in three columns, names he reads and rereads "horizontally and vertically, from the center outward, from bottom to top, skipping and at random," then laughing and thinking "that the whole thing was a truism, in other words a proposition too obvious to formulate:"

Pico della Mirandola	Hobbes	Boecio
Husserl	Locke	Alexander of Hales
Eugene Fink	Erich Becher	Marx
Merleau-Ponty	Wittgenstein	Lichtenberg
Bede	Llull	Sade
St. Bonaventure	Hegel	Condorcet
John Philoponus	Pascal	Fourier
Saint Augustine	Canetti	Lacan
Schopenhauer	Freud	Lessing[11]

Amalfitano's supplemental mapping and "proposition" of the field and history of philosophy notwithstanding, a very personal, father-inflected voice returns, in the section immediately following, to pose to Amalfitano the question their previous exchange had only implied: "Queer? asked Amalfitano. Yes, queer, faggot, cock-sucker, said the voice. Ho-mo-sex -u-al, said the voice." Responding to Amalfitano's reply that he is not, the voice speaks again in terms that link questions concerning relationships, gender, and sexual orientation to questions of genre: "There is no friendship, said the voice, there is no love, there is no epic, there is no lyric poetry that isn't the gurgle or chuckle of egoists, the warble of faggots." Yet again, he insists that he has nothing "against homosexuals," that he is speaking "figuratively." Asked by the voice if he has thought about his daughter "and about the murders committed daily in this city, and about Baudelaire's faggoty (I'm sorry) clouds" but not "about whether your hand is a hand," which Amalfitano claims "isn't true," Amalfitano is positioned once again between philosophy and poetry.[12] Recalling the final line of the opening prose poem of *Le Spleen de Paris,* "L'Étranger," which prominently figures the poetic as such in *By Night in Chile,* the voice's reference to "Baudelaire's faggoty (I'm sorry) clouds" in addressing Amalfitano, the philosopher, further contributes to aligning poetry and philosophy with each other, a discursive alliance in play, with very different emphases and inflections, in both *2666* and *True Policeman.*[13]

Amalfitano figures not only the confusion of poetry and philosophy he finds in Rafael Dieste's *Testamento geométrico,* where "poetic creation and speculative creation are focused on a single object," but a connection between both poetry and philosophy and being queer.[14] Figuratively speaking, queerness manifests itself in the connection the narrative subsequently begins to establish between Amalfitano and the Dean's son Marco Antonio Guerra at a dinner "at the house of the rector of the University of Santa Teresa, the august Dr. Pablo Negrete."[15] Marked by a relationship with his father as antagonistic as Amalfitano's with his own, Guerra finds an affinity between the two of them that once again brings poetry and philosophy into a proximity verging on complicity, particularly with respect to figurative and literal understandings of being queer.

Recalling the beating delivered by Espinoza and Pelletier to the Pakistani cab driver in "The Part about the Critics," the violent rage of the Dean's unhappy, stifled son opens paradoxically onto the supposed purity of poetry: "I used to read everything, Professor ... Now all I read is poetry. Poetry is the only thing that isn't contaminated, the one thing that isn't part of the game ... Only poetry—and let me clear, only some of it—is good for you, only poetry isn't shit" ("Antes leía de todo, maestro, y en grandes cantidades, hoy sólo leo poesía. Sólo la poesía no está contaminada, sólo la poesía está fuera del negocio... "Sólo la poesía, y no toda, eso que quede claro, es alimento sano y no mierda").[16] Although Guerra clarifies that "only some" poetry qualifies, the association of such a violent character with poetry hardly recommends it as a non-instrumentalizing, non-commercial discourse to embrace and endorse for its ethical, political value. Recalling the ambiguous closing affirmation of poetry, of "song" ("ese canto"), at the end of *Amulet,* the farcical hallucination at the end of

"The Part about Amalfitano" invoking Boris Yeltsin as the drunken, singing "last Communist philosopher" figures the wobbly transition to a "New World Order" after the Fall of the Berlin Wall from a twentieth century dominated by violent ideological confrontations, the "real combat of isms" at once aesthetic and political, including World War II, the shaping event of Archimboldi's life and the focus of *2666*'s fifth and concluding part. While the post–World War II, post–Cold War transition did not lead, as once optimistically predicted, to an "End of History," or of ideology, it did lead Bolaño to a recognition, in *2666*, that one narrative of history had been radically changed, and that a different, if not entirely new narrative had begun.

Race, News, Print—The Part about Fate

Where "The Part about Amalfitano" links together styles of writing, history, and politics, focused especially on philosophy and poetry, with inconclusive consequences reflecting the end of the Cold War and its aftermath, "The Part about Fate" investigates, through the trope of a journalistic investigation, the landscape of multiculturalism, race, and ethnicity that emerged as the central issue in the Americas, increasingly in Europe as well, in the 1990s.[17] Against the backdrop of the focus on literary criticism and the novel in "The Part about the Critics," and on philosophy and poetry in "The Part about Amalfitano," the shift of focus to journalism in "The Part about Fate," and what Fate's skeptical New York editor dismissively calls "*reportage,*" marks a fundamental turn in Bolaño's work from a meta-focus on poetry and its discursive others, including especially the novel, to a focus on the novel itself and its relation to "extra-literary" forms of writing, including journalism and what has come to be called "creative non-fiction," forms focused more centrally on "real world" events and content, on what is "outside" philosophy, "outside" poetry, in this case strongly connected to questions of race, ethnicity, gender, sexuality, and violence. "The Part about Fate" picks up where "The Part about Amalfitano" leaves off in developing, through Fate's investigation, the "real world" basis for the fears driving Amalfitano mad concerning what might happen to his daughter, Rosa, in relation to which Yeltsin's singing registers as a drunken consolation, a drowning of sorrows. Moving beyond the context of the Cold War, including the Pinochet dictatorship and its aftermath, which figures so prominently in Bolaño's earlier novels, *2666* pivots to journalism as a new genreless genre that nevertheless brings with it its own set of protocols and conventions, its own discursive, disciplinary stakes and orientation, in this respect no less aesthetic and political, a non-genre that is still, for all that, a, and in, genre.

First appearing in 1862, the proto-"visceral realist" prose poems of Baudelaire's *Le Spleen de Paris* aspired too to be both a genreless genre and a "real world" genre, a genre closely aligned with journalism, with documentary "*reportage,*" in this sense, both in Baudelaire's initial choice of *La Presse* as a venue for publication of the new genre and in the latter's dialectic of form and content, combining the prose format of the newspaper with prosaic, everyday subject matter, its play with, on, and against what today we would call "human-interest" stories, a genre at once literary and non-literary that could compete with both the then new medium's *faits divers* and its serialized novels (3).[18] In *2666* this imperative manifests anew, at the threshold of the new millennium, in Fate's desire not merely to be a sports journalist, but to do what would now be called "hard news" stories. Exemplifying Bakhtin's contention that every character in a novel is an ideologue, and that each character's ideology is aligned with and articulated in and through specific discourses or speech genres, "The Part about Fate" tells the story in part of two closely linked characters, an ex-boxer and former member of the Black Panthers named Barry Seaman and an aging left-wing radical/intellectual, Antonio Ulises Jones.[19] Providing historical context for Fate's work as an African-American reporter in the 1990s, Bolaño traces in reverse, through these two synecdochic figures, recalling among others Bobby Seale and Amiri Baraka (Leroi Jones), three generations of political activism at the intersection of African-American and Marxist thought and practice, from the 1930s to the 1960s to the 1990s. Opening onto an entire history of Cold War and post-Cold War issues for the "fate" of Western Marxism from a specifically leftist, African-American perspective, Jones serves as a figure of transition from the Cold War to the post-Cold War period, from a pre- to a post-1989 frame of reference where the ideological battles of the twentieth century give way to those of race, ethnicity, gender, and technology that have increasingly come to define the twenty-first.

Updating the history of the relation between poetry and prose fiction at the heart of *The Savage Detectives*, Part IV's sweeping historical, literary-historical summary provides a panoramic frame within which to understand the changed context for print media as it was then emerging at the time of the novel's writing between 1999 and 2003. With its telescopic history moving from "the Greeks" forward through the past four centuries, the narrative offers a powerful distillation of how "Everything" has changed from the beginnings of literacy in the West to the present. Referencing "society," "words," "Reading news, stories," "crime," "merchandise," "every slave ship," "dark-skinned people," "headlines in the Virginia papers" of a "plantation owner, and the murder of a "neighbor," a "wife," as well as news of "the Paris Commune of 1871" (recalling Rimbaud's turn to the prose poem and the story of his alleged rape in *The Savage Detectives*) where "thousands of people were killed," "The Part about Fate" throws into sharp relief questions concerning what counts as news and what doesn't, who is considered part of society and who isn't, who and what are visible and invisible, legible and what illegible, questions *2666* understands are as urgent for poems and novels as for newspapers, whether in print or electronic media, in all of which words may be used, as the narrator puts it, more "in the art of avoidance" than "of revelation" ("más en el arte de esconder que en el arte de develar").[20]

Tracing Fate's travels to Tucson, Arizona to cover the sports story he wants to be released from to cover the more urgent story of serial murders of women in northern Mexico, "The Part about Fate" marks the precise moment of Bolaño's transition in *2666* from its focus on literary criticism and literary history, in "The Part about the Critics," to poetry, philosophy, and history in "The Part about Amalfitano," to journalism, print. and visual media. Talking to Fate about "the end of the sacred," about film, the coming of VCRs, and the difference between watching movies on TV and watching them on a movie screen, the "video King" Charly Cruz, figures both as a rival for Fate's interest in Amalfitano's daughter, Rosa, erstwhile lover of poetry, and as a synecdochic representation of visual media's increasing threat to print, both to the novel, and to prose fiction generally, and to serious investigative "*reportage.*"[21] What risks getting lost in the privileging of entertainment over hard news is the story of the "more than two hundred" women who have vanished without a trace, "here one minute, gone the next," their bodies turning up "after awhile in the desert," a "hard news" story Fate's editor rejects as he had previously rejected others, "about a political group in Harlem, the Mohammedan Brotherhood . . . groups of Arabs, New York lefties, new anti-globalization activists," until "the Mohammedan Brotherhood caught his attention . . . marching under a big poster of Osama bin Laden."[22] In Guadalupe Roncal, by contrast, the reporter from Mexico City with whom Fate and Rosa Amalfitano travel to Tucson to interview the "suspected killer" later identified as Klaus Haas, Fate finds a kindred journalistic spirit interested in investigating the killings she says (or Rosa says, or maybe "the suspected killer"—Fate isn't sure he remembers which one) "No one pays attention to," killings in which "the secret of the world is hidden."[23]

Death Is a Prose Poem in Santa Teresa—The Part
about the Crimes

With its pervasive references to television, pornography, VCRs, movies, videos, email, video stores, and cybercafés, "The Part about Fate" opens onto the changing discursive environment for journalism, as for the novel, as for print media generally at the turn of the new millennium, an environment Part V, "The Part about the Crimes," continues to explore. Paralleling the increasingly global saturation of the marketplace by visual, electronic, and digital media in the decade following the Fall of the Berlin Wall, the murders of women in and around Santa Teresa (Juárez) date back to the early 1990s. Sustained through Bolaño's characteristic construction of lengthy, digressive narratives by means of a seemingly endless series of brief, prose-poetic texts, it offers an overwhelming number of self-contained, proto-visceral realist exhibits that draw the form and content of the prose poem and its legacy into close proximity with the sacredness of literary elegy and its prosaic, profane, mundane, extra-literary, journalistic cousin, the obituary, as well as investigative reporting. Extending across 350 pages in the original, the account or accounting, plot and emplotment of murder after murder in "The Part about the Crimes," the novel's single longest section, poses serious ethical and political questions, questions as well of literary economy, both literally and figuratively, for the novel's readers. Faced with such a gruesome narrative agenda, how should readers respond? With empathy or with disgust, with a desire to read on as co-investigators to discover the source of the killings, or a sense that enough is enough, that each sensational murder is at once more sadistic than the next, that what initially provoked interest and outrage has become, after sum-maries of so many killings, either a masochistic exercise or a sadistic indulgence, that Poe's "The Poetic Principle" and "The Philosophy of Composition"—"Beauty is the sole legitimate province of the poem"; "The death of a beautiful woman is, unquestionably, the most poetical topic in the world"—have in the relentlessly prosaic, visceral realist prose of *2666* come to their horrifically sadistic, misogynist end.

Or on the contrary, inviting the reader to participate in act after act, account after account, of such an aesthetics and poetics as complicit voyeur, does *2666* merely spotlight this principle and its consequences for all to see?[24] With the prose poem's characteristic, self-contained brevity and intensity, recalling as well its family resem-blance to what Bolaño understood with Baudelaire to be the prose poem's cognate journalistic forms—*faits divers,* police reports, obitu-aries, human-interest stories, op-eds—here are but two early exam-ples in full, each a single paragraph, each set off by an extra line of white space (in Wimmer's translation by a single dot with an extra line of white space) before and after from the paragraphs preceding and following:

A mediados de febrero, en un callejón del centro de Santa Teresa, unos basureros encontraron a otra mujer muerta. Tenía alrededor de treinta años y vestía una falda negra y una blusa blanca, escotada. Había sido asasinada a cuchilladas, aunque en el rostro y el abdomen se apreciaron las contusiones de numerosos golpes. En el bolso se halló un billete de autobús para Tucson, que salía esa mañana a las nueve y que la mujer ya no iba a tomar. También se encontró un pintalabios, polvos, rímel, unos pañuelos de papel, una cajetilla de cigarrillos a medias y un paquete de condones. No tenía pasa-porte ni agenda ni nada que pudiera identificarla. Tampoco llevaba fuego.

Midway through February, in an alley in the center of the city, some garbagemen found another dead woman. She was about thirty and dressed in a black skirt and low-cut white blouse. She had been stabbed to death, although contusions from multiple blows were visible about her face and abdomen. In her purse was a ticket for the nine a.m. bus to Tucson, a bus she would never catch. Also found were a lipstick, powder, eyeliner, Kleenex, a half-empty pack of cigarettes, and a package of condoms. There was no passport or appointment book or anything that might identify her. Nor was she carrying a lighter or matches.[25]

El asesinato de Isabel Urrea, aireado los primeros tres días por su emisora de radio y por su periódico, se atribuyó a un robo frustrado, obra de un loco o de un drogadicto que seguramente quería apropiarse de su coche. También circuló la teoría de que el autor del crimen podía ser un centroa-mericano, un guatemalteco o salvadoreño, veteran de las guerras de aquellos países, que recaudaba dinero por cualquier medio antes de desplazarse a los Estados Unidos. No hubo autopsia, en deferencia a su familia, y el examen balístico no se dio a conocer jamás y en alguna ida y venida entre los juzgados de Santa Teresa y Hermosillo se perdió definitivamente.

The murder of Isabel Urrea, covered the first three days by her radio station and paper, was explained as frustrated robbery, the work of a lunatic or drug addict who probably meant to steal her car. The theory also circulated that the perpetrator might be a Guatemalan or Salvadorean veteran of the wars in Central America, someone desperate to get the money to move on to the United States. There was no autopsy, in deference to the family, and the ballistic analysis, which was never made public, was later lost for good some-where in transit between the courts of Santa Teresa and Hermosillo.[26]

Accepting the invitation to read each gruesome, condensed, prose-poetic verbal spectacle, each proto-journalistic, obituary sketch—the most viscerally prosaic of all prose poems—further distilling, captioning, freezing each cold case, counting, recounting, and accounting for each—"Total murders in *2666*: 109 (case 71 is a suicide)"—as Chris Andrews does in what is clearly intended as an act of remembrance and testimonial across the twenty-five final, unnumbered pages of *Roberto Bolaño's Fiction: An Expanding Universe?*[27]—What are the literary and general economies, the economics and purposeless purposes, of such representations, of Bolaño's and of our own? What are their implications for how we understand the relation between *poiesis* and *aesthesis*? Should they induce us to put down the book and rise up to engage in activism against similar events in real life that have given rise to, that have inspired, such fiction? If that is the goal, how many accounts of how many murders will suffice? Would it be preferable to approach them affectively or conceptually? What relation between these binary terms do they encourage us to entertain, to take seriously? Would one or two, succinctly drawn, prove less effective and affecting, than dozens, a hundred, a thousand or more? When will it all stop, we might ask ourselves as readers, and shouldn't we want it to? As effective mimesis of a horrific reality, should the narrative run the full length of "The Part about the Crimes," as is, at 350 pages? Should it stop at 150? At 100? At 50? At 25? At 1? How might gender and sexual orientation figure into the aesthetic, prose-poetic play of such questions, in *2666*, as in Bolaño's work generally?

Faced with the narrative's relentless accumulation of so many condensed, tragic narratives, all within the prose poem's average formal range of a half to several pages, we find ourselves as readers in an increasingly uncomfortable position, as much vicarious voyeurs as investigators. The awareness settles in that to read on is to agree to become involved, even to become complicit, in the pursuit of an inquiry at once literary-historical and political—novelistic, prose-poetic, journalistic—into the prose poem's core concerns about the policing of the boundaries of the poetic and the prosaic, of the literary and extra-literary, the aesthetic and extra-aesthetic; about economies of pleasure and pain, empathy and analysis, inertia and activism, ideology and representation; about the nature of the modern and contemporary, including its, and our, mediations and forms of response; about contexts and environments of production and reception, distribution and circulation; about speech genres, discourses, disciplines, and what Volosinov/Bakhtin called "verbal interaction," the ways we are aligned, as readers and writers, with such crimes against humanity, how we are situated in relation to them, how we participate in or challenge, contest, affirm, embrace, a text's local and global economy in every sense, within and beyond its borders.[28]

Heir to the prose poem's blurring and dismantling of the boundary between prose and poetry, "The Part about the Crimes" conveys Bolaño's powerful sense of the extent to which boundaries between the novel and journalism, the literary and the extra-literary, had become unthinkable and inextricable over the course of the 1990s apart from questions of electronic and digital media. As Baudelaire understood more acutely than any other poet in the nineteenth century the threat to poetry's prestige posed by the emergence of the novel (the central concern of his pitch for the first prose poems published in *La Presse*), Parts III and IV of *2666* convey Bolaño's growing sense of the extent to which the novel's own prestige and function had come to be radically reframed and reconfigured by Charly Cruz's video stores, by Rosa Amalfitano's beloved movies and thrillers, by the porn Oscar Fate looks for in his hotel room in Detroit, by email and cybercafés. What would it mean, the text asks, in our increasingly hyper-mediated context, to continue to embrace, or rather to give up, not just poetry, or verse poetry (the central question of *The Savage Detectives*), but literature? While poetry's, fiction's, all literature's relations with other media, not merely print media but film, are an integral concern of Bolaño's, as we have seen, from the beginning, in *Antwerp, Monsieur Pain, The Third Reich, Distant Star*, Parts III and IV of *2666* figure the extent to which such intermedial concerns have become for the novel, as for journalism, poetry, philosophy, print media in all its forms, by the turn of the millennium, what Sartre said Marxism had become in the first years of the Cold War period: the "unsurpassable horizon of our time" ("l'horizon indépassable de notre temps") (33).[29]

Where "The Part about Fate" questions the novel's privilege by focusing on print journalism, race, and gender through the love story of Fate and Rosa, "The Part about the Crimes" expands and deepens *2666*'s inquiry into the relation between journalism and the novel, in particular the detective novel, through its relentlessly sustained, unflinchingly detailed investigation of the serial murders of women in and around Santa Teresa. In its representation of the potential of violence, and of violence against women in particular, not merely to entertain, or to interest, but even to arouse, *2666* places its readers, who have by this point been exposed to one graphic murder of a woman after another, in an increasingly troubled and troubling, untenable position (340).[30] Exploring further not only the relation between journalism and the novel but also the ways print media of all kinds are increasingly configured in broader intermedial environments, "The Part about the Crimes" focuses on Florita Almada, a "seer" known to her few followers as "La santa" ("The Saint") who appears on "Sonora TV" on the "lovely show" of the gay TV celebrity Reinaldo "so fittingly called *An Hour with Reinaldo*, a nice, wholesome program." Through the figures of Almada and Reinaldo, *2666* opens the relation between journalism and the novel onto the relation of both to electronic, visual media in a way that suggests how ubiquitous, by the mid-to-late 1990s, intermediality had become. Where in *Antwerp*, two decades earlier, Bolaño demonstrates a clear understanding of the extent to which poetry, the novel, detective fiction, and literature generally had already come to be mediated by film, and where by 1996, in *Distant Star*, Wieder's apprenticeship in poetry leads eventually to a proto-surrealist photography exhibit equally marked by violence toward women, "The Part about the Crimes" marks a new level of awareness in Bolaño's oeuvre of the intermedial environment in which all violence, and all acts of writing—poetry, novels, literary criticism, philosophy, sports journalism, serious "reportage"—had become situated by the turn of the millennium. The topicality associated with journalism and the more enduring value associated with literature must be understood in this context in relation to the mediascape that defines, shapes, and overdetermines both. Like Charly Cruz, the "Video King" owner of a video store, like Kessler, the investigator who has ties to mass media through the film industry that blur the border between "business," "crime," and "the movies," the "suspected killer" at the heart of the investigation, the German "giant" Klaus Haas, has his own connections to technology and electronic media. Keenly aware of the media's role, he calls press conferences to influence public opinion, the first causing a "minor scandal," the second drawing fewer reporters.[31] Is the murder of women, pace Poe, in that expanded context, more a poetic subject or a philosophical one, more a matter of history or literary history, fiction or journalism, economics or politics, *poiesis* or *aesthesis*? How should we as "readers" respond?

Novel(izing) Histories—The Part about Archimboldi

Having expanded the scope and scale of its multi-discursive investigation from the novel, literary criticism, and literary history, in Part I, to philosophy, poetry, and history, in Part II, to journalism, print and electronic media, and popular culture in Parts III and IV, Part V, "The Part about Archimboldi," focuses on the novel, twentieth-century European history and literary history, and the German novelist in particular to whom the four European critics of Part I have dedicated their careers. Where *The Savage Detectives* expands and ultimately breaks the frame of its visceral realist, prose-poetic inquiry into the relation between poetry and the novel, "The Part about Archimboldi" concludes *2666* with the most explicit, sustained narrative of Bolaño's career affirming the centrality of the novel to his prose-poetic, fictive, literary-historical imaginary, as both a reader and writer, even as it challenges in important ways the novel's past and present value.

Arcing back to the German Romantic literary tradition of the late-eighteenth and early nineteenth centuries, and situated in the context of the emerging *Nazizeit* of the Germany of the 1920s and 1930s, "The Part about Archimboldi" begins its meta-*Bildungsroman* about Archimboldi's life and career as a novelist with a fairy tale, or *Märchen*, recalling the origins of the modern German novel, most explicitly through allusions to Goethe's *Werther* (which figures in a similar role, as we have seen, in *The Third Reich*), Novalis' *Heinrich von Ofterdingen*, and one of the foundational literary texts of German national (and national socialist) mythology, *Parzival*, by the medieval Bavarian knight and poet Wolfram von Eschenbach. Interweaving individual and collective stories, history and literary history, with equal measures of seriousness and parody, in ways that more than fulfill expectations of the kind of epic ambition with which the novel tends to be associated, "The Part about Archimboldi" traces Archimboldi's life and career from his birth in 1920 to the first few years of the twenty-first century, when Archimboldi is in his early eighties, a period encompassing the three decades of Bolaño's parents' generation prior to his birth, in 1953, through Bolaño's death, at the age of fifty, in 2003.

Extending across 326 pages in the original, second in length only to the preceding "The Part about the Crimes," of a comparable length at 350 pages, approaching twice as long as "The Part about the Critics" (194 pages), four times as long as "The Part about Amalfitano" (82 pages), and more than twice the length of "The Part about Fate" (147 pages), "The Part about Archimboldi" builds a case for its central protagonist as a synecdochic figure of the crucial events of European history and literary history, including the history of the novel, in which the role of Germany proved so tragically and traumatically central. Reprising and bringing to term Bolaño's lifelong preoccupation with the legacy of German history and literature in Europe and the Americas—in *The Third Reich*, in the second-coming of German fascism in *Nazi Literature in the Americas, Distant Star*, and *By Night in Chile*—"The Part about Archimboldi" elaborates a *Bildung* of its central character that is also a dismantling, a history of the life and legacy of an imaginary novelist whose experiences and career allow Bolaño to map the shaping, overdetermining historical and literary-historical influences of his parents' generation and his own. A masterful example, in effect, of the kind of traditional novel Bolaño might have written much earlier had he not wanted not to write precisely that kind—producing instead in the experimental prose poem novel *Antwerp* a form of resolutely "Undisciplined writing" that dismantled the ambition of writing such a novel even as it served as a form of apprenticeship into that very form—"The Part about Archimboldi" offers an uncomplicatedly linear, chronological narrative that meets all the expectations readers might have of a conventional novel.

Divisible into three shorter periods—1920–1936, 1936–1939, and 1939–1945—the periods, respectively, of 1) Hans Reiter's youth at home in Paderborn from birth to the age of 16; 2) his adolescence away from home and first jobs, ages 16–19, during the German build-up to the war; and 3) his experience as a soldier in the German army and eventually as a member of the SS, ages 19–25—the narrative chronicling the years from 1920 to 1945 begins with a description of the protagonist's early childhood that oscillates among fantastical, literary-historical, and historical frames. In its opening movement from Hans Reiter's birth in 1920 through his release from employment as a servant at the closing of the baron's house in 1936, "The Part about Archimboldi" intertwines its narrative of Reiter's early literary-historical *Bildung* with the historical, political narrative of Hitler's rise to power. Through its allusions to the Nazi book burnings, and the narrator's assessment of the protagonist's capacities as an intellectual, Reiter's story calls into question the value of German literature and culture, synecdochic of all literature and culture, in the face of the murderous atrocities in which Reiter would soon participate as a German soldier.

Against the background of this profanation of the poetic and of the literary as such, Reiter's furlows allow him to return to the innocence of "long periods with his sister, Lotte, who was ten by then and adored her brother," and soon to find his first love, "Ingeborg Bauer," a girl who "couldn't have been more than sixteen," whose name recalls the poet Ingeborg Bachmann and whose first exchange with Reiter reprises the haunting series of questions with which "L'Étranger" launches the prose poems of *Le Spleen de Paris*, questions their exchange recasts poignantly and ironically in the context of the looming disaster of Nazi ideology and Germany's short-lived European occupations.[32] Reduced to "'only Nazi politics, Nazi politics, Nazi history,' Nazi economics, Nazi mythology, Nazi poetry, Nazi novels, Nazi plays," the German Enlightenment, Romantic, Idealist, more broadly humanist legacy of German literature and culture that had provided the foundation for Reiter's early *Bildung*, as of German *Bildung* in general and the *Bildungsroman* in particular, soon gives way in the narrative to Reiter's participation as a combatant in the disastrous opening up of the Russian front in 1941, and to his reflections on the history of that failed legacy in the wake of the German army's defeat, reflections that set the stage for his future success as a novelist under the name Benno von Archimboldi.

Nowhere does Bolaño remind his readers more profoundly than in *2666*, at the height of his fame and with his health rapidly deteriorating, that such success carries within it the seeds of its own unraveling, a process of becoming historical that continues to pose unrelentingly to all literature the question of value, with no guarantees across time.[33] Seeing in Reiter's blue eyes "the eyes of a young poet," the figure from whom Reiter rents his first typewriter, an old man who is himself an ex-writer, epitomizes the disillusionment of a son who himself received the same typewriter as a gift from his father, an "affectionate and cultured man . . . who believed in progress . . . and of course in the intrinsic goodness of human beings."[34] A template for the "good German" who would perhaps "burst into song or hum some Beethoven," the old man's father occasions pivotal reflections the old man shares with Reiter at the very moment he is about to embark on his career under the name of Archimboldi. Challenging the distinction between major and minor works, he finds the answer to literature's value not in the act of writing, but in reading, an act he identifies above all with "knowledge and questions" in contrast to the "*nothing* in the guts of the man who sits there writing" as if under hypnosis, "like someone taking dictation," his novel or book of poems, however "decent, adequate," arising "not from an exercise of style or will, as the poor unfortunate believes, but as the result of an exercise of concealment.'" Having abandoned writing himself when he realized that "Every book that isn't a masterpiece is cannon fodder," the old man tells Archimboldi that doing so was "in no way traumatic but rather liberating," that it was on the contrary "a relief to give up literature, to give up writing and simply read!" ("Todo libro que no sea una obra maestro es carne de canon . . . No hay trauma . . . sino liberación . . . ¡Un alivio, dejar la literatura, es decir dejar de escribir y limitarse a leer!").[35]

Unsentimental about technology as a tool for writing, although "For a long time, he wouldn't buy a computer," when "laptop computers appeared" Archimboldi would "sometimes" spend "hours on the Internet," eventually flinging his typewriter "off a cliff onto the rocks!" Figuring the potential of literature to fall off a cliff in an age no longer bound up with literature's residual aura in the age of the typewriter—an epoch-defining instrument, as Friedrich Kittler has argued, which Bolaño understood was in the process of being supplanted in the 1990s—"The Part about Archimboldi" moves toward its conclusion through two scenes focusing on the consequences of such technological shifts for the fate of literature.[36] Visiting an asylum of vanished European (especially French) writers—figuring the risk of European literature, by implication of all literature, vanishing or at least receding from visibility and con-sequentiality in an age increasingly dominated by visual media— Archimboldi discovers in the "TV room" writers of all genres, including both poetry and the novel, forgotten and languishing. Now in his seventies, neither watching television, listening to the radio, nor reading the papers in the years immediately following "the fall of the Berlin Wall," he subsequently returns to Germany to find that his publisher and former lover, the Baroness Von Zumpe, who has decidedly non-literary reading habits and no commitment to "serious" literature of any kind, is preparing to hand over the reins to "a young man of twenty-five . . . a poet and an assistant professor at Göttingen" to whom she had previously assigned "the house's poetry list." Talking to Archimboldi "about the Nobel Prize," and complaining bitterly about the legions of vanished writers she hopes Archimboldi will not join, the baroness makes possible a reunion with his sister, who only learns that her brother Hans Reiter is a writer when she comes across the last of his novels, *The King of the Forest*, "at the Frankfurt airport for the flight to L.A." on her way to visit, in 2001, for the first time since two prior visits in 1998, her son Klaus Haas, Archimboldi's nephew, still in prison in Mexico following a retrial in 1999.[37] Having bought "by mistake or because she was in a hurry not to miss her flight . . . a book called *The King of the Forest*, by someone called Benno von Archimboldi," a book "no more than one hundred and fifty pages long," Lotte is struck by how its stories "followed one after another" but "didn't lead anywhere." Placing in an airport bookshop Lotte's crucial discovery of such a "serious" work of literature as *The King of the Forest*, one characterized by a "strange," condensed, discontinuous form that invites the reader to read, as Lotte reads, by "skipping around," Bolaño gestures toward affirming, as he nears the conclusion of *2666*, not so much the forms of more traditional novels, including to a certain extent those that brought him literary fame, as the early non-commercial, experimental, disjointed, prose-poetic style and interactive relation with the reader of *Antwerp*, the novel that doesn't look and read like a novel at the foundation of his career.[38]

As a portal through which to situate that career's arc and trajectory, in relation to German and Russian traditions especially, with nods as well in the direction of other European—Italian (Canetti), Spanish (Cervantes), English (Dickens)—as well as Latin American influences, "The Part about Archimboldi" offers a displaced parable, as the title *The King of the Forest* suggests, of Bolaño's own increasing literary stature and celebrity. In its closing pages, *2666* challenges the assumptions of writers and readers alike about literary value, or at least the value of the monumental literary ambitions of the novel as form so manifestly on display in *2666* itself. Set off by a double-spaced indentation and given a line to itself, the proper name "Fürst Pückler" prefaces, in effect titles, the two-page prose poem anecdote with which *2666* will conclude. As the closing frame of the most monumental of Bolaño's fictions, "Fürst Pückler" concludes *2666*, para-doxically yet fittingly, in the oxymoronic register that is the prose poem's most characteristic gesture, in a way that both echoes and replies to the prose-poetic preface, dedication, and sales pitch to his prospective pub-lisher, Arsène Houssaye, with which Baudelaire launched the invention of the modern prose poem in *Le Spleen de Paris*. Recounting Archimboldi's encounter with "Alexander Fürst Pückler"—his first name recalling per-haps, in the context of the Russian novel from World War II through the post-Cold War period, Alexander Solzhenitsyn—a "gentleman of advanced age, though not as old as Acrhimboldi," the anecdote tells the story of the gentleman's "forebear," the "very brilliant Fürst Pückler" ("un Fürst Pückler muy brillante"), inventor of "an ice cream in three flavors, but not just any three flavors, only chocolate, vanilla, and strawberry," that has come to bear his name. Having caught the descendant's attention as he was "was about to finish" a "Fürst Pückler" he had ordered in Hamburg en route to catching "a direct flight to Mexico" to fulfill his sister's request that he address the situation concerning her son, his nephew, Archimboldi is asked by the descendant "whether he liked it," to which he replies, "I did." Listening to the story of the literary career of the descendant's forebear, the "creator of this ice cream" (after all the novel's complications!), who was also "a great traveler, an enlightened man, whose main interests were botany and gardening," Archimboldi learns that Fürst Pückler thought he would be remembered for some of the many small works he wrote and published, mostly travel chronicles, though not necessarily travel chronicles in the modern sense, but little books that are still charming today and, how shall I say, highly perceptive, anyway as perceptive as they could be, little books that made it seem as if the ultimate purpose of each of his trips was to examine a particular garden, gardens sometimes forgotten, forsaken, abandoned to their fate, and whose beauty my distinguished forebear knew how to find amid the weeds and neglect. His little books, despite their, how shall I say, botanical trappings, are full of clever observations and from them one gets a rather decent idea of the Europe of his day, a Europe often in turmoil, whose storms on occasion reached the shores of the family castle, located near Görlitz, as you're likely aware.

por alguno de los muchos opúsculos que escribía y publicó, crónicas de viaje mayormente, pero no necesariamente crónicas de viaje al uso, sino libritos que aún hoy resultan encantadores, y muy, ¿cómo llamarlo?, lúcidos dentro de lo que cabe, libritos en donde pareciera que el fin último de cada uno de sus viajes fuera examinar un determinado jardín, en ocasiones jardines olvidados, dejados de la mano de Dios, abandonados a su suerte, y cuya gracia mi ilustre antepasado sabía encontrar en medio de tanta maleza y tanta desidia. Sus libritos, pese a su, ¿cómo llamarlo?, revestimiento botánico, están llenos de observaciones ingeniosas y a través de ellos uno puede hacerse una idea bastante aproximada de la Europa de su tiempo, una Europa a menudo convulsa, cuyas tempestades en ocasiones llegaban hasta las orillas del castillo de la familia, ubicado, como usted sabrá, en las cercanías de Görlitz.[39]

Recalling the distinguishing textual features of the "*Petits* poèmes en prose" of *Le Spleen de Paris* not only in the anecdote's prose-poetic form and emphasis on brevity— "the many small works he wrote and published ... little books that are still charming ... little books ... whose beauty .... little books ... full of clever observations"—but in the unexpected capacity of a "little," "small," "charming" work to give, as do the prose poems of *Le Spleen de Paris*, a "rather decent idea of the Europe of his day, a Europe often in turmoil," "Fürst Pückler" deflates by implication the grandiose desires of writers of all genres for impact and immortality even as it brings to a close the most ambitious novel of Bolaño's career. Affirming the forgotten charms, insights, and cultural significance of "opúsculos" and "libritos," what the nameless old man and ex-writer who rented Archimboldi his first typewriter called "obras menores" ("minor works"), Bolaño concludes *2666*, in a register at once ironic, comical, and completely serious, with a dialectical Baudelairean turn at the level of both the content of the form and the form of the content that complicates and challenges the disappointment earlier expressed in "The

Part about Amalfitano" about the contemporary tendency to prefer shorter, minor works over longer, major ones.

Concluding *2666* with a fundamentally anti-literary celebration of how much more memorable a contribution a particular blend of ice cream might prove to be than the writing for which writers might hope to be remembered, Bolaño affirms the value of small works and little books, and of the extra-literary over the literary, with consummate irony precisely in the form of his most ambitious work, a novel acutely aware, as Bolaño's *oeuvre* is at virtually all points, of questions of scale, of invention, of literary evolution and change. It is certainly striking, but should not be surprising given the investments of Bolaño's career from the outset and the many varied forms of his prose poem novels, that the singular novel *2666* (or is it five novels in one?), which appears to be all about maximal scale, should conclude, only apparently paradoxically, with a reaffirmation of the small and the little, in the term that defined the modern prose poem at its beginnings with *Le Spleen de Paris,* the "petit." Recalling in its first name the monumental Goethe of that archetypal striver, *Faust,* "Fürst Püchler" turns *2666* away from such monumentality in the end toward the co(s)mic irony of a joke on "Würst," as on pucker, puker, and poker, suggesting not the name of a great novelist after all, perhaps (like the grandiloquent "Archimboldi"), but rather that of what Wallace Stevens—that *"Whitest"* of poets, *"the alabaster banker,"* as *True Policeman* calls him—calls "The Emperor of Ice Cream," creator of "concupiscent curds" (349). Echoing the mischievous provocations of such prose poems of Baudelaire as "Perte d'auréole" ("Loss of a Halo") against more familiar, "serious," "poetic" literary aspirations—" . . . think of some bad poet picking it up and brazenly putting it on . . . Think of X! Think of Z! Don't you see how amusing it will be? (" . . . je pense avec joie que quelque mauvais poëte la ramassera et s'en coiffera impudemment . . . Pensez à X, ou à Z! Hein! Comme ce sera drôle!"—Bolaño affirms through "Fürst Pückler" simpler, extra-literary pleasures, those of ice cream and, in Lotte's words, "nice people," as a contribution to humanity over the portentous complications, the necessary and gratuitous convolutions, that poetry, fiction, literature, including even prose poems, including even prose poem novels, might offer, not least the kinds of "'difficult' or 'dark'" novels" for which *2666* could serve as synecdoche, the kinds both Archimboldi's beloved sister, Lotte, and his sophisticated yet also deeply profane lover, friend, and publisher, the Baroness Von Zumpe, are said to "hardly ever read" ("rara vez leía novelas «difíciles» u «oscuras», como las que él escribía"), the genre of literary monumentality and grandiosity *tout court.*[40]

It is in this sense that the matter of scale, in the end for Bolaño, is perhaps paradoxically at once critical and inconsequential, in "the long and the short of it," in the "grand scheme of things," in both monumental novels and small works and little books, as Baudelaire's prose poem "Un plaisant" puts it, a mere "joke."[41] As Baudelaire's dedication to Arsène Houssaye both prefaces and prefigures, instantiates and exemplifies the prose poems of *Le Spleen de Paris*, so the relatively autonomous, self-contained prose poem "Fürst Püchler" brings "The Part about Archimboldi," and with it all of *2666*, to a close, in the process concluding, yet not quite entirely, a novel that has been presented to the reader—has been published, as such—as a single, whole work of epic scale, a singular novel in the strict sense, divided into five parts, rather than as five relatively autonomous, relatively self-contained novels or novellas that might be perceived as legible, comprehensible, in themselves, apart from the others. Its epic novelistic ambitions undone in the end, along with those of literature generally in whatever genre, of whatever scale, in verse or prose, by Faust's endearingly paronomastic namesake—"Fürst" as in "Würst," for "sausage," suggesting, in the words of *By Night in Chile*, "how literature is made —" "Püchler," forgotten for his well-written, charming-yet-substantial "small works'" and "little books," remembered instead over time for his contributions to humanity (Faust's ultimate goal) not for his writings but for the special brand of ice cream that bears his name, *2666* concludes where the "petit" yet revolutionary *Le Spleen de Paris* begins, with a paratext that is also an integral part of the "text proper."

As a synecdoche of whatever might be thought too unimportant to be made visible in "serious" literature, the closing text's appetizing yet not unserious, casual yet not uncomplicated, seemingly unlikely trope figures at the opposite end of the spectrum of what literature might or should include from the serial murders of women in and around Santa Teresa. "The Part about Fate" approaches the murders, through its literary lens, as a subject perhaps more appropriate for investigative journalism, but "The Part about the Crimes" then goes on exhaustively and exhaustingly to explore it. Eliciting a far greater measure of disgust, in what can only strike readers, as the reading progresses, as an overwhelming accumulation of mind- and heart-numbing accounts—each, like "Fürst Püchler," of prose-poem length—the proliferation of at first sympathetic yet ultimately merciless, unrelenting, sensationalist, voyeuristic, even sadistic representations of murdered women, once read, cannot be forgotten, as the charming, well-written small works and little books of Fürst Püchler are said to have been. And yet, where the barrage of accounts in "The Part about the Crimes" cannot help but remain indelible in memory, threatening to overwhelm all other narratives, so too does the light-hearted Baudelairean, Borgesian, Bolañoesque prose poem—affixed in its place of honor at the conclusion of that arch, bold narrative of a "candidate for the Nobel"— that brings to a close the epically Faustian, mischievously Mephistophelian contract between the Reading and Writing of Novels that is *2666*.

From the Known to the Unknown University

The centrality of the prose poem in Bolaño's imaginary lay in large measure in his understanding of it as precisely that literary-historical "dwarf," positioned from the beginning of the history of modern poetry against the novel's growing hegemony, that figured both formally and conceptually as a reminder that literary histories of the future may not have to be those of the victors.[1] This is the literary history "de otra manera" toward which Bolaño's work points the way. If he was in the end one of the victors himself, his literary celebrity nevertheless arrived only as he was running out of time (352). Whatever the fate of his work, he understood better than anyone that he could not know whether its reception would rise or sink.

For Bolaño, a novelist who began as a poet and never ceased wanting to be one, the impact of Baudelaire's exemplary turn from poetry to prose remained pivotal. One of the central insights Bolaño inherited from the prose poem is that what is called poetry risks confining itself to irrelevance to the extent that it remains a discourse of the self, by the self, and for the self, incapable of calling itself into question. Recognizing that the increasingly intermedial frames of the last two decades of the twentieth and first few years of the twenty-first century made the competition Baudelaire saw emerging as primarily between poetry and the novel seem at once quaint and outdated and more relevant than ever, Bolaño figured into his work a profound sense of the becoming historical of all literature (354). Faced with the growing ubiquity and hegemony of screens all kinds, of all shapes and sizes, of monitors and the monitoring, or "sharing," of endlessly proliferating forms and contents, of webs and connectivities without end, understanding himself as a writer struggling to survive and continue to be productive in increasingly challenging times for literature in all genres, Bolaño seems to have taken on the responsibility of reading, very nearly, everything, even including works never or not-yet written, a responsibility he understood to be that much greater at a time when literature itself had come to seem increasingly embattled on all sides.

Framing his short story "The Man of the Crowd," that "famous tale," as Benjamin put it, which Baudelaire condensed into the prose poem "Les Foules" and that Benjamin describes as "something like an X-ray of a detective story," Poe begins with a German phrase he cites and translates in the text's opening sentence, then repeats untranslated at its close: "'er lasst sich nicht lesen'—it does not permit itself to be read."[2] From "distant" to "lyric" to "surface" to "postcritical" reading,[3] the early twenty-first century has seen a surge of interest in developing new modes of reading, new methodologies for understanding what acts of reading involve. For all their contributions, what is perhaps most surprising about these approaches is the extent to which they have recourse to a logic of either/or binaries even as they invert the received privilege of one term over the other (surface/depth, distant/close). While such inversions have been productively complicated by among others N. Katherine Hayles and Rebecca Walkowitz, who propose both/and logics that value a certain complementarity rather than exclusivity of perspectives associated with each term, it is striking, given the proliferation of so many diverse reading technologies in the last several decades of the twentieth century, to see the return of a logic of binary tropes for reading, even in inverted form, that might have seemed more at home in the criticism of an earlier era.[4]

Reading in the "huge library" of a Prussian baron near the beginning of the fifth and concluding part of Bolaño's *2666*, "The Part about Archimboldi," the young Hans Reiter, the future novelist Benno von Archimboldi, comes to understand that while the "love of books" he learns there didn't translate "into reading" among the baron's descendants, in the years the Nazis were seizing power in Germany, "it did translate into the preservation of the library."[5] It was during the same period Bolaño describes, in the 1930s, at what Benjamin called a "moment of danger," that Erich Auerbach, that most exemplary of readers and literary historians, proved to be one of the twentieth century's indispensable literary detectives.[6] Through his synecdochic readings of two dozen synecdochic works, in *Mimesis: Representations of Reality in Western Literature*, Auerbach set out to preserve Western literature at a moment when whole libraries were literally going up in flames. Like Benjamin, whose reading and writing came to an end at the Spanish border in the Pyrenees, and like Bolaño, for whom Spain—"Far from the Southern Hemisphere"—became the safe place it did not for Benjamin to pursue a life-long literary-historical "Stroll," Auerbach understood from his exile in Istanbul that reading, writing, and the preservation of libraries are more than just a literary matter, that literary history, history, and politics are inextricably intertwined.[7]

Synecdochic Bolaño

Beyond the persuasive power of any one of *Mimesis*'s twenty chapters, what has remained most influential is its immanentist, synecdochic procedure, the methodological brilliance of defining and elaborating a text's significance for a large expanse of literary history by means of the "telling example"—a single representative passage, from a single text, by a single author—that can give, as the conclusion of *2666* has it, "a rather decent idea" of an entire era?[8] As untimely today in the Nietzschean sense of Agamben's "What Is Contemporary?" as it was on first appearing in 1946 (in English only in 1953), *Mimesis* serves still as a reminder that reading and writing decisions remain always to be made, that literary histories by whatever means are as necessary as ever in an age where literature itself is continually reconfigured through electronic devices.[9]

Whatever other candidates one might offer in both cases, and beyond the question of any single author's or literary critic's, historian's or theorist's exemplary, representative, synecdochic status, beyond his or her current place "in the canon," what makes Auerbach's synecdochic procedure as vital as ever, unlikely to be supplanted by new and evolving critical approaches, is that it is arguably unavoidably, necessarily, what we do. While few in literary studies would seriously oppose, for example, Hoyos' affirmation, which I obviously share, of the continuing need for a combination of "close reading, theoretical consideration, and cultural critique"—certainly not Moretti, whose contributions, as *The Bourgeois: Between Literature and History* reminds us, are too complex, substantive, subtle, and various to warrant caricature—it is obviously the case that "close" and "distant" reading are neither incompatible nor mutually exclusive (366).[10] On the contrary, as distant reading holds the promise of fulfilling in certain ways the ambitions of earlier structuralist and post-structuralist practices, so close reading may encompass lyrical, surface, and postcritical reading, all of which are in the end, after all, however heuristically useful, metaphors, ways of approaching literary texts that inevitably attend to certain stakes and perspectives while excluding and marginalizing others. For all their worthwhile contributions, the central problem that remains unsurpassable is that of constructing a literary history that would ultimately be anything other than a series of possible synecdoches, representative examples, exemplarities. However much data we accumulate, however much information we have about audiences and sales, questions of value(s) remain, as for example in Benjamin's still resonant question, now more than ever: "How, in this day and age, can one read lyric poetry [or the novel, or the prose poem novel] at all?"[11] The search for synecdochic figures, for representativeness, for exemplarity, remains integral, and not only for literature.

The best way to define something, in a fundamental sense the only way to define anything, we learn from Wittgenstein, whom Bolaño called "the greatest philosopher of the twentieth century" ("el más grade filósofo del siglo XX"), is by example.[12] But what counts as exemplary? And to whom? For how long? Within what frames, in what contexts, always changing? Such questions may be approached as a matter of person or poem, of identity or genre, whether for example as poem, novel, or prose poem novel, to exemplify or depart from certain norms, to perform or resist certain normative features, to hybridize the normative and the non-normative, to wear the mask of a deceptively descriptive imperative or openly manifest a prescriptive stance, to mask, conceal, reveal, or in Rancière's terms make visible, the tension between normativity and anomaly. Bolaño is a synecdochic figure precisely to the extent that he does all the above, and does so throughout his career with increasing sophistication, variety, innovation, flexibility, purposiveness, range, courage, and adventurousness.

Whatever Bolaño's future reception might prove to be, a certain undeniable consensus has emerged over the past two decades as to Bolaño's significance. While no author's status is secure, Bolaño has become for our time, as much as any writer of his or any other generation, an exemplary, synecdochic figure, not least for the question of exemplarity, of synecdoche itself and what makes a work truly contemporary.[13] One of the fundamental questions his belated, now posthumous celebrity poses, a question his work itself raises at its core, is that of the search for synecdoche as a feature of literature itself. In his emphasis on the becoming historical of all writers, all literature, Bolaño builds into his work a certain autoimmunity, a disarming awareness of the unreliability of all authorial "success." As his phenomenal worldwide reception continues to grow, there is increasing evidence of his importance well beyond Europe and the Americas. In the end, of course, questions of value are not questions merely of the "popular." What is popular, or for that matter critically accepted, and what is of enduring value, as Bolaño reminds us again and again, can never be assumed to be the same. But to negotiate popularity and value effectively, as he also understood, involves a keen sense of the relation between the two.

Becoming Historical, or, What Is Contemporary?

What makes an author exemplary, representative, what makes for synecdochic reading, is not just the work itself, but the kinds of readings it invites, the range of audiences and readers, methodologies and approaches it seems to welcome, all of which are inseparable from one another. Where Andrews' approach to his reading of Bolaño is framed, for example, in predominantly psychological, ethical-philosophical, moral terms, Hoyos' reading of Bolaño, and of the small canon of contemporary Latin American novelists he reads along with him, is closer to my own in its indebtedness to the Frankfurt School and a similar emphasis on the still fundamental importance of close reading that Andrews shares as well. One of the intriguing questions that arises in Hoyos' continued emphasis on the value of the dialectic, is that of the dialectic's own dialectical, or anti-, or a-dialectical status, a question Rita Felski explores in her inquiry into the possibility and desirability of "postcritical" reading.[14] Whatever stances one may take toward Bolaño's work, what is pervasively clear throughout his career, from *Antwerp* to *2666*, is that he does not understand literature as an object waiting for the critic as subject to unpack it. Like Borges, he does the work himself, the packing and unpacking, the compression and the complication, the explosion and the implosion. In Bolaño's literary worlds, as in Borges', literary history does not take place first and foremost outside the work or on it, but in the works themselves, in all their intricacy and complexity. An integral part of the joke on the critics in Part I of *2666* is that Bolaño is as much a critic as they are. Literary criticism, history, theory are not the others of poetry and fiction, his work tells us, but inextricably bound up with them (375).[15]

The question of the prose poem, in Bolaño's prose poem novels, is the question of literature itself and its synecdochic powers of representation. Bolaño's prose poem novels are continuous with, and a logical amplification of, Baudelaire's prose poems in being at once dialogical, implying a binary dialectic, especially that of poetry and prose, and heteroglossic, opening onto the heterogeneity, variety, and multiplicity of genres, disciplines, and discourses at the center of Bakhtin's late work—and increasingly, at its point of maximum inflection in *2666*, under the name "speech genres." Prose fiction becomes, in Bolaño's recognition of its full potential, the site of a maximum inclusiveness of genres of speech and writing that he gradually, reluctantly came to understand poetry—especially defined in its dominant reception and practice as monological confessional, autobiographical, first-person utterance—virtually by definition by the end of the twentieth century, could not approach. This is the sense in which he understood that the politics of genre—the policing of literary, aesthetic structures of hierarchy and exclusivity, its hatred of democracy—converges with politics in the most inclusive sense. Paralleling the continuity and evolution in Bakhtin's work from the sustained focus on the poetry/prose binary and novelistic heteroglossia in *The Dialogic Imagination* to the more explicit, sustained emphasis on multiple discourses, both intra- and extra-literary, in *Speech Genres and Other Late Essays*[16]—a movement at the heart of the prose poem's cross-genre, interdiscursive, intermedial investigations —the five parts of *2666* thus move from the discourses of 1) the novel and literary criticism; to those of 2) philosophy and poetry, ideology and politics; to 3) race and investigative journalism (sports and politics) in print media; to 4) gender violence and print journalism, including prose-poetic accounts of 109 murdered women (echoing the publication of Baudelaire's first prose poems in the newspaper, *La Presse,* the prose poem's original venue), expanding increasingly into electronic media; to, finally, 5) the novel, history, and literary history—now in the expanded intergeneric, interdiscursive, interdisciplinary, intermedial, at once aesthetic and extra-aesthetic.

Absorbing influences from Europe and the Americas, yet not significantly from Africa or Asia, Bolaño's work is not quite so encompassing as the terms "global novel" or "world literature" might want to allow. These constraints, at once historical and literary historical, must not be ignored any more than the constraints of designating him a "Latin American" or "hemispheric" or "global" writer, whatever these fluid, heterogeneous, contested, complicated terms are taken to involve. In his late short story "Photos," the penultimate text of *Putas Asesinas* (2001, *The Return* 2010), Bolaño offers a glimpse of a growing recognition, near the end of his life, of the extent to which his literary worlds, including his historical and literary-historical imaginary, in both poetry and fiction, had remained limited to Europe and the Americas, more parochial and provincial than it once might have seemed, a recognition figured through the discovery by his most enduring and important protagonist and alter-ego, Arturo Belano, now "lost in Africa" ("perdido en África")—recalling the fate of his name-sake Arthur Rimbaud, after poetry, after literature—of "*La Poésie contemporaine de langue française depuis 1945* ... a compendium of little texts about all the poets writing in French around the world, be it in France or

Belgium, Canada or North Africa, sub-Saharan Africa or the Middle East."
"When it comes to poets," Bolaño writes, in Belano's name—echoing his
emphasis on the pivotal importance of nineteenth-century French poetry
—"give me the French" ("Para poetas, los de Francia, piensa Arturo
Belano").[17]

Published in 1973, the collection prompts Belano to think about his
attempts "to publish a poem, in Mexico, years ago when he lived in Mexico
City," when "he'd had to sweat blood, because Mexico is Mexico ... and
France is France." Struck by the number of poets he encounters in the
anthology from North and sub-Sahara Africa who had been previously
unknown to him, he discovers photos "of Mohammed Khaïr and Kateb
Yacine and Anna Greki and Malek Haddad and Abdellatif Laabi and
Ridha Zili, Arab poets who write in French." Astonished to discover "so
many other faces, faces of poets who write in French," Belano opens out in
a way that is rare for Bolaño, and with a self-conscious exoticization and
sexualization, onto a world beyond Europe and the Americas. Recognizing
belatedly the existence of so many perhaps forgotten, invisible non-
European, non-American poets, the text suggests a growing understanding
of the extent to which the lingering parochialism of Western authors would
become increasingly apparent and untenable (379).[18]

Expanding from the characteristically European-American frames of
Bolaño's prose-poetic, fictive literary histories by other means to more
genuinely global, "planetary" frames, "Photos" recalls what are perhaps the
other two most striking passages in Bolaño's oeuvre exemplifying this not
belated, recognition: the savage beating delivered to the Pakistani cab
driver by the Archimboldi specialists Pelletier and Espinoza in "The Part
about the Critics" in 2666 and the tense exchange between the gay poet
"Pere Girau" and the nameless "North African" ("el magrebí") near the end
of 2666's much abbreviated companion novel (the second to be published
posthumously), Woes of the True Policeman.[19] Revising in the end in effect
his own self-mythologized identification, Bolaño concludes "Photos" with
Belano looking out on "the electroencephalogram trembling on the
African horizon," closing the book, standing up and still holding it, "grateful" for "the book of Francophone poets under his arm" (38).[20] His
continuing voyage having taken him not, finally, like Rimbaud, into
Africa and out of literature, but into the "Unknown University" of writers
previously unread, writers until then invisible to him, Belano continues to
explore in the end, like Baudelaire and Rimbaud in their turn to the prose
poem, like Bolaño in his prose poems novels—"Au fond de l'Inconnu pour
trouver du *nouveau!*"—wherever that voyage might lead (38).[21]

"Where does it lead?" Ernst Bloch asks in his prose-poetic, philosophical "The Twice-Disappearing Frame"—"certainly into a domain of poetic meaning, even if it still hasn't been discerned where this domain lies."[22] Despite Poe's "The Poetic Principle" and "The Philosophy of Composition," despite *Le Spleen de Paris, Une Saison en Enfer* and *Illuminations*, despite Gertrude Stein's *Tender Buttons* (1914) and William Carlos Williams's *Kora in Hell: Improvisations* (1920) and *Spring and All* (1923), it has taken more than a century and a half for the prose poem to establish itself in the United States, as it has at last increasingly over the past several decades, and with increasing prominence and force in such works as Claudia Rankine's *Don't Let Me Be Lonely* (2004) and *Citizen* (2014), both provocatively subtitled *An American Lyric,* with anything like the currency and authority it long since acquired in Europe, in France of course in particular, and in Latin America.[23] As Bolaño understood as acutely as anyone, from the mid-1970s through the first few years of the twenty-first century, much as Poe, Baudelaire, and Rimbaud had understood a century earlier, from the 1830s through the mid-1870s, the times and frames for the reading and writing of literature were rapidly changing, transformed daily in ways that made the demand for poetry to be "absolutely modern," to compete for market-share in the age of "the rise of the novel," seem increasingly quaint and outdated, a source of wistfulness and nostalgia if also of melancholy and mourning, a mere flip of the page, or a blip on the screen, in the eventual disappearance of literature itself.[24]

As reading and writing have moved increasingly from texts to screens, questions of reading seem likely to continue to provoke, perplex, and inspire. At the heart of my own approach, both to Bolaño's work and generally, has been a combined focus on how questions of genre and mediality intersect with history and literary history, aesthetics and politics. What remains clear, in an age of increasing acceleration, with its ceaseless overturnings of scale, is that Bolaño's work speaks passionately against the forgetting and disappearing of the anonymous crowds of authors, and others, who will never be read or made visible, the legions of aspiring poets and novelists he knows will walk into the abyss with only a song as their amulet, without anyone even knowing they're gone.[25] That sustained awareness of the marginal, the neglected, the altogether and sooner or later to be forgotten is one he builds into his work at every turn, a core value that merits affirmation and celebration, merits even, perhaps, a certain recognition as exemplary, as representative, as synecdochic, as of a part searching for a greater, more capacious, more inclusive whole. Bolaño's everywhere manifest double knowledge, doubtless a major source of his empathy and appeal, at once literary and non-literary, aesthetic and political, is that we are always in the process of becoming historical, that wholes are what we cannot see.

Not Between but Among—A Poetics for the Twenty-First Century

No genre is an island. Poems, novels, literary histories, aesthetic and political ideologies produce us as much as, in fact more than, we produce them. When as readers and writers we are working only in, rather than on, genres, genres are working on us. With their ever-evolving commitment to a variety and multiplicity of forms, their movement from a predominantly intra-literary, intra-aesthetic understanding of literature as a binary choice between poetry and prose to a more capacious understanding of literature as a limitless heteroglossic field, Bolaño's prose poem novels carry forward, from *Antwerp* and *Monsieur Pain* to *Woes of the True Policeman* and *2666*, the prose poem's fundamental imperative to open onto "extra-literary" speech genres of all kinds, all lingos and jargons, dialects and idioms. They perform in this sense a radical reclaiming and expansion of what counts as poetry toward its full potentiality as an inexhaustible field of language, restoring poetry's full mobility and capacity for engagement with a maximal range of discourses, disciplines, and media. At their most fundamental level, they understand that the prose poem's legacy has always been the dismantling of binaries, the making visible of the instabilities and historicities of genre identities, their internal fractures, the multiplicities and heterogeneities underlying and informing their dichotomous structures. With profound implications for the relation between aesthetics and politics, this dismantling and making visible encourages not a policing of genres, discourses, and media, but an opening toward the increasingly pervasive intermediality—the "mash-up culture"—Bolaño saw would come to define the twenty-first century.

Recalling the explicit movement of Bakhtin's late essays from the poetry/prose binary to an emphasis on multiple speech genres and discourses, *True Policeman* and *2666* track a shift of emphasis, at once aesthetic, epistemological, philosophical, and political, from ideology to identity, from singularities to multiplicities, an emphasis bound up with the Fall of the Berlin Wall and the post-1989 collapse of the Cold War frame. Capturing the last decade of the twentieth century and the first few years of the twenty-first as above all a time of radical transitions, both novels map and make visible the instability and uncertainty of identities—in flux, internally divided, individual and collective—at a moment when familiar binary choices were breaking apart, when "identity" itself began to stake its claim as a pivotal term of both singularities and multiplicities, of the crisis of AIDS and the promise of multiculturalism, of the "rainbow coalition" and the "Arab spring," the old pull toward binaries—which the prose poem set out explicitly to dismantle—all the while reconfiguring and reasserting itself in the emerging hegemony of binary code.

Divided within and against themselves, "poetry" and "prose" are not closed identities, but ever-changing potentialities. Is it more obvious that prose is heterogeneous and multiple than that poetry is? If that seems to be the case, it will be necessary as always, as with Bakhtin's understanding of poetry as monological, self-expressive lyric, to historicize, to understand that both poetry and prose are mobile and, in Bakhtin's terms, hetero-glossic, composed, at least potentially, of as many genres of speech and writing as can be imagined, virtual and real, existing and yet to come. The opposition "poetry/prose"—or is it a complementarity? and which is the supplement of the other?—understood not ontologically, but historically, cannot simply be wished away. Its consequences will continue to play out. Yet as Baudelaire understood, with Poe, the apparent either/or of poetry and prose remains a false choice, a reductive binary, a regulated, policed economy. Hence the humor in Monsieur Jourdain's famously farcical lesson, in Molière's *Le Bourgeois Gentilhomme* (*The Middle-Class Gentleman*) that we have only two choices, verse and prose. From its inception with Poe, Baudelaire, and Rimbaud, as Bolaño understood better than anyone, the prose poem has only apparently been about binaries. Understanding poetry not as one thing, and prose another, but rather "both" as, in their histories, multiple, the real challenge has always been a reclaiming of heterogeneity, of permeability, of possibility. What is called poetry, prose, is not one thing, Bolaño's prose poem novels teach us, but many things, always in process, always becoming historical, an infinite set of complex, conditional relations. Situated not between but among genres, discourses, media, they encourage and embrace a paradoxical dis-tinction, a poetics not of opposition but of apposition, a poetics for the twenty-first century.

Notes

Introduction

1. Walter Benjamin, "Das Paris des Second Empire bei Baudelaire" (1938), "Über einige Motive bei Baudelaire" (1939), and "Zentralpark" (1939), in *Gesammelte Schriften I.2*, ed. Rolf Tiedemann and Hermann Schweppenhauser (Frankfurt: Suhrkamp, 1977); "The Paris of the Second Empire in Baudelaire," "On Some Motifs in Baudelaire," and "Central Park," in *Selected Writings, vol. 4, 1938–1940*, ed. Howard Eiland and Michael W. Jennings, trans. Edmund Jephcott et al. (Cambridge: Belknap Harvard University Press, 2003); Charles Baudelaire, *Oeuvres complètes*, ed. Claude Pichois, vol. 1 (Paris: Gallimard, 1976); Pascale Casanova, *The World Republic of Letters*, trans. M. B. Debevoise (Cambridge, MA: Harvard University Press, 2004), xii, 115–125 and "Combative Literatures," *New Left Review* 72 (2011): 123–134; Franco Moretti, "The Slaughterhouse of Literature," *Modern Language Quarterly* 61, no. 1 (2000): 207–228; rpt. in *Distant Reading* (London and New York: Verso, 2013), 65–69. Roberto Bolaño, "Encuentro con Enrique Lihn," in *Putas asesinas* (Barcelona: Anagrama, 2001), rpt. in *Cuentos: Llamadas telefónicas / Putas asesinas / El gaucho insufrible* (Barcelona: Anagrama, 2013), 408; "Meeting with Enrique Lihn," in *The Return*, trans. Chris Andrews (New York: New Directions, 2010), 192.

2. Roberto Bolaño, "La literatura no se hace sólo de palabras," in *Bolaño por sí mismo: Entrevistas escogidas*, ed. Andrés Braithwaite (Santiago, Chile: Universidad Diego Portales, 2006), 51–52; "Literature Is Not Made from Words Alone" (Interview by Héctor Soto and Matías Bravo, Capital, Santiago, December 1999), trans. Margaret Carson, *in Robert Bolaño: The Last Interview and Other Conversations* (Brooklyn, New York: Melville House Publications, 2009), 48.

3. See Philippe Lacoue-Labarthe, *Poetry as Experience* (*La Poésie comme expérience*, 1986), trans. Andrea Tarnowski (Stanford, CA: Stanford University Press, 1999." Of the "overly nostalgic Baudelaire," who "sometimes did not understand in understanding himself," Laboue-Labarthes writes, "(though he

did write the prose poems, which redeem all"), 19–20. On the prose poem's transformative, transnational history and legacy, see my *A Poverty of Objects: The Prose Poem and the Politics of Genre* (Ithaca, NY: Cornell University Press, 1987); Friedrich Schlegel, *Athenäums-Fragmente*, in *Charakteristiken und Kritiken I (1796–1801)*, ed. Hans Eichner, vol. 2, *Kritische Friedrich-Schlegel-Ausgabe*, ed. Ernst Behler, vol. 2 (Paderborn: Ferdinand Schöningh, 1967); Charles Baudelaire, *Le Spleen de Paris*, in *Oeuvres complètes*, hereafter referred to as OC; and Arthur Rimbaud's *Une saison en enfer and Illuminations, oeuvres de Rimbaud*, ed. Suzanne Bernard (Paris: Garnier, 1966).

4. Bolaño, *Amberes* (Barcelona: Anagrama, 2002); *Antwerp*, trans. Natasha Wimmer (New York: New Directions, 2010); hereafter cited as A and AN. Rodrigo Fresán, "Pequeño Big Bang" (Rev. of *Amberes*), *Letras.55* (July 27, 2003). Roberto Bolaño, *2666* (Barcelona: Anagrama, 2004); Roberto Bolaño, *2666* (Barcelona: Anagrama, 2004); *2666*, trans. Natasha Wimmer (New York: Picador/Farrar, Straus and Giroux, 2008). Roberto Bolaño and Mónica Maristain, "The Last Interview" (Interview by Mónica Maristain: *Playboy*, Mexico edition, July 2003), in *The Last Interview and Other Conversations*, 117; "La última entrevista a Roberto," in *La última entrevista a Roberto Bolaño y otras charlas con grandes escritores*, ed. Mónica Maristain (2010), 19–36.

5. Bolaño, *2666s*, 1118; *2666*, 892.

6. See Nicholas Birns, Juan E. De Castro, and Thomas Oliver Beebe, eds., *Roberto Bolaño as World Literature* (New York and London: Bloomsbury, 2017); Ignacio López-Calvo, ed., *Robert Bolaño, a Less Distant Star* (New York: Palgrave Macmillan, 2015); Edmundo Paz Soldán and Gustavo Faverón Patriau, eds., *Bolaño salvaje* (Barcelona: Candaya, 2008, 2013); Fernando Moreno, ed., *Roberto Bolaño: La experiencia del abismo* (Santiago, Chile: Lom édiciones, 2011) and *Roberto Bolaño: Una literatura infinita* (Poitiers: Centre de Recherches Latino-américaines, 2005); Felipe A. Ríos Baeza, ed., *Roberto Bolaño: Ruptura y violencia en la literatura finisecular* (Mexico City: Ediciones Eón, 2010); Karim Benmiloud and Raphaël Estève, eds., *Les Astres noirs de Roberto Bolaño* (Bordeaux: Presses Universitaires de Bordeaux, 2007); Ramón González Férriz, ed., *Jornadas homenaje Roberto Bolaño: (1953–2003) Simposio internacional* (Barcelona: Institut Català de Cooperació Iberoamericana. Casa América a Catalunya, 2005); and Patricia Espinosa, ed., *Territorios en fuga. Estudios críticos sobre la obra de Roberto Bolaño* (Santiago, Chile: Frasis, 2003); Celina Manzoni, ed., *Roberto Bolaño: La escritura como tauromaquia* (Buenos Aires, Corregidor, 2002).

7. Gayatri Chakravorty Spivak, *Death of a Discipline* (New York: Columbia University Press, 2003).

8. Roberto Bolaño, "Reading Is Always More Important than Writing" (Interview with Carmen Boullosa, 2002), trans. Margaret Carson, in *The Last Interview*, 53–68, 63; Roberto Bolaño, "Carmen Boullosa entrevista a Roberto

Bolaño," *Cadáver Exquisito* (January 24, 2012), http://micadaverexquisito
.blogspot.com/2012/01/carmen-boullosa-entrevista-roberto.html#.WUl_DM
aZPdQ. On Bolaño's increasingly global reception, see Jeffrey Lawrence,
*Anxieties of Experience: The Literatures of the Americas from Whitman to
Bolaño* (Oxford Studies in American Literary History; Oxford: Oxford
University Press, 2018); *Roberto Bolaño as World Literature*; Héctor Hoyos,
Beyond Bolaño: The Global Latin American Novel (New York: Columbia
University Press, 2015); Rebecca L. Walkowitz, *Born Translated: The
Contemporary World in an Age of World Literature* (New York: Columbia
University Press, 2015); Chris Andrews' *Roberto Bolaño's Fiction: An
Expanding Universe* (New York: Columbia University Press, 2014);
Jean Franco, "Questions for Bolaño," *Journal of Latin American Cultural
Studies* 18, no. 2–3 (2009): 207–217 and *Cruel Modernity* (Durham, NC:
Duke University Press, 2013); Sarah Pollack, "After Bolaño: Rethinking the
Politics of Latin American Literature in Translation," *PMLA* 128, no. 3 (2013):
660–667 and "Latin America Translated (Again): Roberto Bolaño's *The
Savage Detectives* in the United States," *Comparative Literature* 61, no. 3
(2009): 346–365; Ignacio Echevarría, "Bolaño extraterritorial," in *Bolaño
salvaje*; and Bob Thomson, "A Writer Crosses Over," *The Washington Post*,
April 8, 2007.
9. Roberto Bolaño, *Los perros románticos: poemas 1980–1998*; revised from *Los
perros románticos: Poemas 1977–1990*, 1993 (Barcelona: Lumen, 2000); *The
Romantic Dogs*, trans. Laura Healy (New York: New Directions, 2008); *La
Universidad Desconocida* (Barcelona: Anagrama, 2007); *The Unknown
University*, trans. Laura Healy (New York: New Directions, 2012); *Monsieur
Pain* (Barcelona: Anagrama, 1999; *La senda de los elefantes*, 1984, written
1981–1982); *Monsieur Pain*, trans. Chris Andrews (New York: New
Directions, 2010); *El Tercer Reich* (Barcelona: Anagrama, 2010); *The Third
Reich*, trans. Natasha Wimmer (New York: Farrar, Straus and Giroux, 2011).
10. Roberto Bolaño, *Los detectives salvajes* (Barcelona: Anagrama, 1998), 151; *The
Savage Detectives*, trans. Natasha Wimmer (New York: Farrar, Straus and
Giroux, 2007), 154.
11. Edgar Allan Poe, "The Murders in the Rue Morgue," "The Mystery of Marie
Roget," and "The Purloined Letter," "The Man of the Crowd," *Complete
Tales and Poems* (New York: Vintage, 1975); "The Poetic Principle," "The
Rationale of Verse," "The Philosophy of Composition," *Poems and Essays on
Poetry*, ed. C.H. Sisson (New York: Routledge, 1995, 2003). Benjamin, "The
Paris of the Second Empire in Baudelaire," in *Selected Writings, vol. 4*, 23, 27.
12. Walter Benjamin, "Ich packe meine Bibliothek aus," *Gesammelte Schriften* IV,
Denkbilder, 388; "Unpacking My Library," in *Selected Writings, vol. 2*,
486–493.

13. A, x; AN, 10. Baudelaire, "L'Étranger," OC 277; "The Stranger," in *Paris Spleen*, trans. Louise Varèse (New York: New Directions, 1947, 1970), 1, and *Paris Spleen: Little Poems in Prose*, trans. Keith Waldrop (Middletown, CT, 2009), 5. Varèse's and Waldrop's translations will be referred to hereafter as LV and KW, respectively.

14. Baudelaire, "L'Invitation au voyage" and "Le Voyage," *Les Fleurs du Mal*, OC 53–54 and 129–134; "Invitation to the Voyage" and "Travelers" (The Voyage), *Les Fleurs du mal*, trans. Richard Howard (Boston: David R. Godine, 1982), 58–59 and 151–157; "L'Invitation au voyage," OC 301–303; "L'Invitation au voyage," LV 32–34; "Invitation to the Voyage," in KW 33–35.

15. Despite poetry's undeniably central role in Bolaño's fiction, that much more strikingly in his novels—*The Third Reich* and *2666* emerging as the exceptions, as I will argue, that prove the rule—Andrews devotes only minimal attention to it, alluding to Baudelaire only once in passing (with reference to the "symbolist" poetics of the "poètes maudits"), and without mention either of the prose poem in general or the prose poems of Baudelaire or Rimbaud in particular. Reading Bolaño, as Andrews does as well, as the most important literary heir of Borges (to whose influence both Andrews and Hoyos devote a full chapter), Hoyos positions Bolaño as the pivotal figure for the contemporary development of *The Global Latin American Novel*. Although he devotes only a single full chapter to Bolaño, it is striking that he mentions neither poetry in general nor the prose poem in particular. The comparative neglect of poetry's and the prose poem's centrality in Bolaño's fiction by Andrews and Hoyos, among others, is integrally bound up with a broader tendency to undervalue the importance of Bolaño's work in the years leading up to *The Unknown University* and *Nazi Literature*, which I argue are the dual turning points of his career, between 1980 and 1994, especially *Antwerp, Monsieur Pain*, and Bolaño's 1983 *Consejos de un discípulo de Morrison a un fanático de Joyce*, co-written with A.G. Porta (Barcelona: Anthropos, 1984, 2006), the triple "big bang" of works with which his life-long commitment to the development of what I am calling his prose poem novels began.

16. On the novel's hegemony among literary genres, and in relation to poetry in particular, see Franco Moretti, "The End of the Beginning: A Reply to Christopher Prendergast," *Distant Reading* (London and New York: Verso, 2013), 140.

17. "Carnet de baile," in *Cuentos*; "Dance Card," in *Last Evenings on Earth*, trans. Chris Andrews (New York: New Directions, 2006), 398–406. See Juan Villoro, "La batalla futura," in *Bolaño por sí mismo*, also in *Bolaño salvaje*.

18. *Cuentos*, 217–219.

19. Roberto Bolaño, "Literatura + enfermedad = enfermedad," in *El gaucho insufrible* (Barcelona: Anagrama, 2003), 63–75, rpt. in *Cuentos*; "Literature + Illness = Illness," in *The Insufferable Gaucho*, trans. Chris Andrews (New York: New Directions, 2010), 123–246. On the origins of *El gaucho insufrible*, see Gustavo Faverón Patriau, "El rehacedor: 'El gaucho insufrible' y el ingreso de Bolaño en la tradición argentina," in *Bolaño salvaje*.

20. Bolaño, "Literature + Illness = Illness," 130–131.

21. Baudelaire, OC 134.

22. Baudelaire, "Perte d'auréole," OC 352; "Loss of a Halo," LV 94; "Lost Halo," KW 88. Benjamin, "The Paris of the Second Empire," 23; "One-Way Street" ("Einbahnstrasse," 1926, 1928, in *Gesammelte Schriften* IV.1), in *Selected Writings, vol. 1, 1913–1926*; and "Central Park," and "On the Concept of History" ("Über den Begriff der Geschichte," in *Gesammelte Schriften* I.2), in *Selected Writings, vol. 4*.

23. Bolaño, "La literatura no se hace sólo de palabras," in *Bolaño por sí mismo*, 52; "Literature Is Not Made from Words Alone," in *The Last Interview*, 48.

24. Bolaño and Boullosa, "Reading Is Always More Important than Writing," *The Last Interview*, 63.

25. Bolaño, "Prólogo: Consejos sobre el arte de escribir cuentos," *Cuentos*, 7–8, rpt. in *Entre paréntesis: ensayos, artículos, y discursos (1998–2003)*, ed. Ignacio Echevarría (Barcelona: Anagrama, 2004); "Advice on the Art of Writing Short Stories," in *Between Parenthesis: Essays, Articles and Speeches (1998–2003)*, trans. Natasha Wimmer (New York: New Directions, 2011). See also Bolaño's brief poem, "Biblioteca de Poe" ("Poe's Library"), *The Unknown University*, 128–129.

26. Roberto Bolaño, "Los mitos de Cthulhu," in *El gaucho insufrible*, 76–85, rpt. in *Cuentos*; "The Myths of Cthulhu," *The Insufferable Gaucho*, 147–164.

27. Bolaño, "The Myths of Cthulhu," *The Insufferable Gaucho*, 147–48, 158; "Los mitos de Cthulhu," in *El gaucho insufrible*, 76–77, 82.

28. Roberto Bolaño, "Derivas de la pesada," in *El secreto del mal*, 23–30, 23, rpt. in *Entre paréntesis*; "The Vagaries of the Literature of Doom," trans. Natasha Wimmer, in *The Secret of Evil*, 67–76, 67.

29. Bolaño, "The Vagaries of the Literature of Doom," *The Secret of Evil*, 67–68, 74; "Derivas de la pesada," *El secreto del mal*, 23–25, 28.

30. Bolaño, "Encuentro con Enrique Lihn," in *Cuentos*, 408; "Meeting with Enrique Lihn," in *The Return*, 192.

31. Bolaño, "Sevilla me mata," *El secreto del mal*, rpt. in *Entre paréntesis*, 312; "Sevilla Kills Me," *The Secret of Evil*, 140. See Hoyos' "Introduction: Globalization as Form" and "Nazi Tales from the Americas at the Turn of the Century," in *Beyond Bolaño* and Andrews' "Duels and Brawls: Borges and Bolaño," in *Roberto Bolaño's Fiction*.

32. "Sevilla me mata," *Entre paréntesis*, 311–314; "Sevilla Kills Me," *The Secret of Evil*, 139–143. See Celina Manzoni, "Ficción de futuro y lucha por el canon en la narrativa de Roberto Bolaño," in *Jornadas homenaje Roberto Bolaño* and *Bolaño salvaje*.

33. Roberto Bolaño, "La novela y el cuento son dos hermanos siameses" (interview with Daniel Swinburn), in *Bolaño por sí mismo*, 74.

34. Roberto Bolaño, "Balas pasadas," in *Bolaño por sí mismo*, 98.

35. Roberto Bolaño, "Un paseo por la literatura" / "A Stroll through Literature," in *Tres* (Barcelona: El Acantilado, 2000), bilingual edition, trans. Laura Healy (New York: New Directions, 2011), 114–173, 142–143. See Raymond Williams, *Marxism and Literature* (Oxford, UK: Oxford University Press, 1977), 108–114, 115–120, and 121–128.

36. Bolaño back jacket-cover statement, *Tres*. On *Amberes* and *Tres, The Return, The Insufferable Gaucho*, and *Between Parentheses*, see Mark Ford, "Bolaño: On the Edge of the Precipice," *The New York Review of Books* 58, no. 15 (October 13, 2011): 33–36;

37. Georg Perec, *La Vie mode d'emploi* (Paris: Hachette, 1978); *Life, a User's Manual*, trans. David Bellos (David R. Godine, 2009). See Fernando Moreno, "Los laberintos narrativos de Roberto Bolaño," in *La experiencia del abismo*; and Enrique Vila-Matas, "La lista de Bolaño y Perec," https://yonosoyfunes.wordpress.com/2013/06/27/la-lista-de-bolano-y-perec/.

38. Bolaño, "A Stroll through Literature," 116–117.

39. *Ibid.*, 12; 128–129.

40. *Ibid.*, 15; 135.

41. Bolaño, "Un paseo por la literatura" / "A Stroll through Literature," in *Tres*, 142–143.

42. Nicanor Parra, *Poemas y antipoemas* (1954); *Obra Gruesa* (1969); and *Artefactos*, in *Obras completas* (Barcelona: Círculo de Lectores, Galaxia Gutenberg, 2006); *Antipoems: How to Look Better and Feel Great: Antipoemas / Antipoems and artefactos visuales / visual artefactos*, bilingual edition, trans. Liz Werner (New York: New Directions, 2004); Roberto Bolaño, *Gente que se aleja / People Walking Away*, in *The Unknown University*; Baudelaire, "À Arsène Houssaye," in OC 275–276; LV i–x and KW 3–4. Ezra Pound, *ABC of Reading* (1934) (New York: New Directions, 1960), 36.

43. Franco Moretti, *The Bourgeois: Between History and Literature* (Brooklyn: Verso, 2013); Ian Watt, *The Rise of the Novel: Studies in Defoe, Richardson, and Fielding* (Berkeley: University of California Press, 1960).

44. See Jacques Rancière, *The Politics of Aesthetics: The Distribution of the Sensible*, trans. Gabriel Rockhill (London and New York: Continuum, 2004).

45. Bolaño, *Amulet*, 159; *Amuleto*, 134.

46. See Robert von Hallberg, *Lyric Powers* (Chicago: University of Chicago Press, 2008); Charles Altieri, *Self and Sensibility in Contemporary American Poetry* (Cambridge: Cambridge University Press, 1984, digital rpt. 2009). See also Walter Kalaidjian, *The Cambridge Companion to Modern American Poetry* (Cambridge: Cambridge University Press, 2015); Jonathan Culler, *Theory of the Lyric* (Cambridge, MA: Harvard University Press, 2015); Jahan Ramazani, *Poetry and Its Others: News, Prayer, Song, and the Dialogue of Genres* (Chicago: The University of Chicago Press, 2014); Marjorie Perloff, *Poetics in a New Key: Interviews and Essays*, ed. David Jonathan Y. Bayot (Chicago: University of Chicago Press, 2014); Christopher Nealon, *The Matter of Capital: Poetry and Crisis in the American Century* (Cambridge, MA: Harvard University Press, 2011); Jennifer Ashton, *From Modernism to Postmodernism: American Poetry and Theory in the Twentieth Century* (Cambridge: Cambridge University Press, 2008) and ed., *The Cambridge Companion to American Poetry since 1945* (Cambridge: Cambridge University Press, 2013); and Mutlu Konuk Blasing, *Politics and Form in Postmodern Poetry* (Cambridge: Cambridge University Press, 1995, 2009) and *Lyric Poetry: the Pain and Pleasure of Words* (Princeton, NJ: Princeton University Press, 2007).

47. Bolaño, *Consejos*, 166. Raymond Queneau, *Exercises in Style* (*Exercises de Style*, 1947), trans. Barbara Wright (New York: New Directions, 1981). See also Patricia Poblete, "Imágenes como flashes sin sonido," in *La experiencia del abismo*.

48. Baudelaire, "À Arsène Houssaye," in OC 275–276; LV i–x and KW 3–4.

49. *Ibid.* See Giorgio Agamben, *The End of the Poem: Studies in Poetics*, trans. Daniel Heller-Roazen (Stanford, CA: Stanford University Press, 1999), *Idea of Prose*, (*Idea della prosa*, 1985), trans. Michael Sullivan and Sam Whitsitt (Binghamton: SUNY Press, 1995), and *The Coming Community* (1993, *La comunità che viene*, 1990), trans. Michael Hardt (Minneapolis: University of Minnesota Press, 1993).

50. Mikhail Bakhtin, *The Dialogic Imagination: Four Essays*, trans. ed Caryl Emerson and Michael Holquist (Austin: University of Texas Press, 1981).

51. Moretti recalls discovering *"the truth of Haldane's famous dictum that 'size is never just size,'"* while working on the last chapter of his *Atlas of the European Novel 1800–1900* (London: Verso, 1998), in "Planet Hollywood," *New Left Review* 9 (2001): 90–101, rpt. in *Distant Reading*, 91. See also Nirvana Tanoukhi, "The Scale of World Literature," *New Literary History* 38 (2008): 599–618.

52. See Jacques Rancière, "Are Some Things Unrepresentable?" in *The Future of the Image (Le destin des images, 2003)*, trans. Gregory Elliott (London and New York: Verso, 2007).

53. See Rimbaud, Letter to Georges Izambard, Charleville, May 13, 1871, in *Rimbaud: Complete Works, Selected Letters*, trans. Wallace Fowlie (Chicago: University of Chicago Press, 1966); Juan Ramón Jiménez, "yo no soy yo," in

Eternidades (1916–1917), *Obras de Juan Ramón Jiménez* (Madrid, Visor, 2008); and Jorge Luis Borges, "Borges y yo" (1960), in *El hacedor, obras completas*, vol. 1 (Buenos Aires: Emecé Editions, 1996, 2005), 197.
54. Bolaño, SVP, 312; TP, 214.

Chapter 1 "Undisciplined Writing"

1. Roberto Bolaño, *Antwerp*, trans. Natasha Wimmer (New York: New Directions, 2010), hereafter cited in the text as AN, x.
2. *Ibid.*
3. AN, 3; Roberto Bolaño, *Amberes* (Barcelona: Anagrama, 2002, written 1980), hereafter cited in text as A, 15. See Franco Moretti, "Markets of the Mind," *New Left Review* 11, no. 5 (2000) and "Planet Hollywood" and "The End of the Beginning," in *Distant Reading* 146 n. 18, 19.
4. Roberto Bolaño, *Nocturno de Chile* (Barcelona: Anagrama, 2000); *By Night in Chile*, trans. Chris Andrews (New York: New Directions, 2003). See Fresán's "Pequeño big bang," 12; Enrique Salas Durazo, "Roberto Bolaño's Big Bang: Deciphering the Code of an Aspiring Writer in *Antwerp*," in *Roberto Bolaño, a Less Distant Star*; Myrna Solotorevsky, "*Amberes* y *la pista de hielo*, dos novelas de Bolaño, dos estéticas contrarias," in *Roberto Bolaño: La experiencia del abismo*; Nora Catelli, "El laboratorio Bolaño," *El País*, September 14, 2002; and Andrews, *Roberto Bolaño's Fiction*, 3, 236.
5. Baudelaire, "Le Mauvais Vitrier," OC 285–287; "The Bad Glazier," LV 12–14 and KW 15–17.
6. AN, 3; A, 15.
7. E.M. Forster, *Aspects of the Novel* (Harmondsworth: Penguin, 1962); Andrews, *Roberto Bolaño's Fiction*, 169–174.
8. AN, 4; A, 17.
9. AN, 5–6. A, 18–20. Ludwig Wittgenstein, *Philosophische Untersuchungen* (Frankfurt am Main: Suhrkamp, 1971; London: Basil Blackwell, 1958); *Philosophical Investigations* (Oxford: Blackwell, 2001), 43, 65–67, 85, 198, and *passim*. In "Literature + Illness = Illness," Bolaño names Wittgenstein's *Tractatus* one of the most influential books of his life, 118.
10. See in this connection Theodor W. Adorno, "Parataxis," in *Notes to Literature*, vol. 2 (New York: Columbia University Press, 1991).
11. AN, 7; A, 21–22. Borges, "Borges y yo," *Obras completas*, 197.
12. See Tzvetan Todorov, "Typologie du roman policier," in *Poétique de la prose* (Paris: Seuil, 1971); Ernst Bloch, "A Philosophical View of the Detective Novel," in *The Utopian Function of Art and Literature: Selected Essays*, trans. Jack Zipes and Frank Mecklenburg (Cambridge, MA: MIT Press, 1988); D.A. Miller, *The Novel and the Police* (Berkeley: University of California Press, 1988).

216 *Notes to pages 27–33*

13. AN, 8; A, 23.
14. Mikhail Bakhtin, *Speech Genres and Other Late Essays*, trans. Vern W. McGee, ed. Caryl Emerson and Michael Holquist (Texas: University Press, 1986); V.N. Volosinov, *Marxism and the Philosophy of Literature*, trans. Ladislav Matejka and I.R. Titunik (Cambridge, MA: Harvard University Press, 1986).
15. AN, 10; A, 25–26.
16. AN, 11; A, 27–28.
17. AN, 12; A, 14.
18. AN, 66; A, 103.
19. AN, 4, 66; A, 17, 103. Baudelaire, OC 275–276; LV i–x and KW 3–4.
20. Bolaño, "Discurso de Caracas," in *Entre paréntesis*; "Caracas Address," in *Between Parentheses*.
21. A, 35–36; AN, 16–17.
22. AN, 18; A, 37.
23. AN, 28; A, 49.
24. A, 50; AN, 29.
25. See Baudelaire, "Au Lecteur," in OC 5–6; "To the Reader," Howard, 6.
26. AN, 30–31; A, 51–52.
27. AN, 32; A, 54–55. Baudelaire, OC 287–288; "One O'Clock in the Morning, LV 15–16; "One A.M.," KW 18–19.
28. AN, 42; A, 68–69. There are striking resonances between Bolaño's "jorobadito" in *Antwerp* and the hunchback in the famous opening section of Benjamin's prose-poetic philosophical "Über den Begriff der Geschichte" (Jephcott's "On the Concept of History," Harry Zohn's "Theses on the Philosophy of History"). Providing the title for the opening section of Hannah Arendt's Introduction to Benjamin's *Illuminations* (Harcourt Brace Jovanovich, 1968), Benjamin's "ein buckliger Zwerg" (693) is translated by Zohn as "a little hunchback" (253), by Jephcott as "a hunchbacked dwarf" (389).
29. AN, 44, 50, 51; A, 72, 80, 82.
30. AN, 52; A, 83–84. Stéphane Mallarmé, *Igitur – Divagations – Un Coup de dés*, ed. Bertrand Marchal (Paris: Gallimard, 2003). See Jacques Rancière, "The Intruder: Mallarmé's Politics" and "The Poet at the Philosopher's: Mallarmé and Badiou," in *The Politics of Literature (Politique de la littérature, 2006)*, trans. Julie Rose (London: Polity, 2011).
31. AN, 56; A, 90–91.
32. A, 92–93; AN, 58.
33. AN, 64; A, 99–100.
34. A, 102–103; AN, 66.
35. A, 107–108; AN, 69.

36. AN, 71; A, 112.
37. A, 115–116; AN, 75–76. See Franco Moretti, *Graphs, Maps, Trees: Abstract Models for Literary History* (New York: Verso, 2007) and *Signs Taken for Wonders* (London/New York 2005).
38. A, 117–118; AN, 77. Walter Benjamin, "The Work of Art in the Age of Its Technological Reproducibility" ("Das Kunstwerk im Zeitalter seiner technischen Reproduzierbarkeit," 1935–1936), in *Selected Writings, vol. 4*; Jasper Bernes, *The Work of Art in the Age of Deindustrialization* (Stanford, CA: Stanford University Press, 2017); Tom Conley, "Cinema and Its Discontents," *Jacques Rancière: History, Politics, Aesthetics*, ed. Gabriel Rockhill and Philip Watts (Durham, NC: Duke University Press, 2009); Susan McCabe, *Cinematic Modernism: Modernist Poetry and Film* (Cambridge: Cambridge University Press, 2005).
39. A, 119; AN, 78. Translation modified. Significantly, Bolaño does not write "Odes" to the human and the divine, but only "To the human and divine."
40. See Thomas Pavel, *Fictional Worlds* (Cambridge, MA: Harvard University Press, 1986); Ruth Rosen, *Possible Worlds in Literary Theory* (Cambridge: Cambridge University Press, 1994); Pascale Casanova, "Literature as a World," *New Left Review* 31 (2005): 71–90; Eric Hayot, *On Literary Worlds* (New York: Oxford University Press, 2012).

Chapter 2   Poetry as Symptom and Cure

1. See Bakhtin, *The Dialogic Imagination*; Franco Moretti, *The Modern Epic: The World-System from Goethe to García-Márquez*, trans. Quintin Hoare (London: Verso, 1996); Massimo Fusillo, "Epic, Novel," in *The Novel, Volume 2*.
2. Poe, "How to Write a Blackwood Article," in *Complete Tales and Poems*; Baudelaire, "Le Mauvais Vitrier," OC 285–287; LV 12–14 and KW 15–17; "À une heure du matin," OC 287–288; "One O'Clock in the Morning," LV 15–16; "One A.M.," KW 18–19. Roberto Bolaño, *Monsieur Pain* (Barcelona: Anagrama, 1999, originally *La senda de los elefantes* [Ayuntamiento de Toledo, Concejalía del Área de Cultura, 1973]); *Monsieur Pain*, trans. Chris Andrews (New York: New: Directions, 2010).
3. Bolaño, "Un paseo por la literatura" / "A Stroll through Literature," in *Tres*, 142–143; See Darío Oses, "El viaje de Pain," and Magda Sepúlveda, "La narrativa policial como un género de la modernidad: La pista de Bolaño," in *Territorios en fuga*; Fernando Iwasaki, "Roberto Bolaño, Monsieur Pain," in *Bolaño salvaje*.
4. Parra, *Poemas y antipoemas; Obra Gruesa*; and *Artefactos*, in *Obras Completas; Antipoems: How to Look Better and Feel Great*.

5. Bolaño, LDS, 151; SD, 154. See Bakhtin, "Discourse in the Novel," *The Dialogic Imagination*, 259–422.

6. Sigmund Freud, *The Interpretation of Dreams* (1900–1901); *Jokes and Their Relationship to the Unconscious* (1905); *Beyond the Pleasure Principle* (1920–1922); and *The Ego and the Id* (1923–1925), in *The Standard Edition of the Complete Psychological Works of Sigmund Freud*, ed. James Strachey (London: The Hogarth Press, 1957–1958; New York: Norton, 1990), vols. IV and V, VIII, XVIII, and XIX. See also Celina Manzoni, "Ciencia, superchería y complot en *Monsieur Pain*," in *Roberto Bolaño: La experiencia del abismo*.

7. MP, 82, MPs 112. See Jacques Rancière, "From the Poetry of the Future to the Poetry of the Past," in *Mute Speech: Literature, Critical Theory, and Politics* (*La Parole muette: Essai sur les contradictions de la littérature*, 1998), trans. James Swenson (New York: Columbia University Press, 2011), 73–85; Martin Puchner, *Poetry of the Revolution: Marx, Manifestos, and the Avant-Gardes* (Princeton, NJ: Princeton University Press, 2006); Peter Bürger, *Theory of the Avant-Garde* (*Theorie der Avantgarde, 1974*), trans. Michael Shaw (Minneapolis: University of Minnesota Press, 1984); Hans Magnus Enzensberger, "Aporias of the Avant-Garde" ("Die Aporien der Avantgarde," 1962), in Hans Magnus Enzensberger, *The Consciousness Industry: On Literature, Politics and the Media*, ed. Michael Roloff (New York: Seabury Press, 1974); André Breton, *Manifestes du surréalisme* (Paris: Gallimard, 1948); *Manifestoes of Surrealism*, trans. Richard Seaver and Helen Lane (Ann Arbor: University of Michigan, 1972).

8. MP 3; MPs 17.

9. See Jacques Rancière, "The Truth through the Window: Literary Truth, Freudian Truth," in *The Politics of Literature and The Aesthetic Unconscious* (*L'Inconscient Esthétique*, 2001; Cambridge: Polity Press, 2009).

10. André Breton, *Nadja* (Paris: Gallimard, 1928); trans. Richard Howard (New York: Grove Press, 1960); Louis Aragon, *Le Paysan de Paris* (Paris: Gallimard, 1926); Bolaño, "The Last Interview," 118.

11. See my "Introduction: The Prose Poem as a Dialogical Genre," in *A Poverty of Objects* and Ramazani, "A Dialogic Poetics: Poetry and the Novel, Theory, and the Law," in *Poetry and Its Others*.

12. See Antoine Ventura, "De la fragmentation et du fragmentaire dans l'oeuvre narrative de Roberto Bolaño," in *Les Astres noirs de Roberto Bolaño*.

13. MP, 82.

14. *Ibid.*, 126–127.

15. *Ibid.*, 45, 116.

16. MPs, 101; MP, 32, 47, 57–58, and 73. Baudelaire, "À Arsène Houssaye," OC 275–276; LV i–x and KW 3–4; "Perte d'auréole," OC 352; LV 94; KW 88. See Jorge Luis Borges, "Las ruinas circulares," *Obras Completas*, vol. 1; "The

Circular Ruins," *Labyrinths: Selected Stories and Other Critical Writings,* ed. Donald A. Yates and James E. Irby (New York: New Directions, 1962, 2007). See also Fernando Moreno, "Los laberintos narrativos de Roberto Bolaño," in *Roberto Bolaño: La experiencia del abismo.*

17. MPs, 53; MP, 30. See Jacques Rancière, *The Emancipated Spectator (Le Spectateur émancipé, 2008),* trans. Gregory Elliott (London and New York: Verso, 2009).

18. MPs, 111, 87, 116; MP, 82, 61, 87, 116.

19. See Benjamin, "Central Park," 535 and 665; Bloch, "A Philosophical View of the Detective Novel," *The Utopian Function of Art and Literature*; and Bruno Bosteels, "The Post-Leninist Detective," in *Marx and Freud in Latin America: Politics, Psychoanalysis and Religion in Times of Terror* (New York and London: Verso Books, 2012).

20. MP, 1, 30–31.

21. *Ibid.,* 57–58, 19.

22. *Ibid.,* 132–134.

23. Bolaño, "Mi carrera literaria" ("My Literary Career"), "La poesía chilena" ("Chilean Poetry Is a Gas"), "Horda" ("Horde"), and "La poesía latinoamericana" ("Latin American Poetry"), in *La Universidad Desconocida / The Unknown University*, in Laura Healy's bilingual edition, vi–vii, 520–521, 522–523, 524–527.

24. Bolaño, *Amuleto* (Barcelona: Anagrama, 1999); *Amulet,* trans. Chris Andrews (New York: New Directions, 2007).

25. MP, 82; MPs, 112.

26. MP, 113, 107–108, 134.

27. *Ibid.,* 134.

28. *Ibid.,* 14–15, 18–20.

29. *Ibid.,* 16.

30. *Ibid.,* 8–9. Friedrich Kittler, *Discourse Networks (Aufschreibesysteme), 1800/ 1900,* trans. Michael Metteer (1985; Stanford, CA: Stanford University Press, 1990), 265.

31. MP, 7.

32. *Ibid.,* 86.

33. *Ibid.,* 23, 29, 49, 33, 73.

34. MP, 53; MPs, 77.

35. William Carlos Williams, "Asphodel, That Greeny Flower," in *Journey to Love (1955), The Collected Poems of William Carlos Williams, vol. 2: 1939–1962* (New York: New Directions, 1988), 318.

36. Jean-Paul Sartre, *What Is Literature?* (New York: Routledge, 2001). See also Moretti, *The Bourgeois* and Michal Peled Ginsburg and Lorri G. Nandrea, "The Prose of the World," in *The Novel, Volume 2.*

37. MPs, 96–97; MP, 69–70.

38. MPs, 153–171; MP, 117–134.
39. MP, 113; MPs, 149.

Chapter 3   The Novel's Regimes Made Visible

1. Roberto Bolaño, *El Tercer Reich* (Barcelona: Anagrama, 2010); *The Third Reich*, trans. Natasha Wimmer (New York: Farrar, Straus and Giroux, 2011). An earlier version of this chapter appears as "Los amores y juegos del joven Berger," in *Bolaño salvaje*, 487–506. See also Carolyn Wolfenzon, "*El Tercer Reich* y la historia como juego de guerra," in *Bolaño salvaje*, 204–228; Edouard Glissant, "A partir d'une situation «bloquée»," *Le Discours Antillais* (Paris: Éditions du Seuil, 1981, rpt. Gallimard, 1997), 13–17; "From a 'Dead-end' Situation," *Caribbean Discourse: Selected Essay*, trans. J. Michael Dash (Charlottesville: University Press of Virginia, 1989, 1992, 1999), 1–3; and Jean-Paul Sartre, *Search for a Method*. trans. Hazel E. Barnes (New York: Vintage, 1968 / Alfred A. Knopf, 1963), 30; "Question de Méthode," *Critique de la raison dialectique*, vol. 1 (Paris: Gallimard 1960), 29.
2. See Amy Hungerford, *Making Literature Now* (Stanford, CA: Stanford University Press, 2016); Paz Soldán, "Roberto Bolaño: Literatura y apocalipsis," in *Bolaño Salvaje*; Samuel Huntington, *The Clash of Civilizations: Remaking of World Order* (New York: Simon and Schuster, 1998); Jean-François Lyotard, *The Postmodern Condition: A Report on Knowledge* (*La Condition postmoderne: rapport sur le savoir*, 1979), trans. Geoff Bennington and Brian Massumi (Minneapolis: University of Minnesota Press, 1984).
3. Bolaño, *Amberes; Antwerp*, hereafter cited as A and AN.
4. Roberto Bolaño, *La literatura nazi en América* (Barcelona: Seix Barral, 1996); *Nazi Literature in the Americas*, trans. Chris Andrews (New York: New Directions, 2008); Roberto Bolaño, *Estrella distante* (Barcelona: Anagrama, 1996); *Distant Star*, trans. Chris Andrews (New York: New Directions, 2004).
5. Immanuel Kant, *Critique of Judgment*, trans. Wener S Pluhar (Indianapolis: Hackett, 1987); "An Answer to the Question: What Is Enlightenment?" in *Political Writings*, trans. H.B. Nisbet, ed. H.S. Reiss (New York: Cambridge University Press, 1991).
6. See Guy Debord, *The Society of the Spectacle* (*La Société du spectacle*, 1967), trans. Donald Nicholson-Smith (Zone Books, 1995, 1999).
7. Roland Barthes, "L'Écrivain en vacances," *Mythologies* (Paris: Éditions du Seuil, 1957); "The Writer on Holiday," in *Mythologies*, trans. Richard Howard (New York: Hill and Wang, Farrar, Straus and Giroux, 2012).
8. Johann Wolfgang von Goethe, *The Sorrows of Young Werther* (*Die Leidungen des Jungen Werthers*, 1774), trans. David Constantine (Oxford: Oxford University Press, 2012).

9. TRs, 336–338; TR, 259–260. Goethe, "Selige Sehnsucht," *West-östlicher Divan: Buch des Sängers* (1814–1818).
10. TR, 251.
11. TRs, 247.
12. Roberto Bolaño, *Amulet* and *Los detectives salvajes* (Barcelona: Anagrama, 1998); *The Savage Detectives*, trans. Natasha Wimmer (New York: Farrar, Straus and Giroux, 2007); *Nocturno de Chile* (Barcelona: Anagrama, 2000); *By Night in Chile*, trans. Chris Andrews (New York: New Directions, 2003). See Giorgio Agamben, "From the Book to the Screen: The Before and After of the Book," in *The Fire and the Tale* (*Il fuoco e il racconto*, 2014), trans. Lorenzo Chiesa (Stanford, CA: Stanford University Press, 2017).
13. TR, 311.
14. Martin Heidegger, "On the Question of Technology" (*Die Technik und die Kehre*, 1954), in *The Question Concerning Technology and Other Essays* (New York: Harper and Row, 1977).
15. Parra, *Poemas y antipoemas; Obra gruesa*; and *Artefactos*, in *Obras Completas*, 1–64, 175–259, and 313–556; *Antipoems: How to Look Better and Feel Great*.
16. TRs, 79–80; TR, 53–54.
17. TR, 216. See Moretti, "Evolution, World-Systems, *Weltliteratur*" and "The Novel: History and Theory," in *Distant Reading*.
18. See Wittgenstein, *Philosophical Investigations*, 43; Julio Sebastián Figueroa Jofré, "Bolaño con Borges: Juegos con la infamia y el mal radical," in *Roberto Bolaño: Ruptura y violencia en la literatura finisecular*; Giorgio Agamben, "What Is an Apparatus?" and "What Is the Contemporary?" in *What Is an Apparatus? And Other Essays*, trans. David Kishik and Stefan Pedatella (Stanford, CA: Stanford University Press, 2009).
19. Bolaño, A, 17; AN, 4.
20. TRs, 337; TR, 260.
21. TRs, 290–291; TR, 222–223.
22. TRs, 324–325. TR, 249–250. See Paul K. Saint-Amour, *Tense Future: History, Modernism, Total War, Encyclopedic Form* (Oxford: Oxford University Press, 2015); Alain Badiou, *The Communist Hypothesis* (*L'Hypothése communiste*, 2008), trans. David Macey and Steve Corcoran (London and New York: Verso, 2010); Lionel Ruffel, ed. *Qu'est-ce que le contemporain?* (Nantes: Éditions Cécile Defaut, 2010).
23. TR, 6–7. See Jacques Rancière, *Aisthesis: Scenes from the Aesthetic Regime of Art*, trans. Zakir Paul (New York and London: Verso, 2013) and "Is History a Form of Fiction?" in *The Politics of Aesthetics*.
24. Bolaño, *Entre paréntesis; Between Parentheses*.
25. See Michael W. Clune, *American Literature and the Free Market, 1945–2000* (Cambridge: Cambridge University Press, 2010); Annie McClanahan, *Dead*

Pledges: Debt, Crisis, and Twenty-First-Century Culture (Stanford, CA: Stanford University Press, 2017).

26. Ernst Bloch, *Traces*, trans. Anthony A. Nassar (Palo Alto, CA: Stanford University Press, 2006); *The Principle of Hope*, vol. 3, trans. Neville Plaice, Stephen Plaice, and Paul Knight (Cambridge, MA: MIT Press, 1995; Basil Blackwell, 1986); and *The Spirit of Utopia*, trans. Anthony A. Nassar (Palo Alto, CA: Stanford University Press, 2000); and Fredric Jameson, *Archaeologies of the Future: The Desire Called Utopia and Other Science Fictions* (London: Verso, 2005). In Moretti's *The Novel, Volume 1*, see Andreas Gailus, "Form and Chance: The German Novella"; in *Volume 2*, see Fredric Jameson, "A Businessman in Love," and Thomas Pavel, "The Novel in Search of Itself: A Historical Morphology." In *Roberto Bolaño as World Literature*, see José Enrique Navarro, "Global Bolaño: Reading, Writing, and Publishing in a Neoliberal World" and Sharae Deckard, "Roberto Bolaño and the Remapping of World Literature."

Chapter 4 Poetry at the Ends of Its Lines

1. See Williams, *Marxism and Literature*, 108–128; Walter Benjamin, "Commentary on Poems by Brecht" ("Kommentare zu Gedichten von Brecht," 1938/1939), "The Paris of the Second Empire in Baudelaire," "On Some Motifs in Baudelaire," and "Central Park," in *Selected Writings, vol. 4*; Roman Jakobson, "Linguistics and Poetics," in *Style and Language*, ed. Thomas Sebeok (Cambridge, MA: MIT Press, 1966); Theodor W. Adorno, "On Lyric Poetry and Society" ("Rede über Lyrik und Gesellschaft," 1958), trans. Shierry Weber Nicholsen, *Notes to Literature*, vol. 1 (New York: Columbia University Press, 1991). See also Walter Kalaidjian, "Left Poetry," in *A Companion to Modernist Poetry*, David E. Chinitz and Gail McDonald, eds. (Chichester, West Sussex, UK: Wiley Blackwell, 2014), 267–228 and Christopher Nealon, "Camp Messianism, Or, the Hopes of Poetry in Late-Late Capitalism," *American Literature* 76, no. 3 (September 2004).

2. Roberto Bolaño, *La Universidad Desconocida* (Barcelona: Anagrama, 2007); *The Unknown University*, trans. Laura Healy (New York: New Directions, 2013), hereafter cited in the text as UU. See Rodrigo Fresán, "El samurai romántico," in *Bolaño salvaje*; Patricia Espinosa, "Tres libros de poesía del primer Bolaño: *Reinventar el amor, Fragmentos de la Universidad Desconocida y el último salvaje*," in *La experiencia del abismo*; Bruno Montané Krebs, "Prefiguraciones de la Universidad Desconocida," in *Jornadas homenaje Roberto Bolaño*; José Promis, "Poética de Roberto Bolaño," in *Territorios en fuga*; and Matías Ayala, "Notas sobre la poesía de Roberto Bolaño," in *Bolaño salvaje*.

3. Bolaño, *Amuleto*, 134; *Amulet*, 159. Parra, *Poemas y antipoemas; Obra Gruesa*; and *Artefactos, Obras; Antipoemas: How to look better and feel great*.

4. Roberto Bolaño, *La literatura nazi en América* (Barcelona: Seix Barral, 1996); *Nazi Literature in the Americas*, trans. Chris Andrews (New York: New Directions, 2008), hereafter cited in the text as LNA and NLA. See Karim Benmiloud, "Transgresión genérica e ideológica en *La literatura nazi en América*," in *Roberto Bolaño: La experiencia del abismo*, 119–131; Willy Thayer, "El Golpe como consumación de la vanguardia," in *El fragmento repetido: Escritos en estado de excepción* (Santiago, Chile: Metales, 2006); Celina Manzoni, "Biografías mínimas/ínfimas y el equívoco del mal," in *Roberto Bolaño: La escritura como tauromaquia*, 17–32;

5. Fredric Jameson, *The Political Unconscious* (Ithaca, NY: Cornell University Press, 1981), ix, 62. See also Oswaldo Zavala, "The Repoliticization of the Latin American Shore: Roberto Bolaño and the Dispersion of 'World Literature,'" in *Roberto Bolaño as World Literature*, 79–97. On the "common grounds" approach to what Jeffrey Lawrence calls "patterns of mutual influence and shared aspirations across the hemisphere," see Lois Parkinson Zamora and Silvia Spitta's introduction to *The Americas, Otherwise* (*Comparative Literature*, 2009), which urges "Americanists and Latin Americanists alike," to "overcome the North-South divide" (*Anxieties of Influence*, 18).

6. López, Óscar, "Breva historia del libro"; "Brief History of the Book," in UU, 816–822, 817.

7. *Ibid.*, 816–817.

8. *Ibid.*, in UU, 819.

9. Bolaño, "Los perros románticos" / "The Romantic Dogs," 818–819; "Gente que se aleja" / "People Walking Away," in UU, 818–819, 388–389.

10. López, "Brief History of the Book," in UU, vi–vii.

11. Bolaño, SVP, 131–134; TP, 89–91.

12. López, "Brief History of the Book," UU, 820. "Retrato en mayo, 1994" / "Portrait in May, 1994" (800–801), "Musa" / "Muse," UU, 804–811; "Policías" / "Police," UU, 600–603; "Los detectives" / "The Detectives," UU, 604–605; "Los detectives perdidos" / "The Lost Detectives," UU, 606–607; "Los detectives helados" / "The Frozen Detectives," UU, 608–609.

13. NLA, 14, 205–227, 137–140, 161, 170; "Gente que se aleja" / "People Walking Away," UU, 812–813; "Apuntes de una castración" / "Notes on a Castration," UU, 436–439; "La Victoria" / "Victory," UU, 444–445.

14. See Francine Masiello, *The Art of Transition: Latin American Culture and Neoliberal Crisis* (Durham, NC: Duke University Press, 2001).

15. Baudelaire, OC 275–276; LV i–x and KW 3–4.

16. See Borges, *Historia universal de la infamia, Obras completas*; Bolaño and Braithwaite, *Bolaño por sí mismo*, 42; Andrews, "Duels and Brawls: Borges and Bolaño," in *Roberto Bolaño's Fiction*; Hoyos, "Introduction: Globalization as Form" and "Nazi Tales from the Americas at the Turn of the Century," in *Beyond Bolaño*.

17. NLA, 179.

18. Roberto Bolaño, "Un paseo por la literatura" / "A Stroll through Literature," in *Tres*, 128–129. See Helen Usandizaga, "El reverso poético en la prosa de Roberto Bolaño," in *Jornadas homenaje Roberto Bolaño*, and "Poesía y prosa en la obra de Roberto Bolaño," in *Roberto Bolaño. Estrella cercana. Ensayos sobre su obra*, ed. Augusta López (Madrid: Verbum, 2012), 377–404.

19. NLA, 171 and 181–183.

20. *Ibid.*, 17.

21. See Theodor Adorno, *The Jargon of Authenticity* (London: Routledge, 1973, 2003) and Bakhtin, *The Dialogic Imagination,* 289. See also Robert Kaufman, "Adorno's Social Lyric and Literary Criticism Today," in *The Cambridge Companion to Adorno*, ed. Tom Huhn (Cambridge: Cambridge University Press, 2004).

22. NLA, 152; LNA, 162.

23. Bolaño, SVP, 146, 283; TP, 75–76, 187, 218–219.

24. NLA, 14, 205–227, 137–140, 161, 170.

25. *Ibid.*, 7, 11, 8; Edgar Allan Poe, "Philosophy of Furniture," *Complete Tales and Poems*.

26. *Ibid.*, 144–145.

27. See Jorge Luis Borges, "Deutsches Requiem" and "El Aleph" (1949), in *El Aleph*, in *Obras completas*, vol. 1; "Deutsches Requiem" and "The Aleph," in *The Aleph and Other Stories*, trans. Andrew Hurley (New York: Penguin, 1998, Viking Penguin, 1998). Mallarmé of course offers his enormously influential "Donner un sens plus pur aux mots de la tribu" ("To purify the language of the tribe") precisely in his 1876 homage to Poe, "Le Tombeau d'Edgar Poe," in *Oeuvres complètes* (Paris: Gallimard, 1945, 1998). On the phrase's continuing importance and inflection in contemporary poetry, see Cole Swenson's "Introduction" to *American Hybrid: A Norton Anthology of New Poetry*, ed. Cole Swenson and David St. John (New York, Norton, 2009), xvii–xxvi.

28. Baudelaire, "Sonnet pour s'excuser de ne pas accompagner un ami à Namur," OC 978; "Á une heure du matin," OC 287–288; LV 15–16; KW 18–19; Bolaño, *UU*, "La novela-nieve" / "The Snow-Novel," 2–68; "Tres Textos" / "Three Texts," 91–302; "Nel, majo" / "Fat Chance, Hon," 290–291; "El inspector" / "The Inspector," 292–295; "El testigo" / "The Witness," 296–299; "Prosa del otoño en Gerona" / "Prose from Autumn in Gerona," 449–520. Bolaño, *Between Parentheses*.

29. Baudelaire, "Á une heure du matin," OC 288.
30. UU, 812–813.
31. *Ibid.*, 620–621.
32. *Ibid.*, 22–23.
33. *Ibid.*, 128–129.
34. Aimé Césaire, "Le Verbe maronner (à René Depestre)," in *Aimé Césaire: The Collected Poetry*, trans. Clayton Eshelman (Berkeley: University of California Press, 1983), 368–371.
35. NLA, 132–134; LNA, 142–143.
36. UU, 671, 675–681, 797.
37. Ezra Pound, "A Retrospect," in *Literary Essays of Ezra Pound*, ed. T.S. Eliot (New York: New Directions, 1935, 1968), 3.
38. Agamben, *The End of the Poem*, 115.
39. Baudelaire, OC 275.
40. UU, 817.
41. *Ibid.*, 8–9.
42. *Ibid.*, 13.
43. Friedrich Nietzsche, *On the Uses and Disadvantages of History for Life*, in *Untimely Meditations* (*Unzeitgemässe Betrachtungen. Zweites Stück: Vom Nutzen und Nachtheil der Historie für das Leben*, 1874), ed. Daniel Breazeale (Cambridge: Cambridge University Press, 1997, 2003), 57–123, 72–77.
44. *Ibid.*, 92–93, 444–445, 186–187, 556–557, 682–685, 656–657, 702–703.
45. *Ibid.*, 736–737, 746–747, 750–751, 774–775.
46. *Ibid.*, 804–811.
47. Baudelaire, "L'Étranger," OC 277; LV 1 and KW 5.
48. UU, 4–5.
49. *Ibid.*, 285.

Chapter 5   Post-Avant Histories

1. Roberto Bolaño, *Estrella distante* (Barcelona: Anagrama, 1996); *Distant Star*, trans. Chris Andrews (New York: New Directions, 2004), hereafter cited in the text as ED and DS.
2. DS, 13.
3. *Ibid.*, 14.
4. *Ibid.*, 6.
5. *Ibid.*, 10.
6. See Cole Swenson, "Introduction," *American Hybrid: A Norton Anthology of New Poetry*, ed. Cole Swenson and David St. John (New York: Norton, 2009), xxi–xxv.

7. ED, 24–25. Bolaño, "Encuentro con Enrique Lihn," in *Cuentos,* 408; "Meeting with Enrique Lihn," in *The Return,* 192. On Bolaño, Lihn, Parra, and Neruda, see Chiara Bolognese, "Fantasmas de poetas en algunos textos de Roberto Bolaño," in *Roberto Bolaño: La experiencia del abismo.*

8. Charles Bernstein, *Attack of the Difficult Poems* (Chicago: University of Chicago Press, 2011). See also Kenneth Goldsmith, *Uncreative Writing: Managing Language in the Digital Age* (New York: Columbia University Press, 2011); and Brian Reed, *Nobody's Business: Twenty-First Century Avant-Garde Poetics* (Ithaca, NY: Cornell University Press, 2013).

9. See Slavoj Žižek, *First as Tragedy, Then as Farce* (New York and London: Verso Books, 2009); Wendy Lesser, "The Mysterious Chilean," *The Threepenny Review. Spring* 26 (2007); Gerald Martin, "The Novel of a Continent: Latin America," in *The Novel, Volume 1: History, Geography, and Culture* (Princeton, NJ: Princeton University Press, 2006); Walter Mignolo, *The Idea of Latin America* (Oxford: Blackwell, 2005); Iván Quezada, "La caída de Chile," in *Territorios en fuga*; Yvonne Unnold, *Representing the Unrepresentable. Literature of Trauma under Pinochet in Chile* (New York: Peter Lang, 2002); Ignacio López-Calvo, *Written in Exile: Chilean Fiction from 1973–Present* (London and New York: Routledge, 2001); Alegría Fernando, "Antiliteratura," in *América latina en su literatura,* ed. César Fernández Moreno (Mexico City: Siglo WWI, 2000); Raúl Zurita, *Anteparadise (1982)*; bilingual edition, trans. Jack Schmitt (Los Angeles and Berkeley: University of California Press, 1986).

10. Nietzsche, *On the Uses and Disadvantages of History for Life,* in *Untimely Meditations,* 72–77. See Hoyos, *Beyond Bolaño*; Maria Luisa Fischer, "La memoria de las historias en *Estrella distante* de Roberto Bolaño," in *Bolaño salvaje*; José de Piérola, "El envés de la historia. (Re)construcción e la historia in *Estrella distante* de Roberto Bolaño y Soldados de Salamina de Javier Cercas," *Revista de Crítica Literaria Latinoamericana* 33, no. 65 (2007): 241–258; 660–667; and Caroline Lepage, "Littérature et dictature: lecture croisée de trois romans de Roberto Bolaño (*Estrella distante – Amuleto – Nocturno de Chile*)," in *Les Astres noirs,* 67–90.

11. DS, 29; ED, 39–40.

12. DS, 33.

13. See Peter Boxall, "A Curious Knot: Terrorism, Radicalism and the Avant-Garde," in *Twenty-First Century Fiction: A Critical Introduction* (Cambridge: Cambridge University Press, 2013); Fernando J. Rosenberg, *The Avant-Garde and Geopolitics in Latin America* (Pittsburgh: University of Pittsburgh Press, 2006); Willy Thayer, "El golpe como consumación de la vanguardia," in *El fragmento repetido: Escritos en estado de excepción* (Santiago, Chile: Metales, 2006);

Hermann Herlinghaus, "Literature and Revolution in Latin America," in *Literary Cultures of Latin America: A Comparative History*, ed. Mario Valdés and Djelal Kadir, vol. 3 (Oxford: Oxford University Press, 2004).

14. DS, 6, 8, 21.
15. *Ibid.*, 15.
16. *Ibid.*, 24.
17. ED, 31–36; DS, 25–29. See Luis Bagué Quílez, "Performing Disappearance: Heaven and Sky in Roberto Bolaño and Raúl Zurita," in *Roberto Bolaño, a Less Distant Star*; Ina Jennerjahn, "Escritos en los cielos y fotografías del infierno. Las 'acciones de arte' de Carlos Ramírez Hoffman, según Roberto Bolaño," *Revista de crítica literaria latinoamericana* 56 (2002); and Silvana Mandolessi, "El arte según Wieder: estética y política de lo abyecto en *Estrella distante*," *Chasqui* 40, no. 2 (2011).
18. DS, 20–21.
19. *Ibid.*, 35–37.
20. DS, 46; ED, 56.
21. DS, 65.
22. Baudelaire, "Au Lecteur," OC 5–6. See Jeremías Gamboa, "¿Dobles o siameses? Vanguardia y postmodernismo en *Estrella distante*," in *Bolaño salvaje*.
23. DS, 47–48.
24. See Rory O'Bryen, "Writing with the Ghost of Pierre Menard: Authorship, Responsibility, and Justice in Roberto Bolaño's *Distant Star*," in *Less Distant Star*; Camilo Marks, "Roberto Bolaño, el esplendor narrativo finisecular," in *Territorios en fuga*; Zavala, "The Repoliticization of the Latin American Shore," Federico Finchelstein, "On Fascism, History, and Evil in Roberto Bolaño," and Will H. Corral, "Bolaño, Ethics, and the Experts," in *Roberto Bolaño as World Literature*.
25. DS, 50.
26. *Ibid.*, 54–55.
27. *Ibid.*, 57.
28. *Ibid.*, 68.
29. DS, 71; ED, 80.
30. DS, 76.
31. ED, 89–91; DS, 81–82.
32. See Rancière, "From the Poetry of the Future to the Poetry of the Past," in *Mute Speech*; Agamben, "What Is the Contemporary?" in *What Is an Apparatus?*
33. DS, 83.
34. *Ibid.*, 88.
35. *Ibid.*, 103–104.

36. *Ibid.*, 107–111. See Jean Franco, "Killers, Torturers, Sadists, and Collaborators" and "Afterword: Hypocrite Modernity," in *Cruel Modernity*; Carmen De Mora, "Los espacios del horror en Roberto Bolaño," in *Roberto Bolaño: La experiencia del abismo*, 7; Daniuska González, "Roberto Bolaño: La escritura bárbara," in *La experiencia del abismo*; Ainhoa Vásquez Mejías, "Ritual del bello crimen. Violencia femicida en *Estrella distante*," in *Roberto Bolaño: Ruptura y violencia en la literatura finisecular*; Ignacio López-Vicuña, "The Violence of Writing: Literature and Discontent in Roberto Bolaño's 'Chilean' Novels," *Journal of Latin American Cultural Studies* 18, no. 2 (2009).
37. Roberto Bolaño and Eliseo Álvarez, "Positions Are Positions and Sex Is Sex" (interview by Eliseo Álvarez, first published in *Turia*, Barcelona, 2005), in *The Last Interview*, 78–79.
38. Bolaño and Maristain, "The Last Interview," *The Last Interview and Other Conversations*, 103.
39. Bolaño and Óscar López, "Claro: Necesito fumar" (Interview in *Qué Leer*, Barcelona, September 1999), in *Bolaño por sí mismo*, 54–56.
40. Bolaño and Maristain, "The Last Interview," 87.
41. DS, 98.
42. *Ibid.*, 122, 111; ED, 131, 120.
43. *Ibid.*, 123, 124–125.
44. *Ibid.*, 130, 132–133, 134–135.
45. *Ibid.*, 147, 149.

Chapter 6   Dismantling Narrative Drive

1. Roberto Bolaño, *Los detectives salvajes* (Barcelona: Anagrama, 1998); *The Savage Detectives*, trans. Natasha Wimmer (New York: Farrar, Straus and Giroux, 2007). Hereafter cited in the text as LDS and SD. On *The Savage Detectives* and Bolaño's burgeoning reception in English, see Nicholas Birns and Juan E. De Castro, "Introduction: Fractured Masterpieces," and Patricia Espinosa, "Considerations on the Real and Reality in Juan Luis Martínez's *La nueva novela* and in Roberto Bolaño's *The Savage Detectives*," in *Roberto Bolaño as World Literature*; Martín Camps, "'Con la cabeza en el abismo': Roberto Bolaño's *The Savage Detectives* and *2666*. Literary Guerrilla, and the Maquiladora of Death," in *Roberto Bolaño, a Less Distant Star*; Raúl Rodríguez Freire, "Ulysses's Last Voyage: Bolaño and the Allegorical Figuration of Hell," in *Less Distant Star*; Sarah Pollack, "Latin America Translated (Again): Roberto Bolaño's *The Savage Detectives* in the United States"; Wilfrido H. Corral, "Bolaño en inglés: La 'nueva literatura' y el apostate," in *La experiencia del abismo*; Don Anderson, "Visceral Realism in Bolaño's Sea of Seeming," *The Australian* (January 10, 2009); Daniel Zalewski,

"Vagabonds: Robert Bolaño and his fractured Masterpiece, *The New Yorker* (March 26, 2007); "The Ten Best Books of 2007," *The New York Times. Sunday Book Review* (December 9, 2007); Ilan Stavans, "Willing Outcast: How a Chilean-Born Iconoclast Became a Great Mexican Novelist," *The Washington Post* (May 6, 2007); James Wood, "The Visceral Realist," *The New York Times* (April 15, 2007).

2. Bolaño, "Discurso de Caracas (aceptación del Rómulo Gallegos)," in *Bolaño salvaje*. On questions of narrative in and around *The Savage Detectives,* see Luis Bagué Quílez and Luis Martín-Estudillo, "Hacia la literatura híbrida: Roberto Bolaño y la narrativa española contemporánea," in *Bolaño salvaje*; Alexis Candia, "Espadas rotas: la 'épica sórdida' en *Los detectives salvajes,*" in *La experiencia del abismo*; Juan Carlos Galdo, "Roberto Bolaño y la configuración del canon narrativo hispanoamericano contemporáneo," in *La experiencia del abismo*; Julia Elena Rial, "Los no lugares y el desarraigo en *Los detectives salvajes* de Roberto Bolaño," in *La experiencia del abismo*; Diego Trellez Paz, "El lector como detective en *Los detectives salvajes* de Roberto Bolaño," in *Roberto Bolaño: Una literatura infinita* and in *Hispamérica* 34, no. 100 (April 2005): 141–151, and *La novela policial alternativa en Hispanoamérica: Detectives perdidos, asesinos ausentes y enigmas sin respuesta* (Austin: The University of Texas at Austin, 2008); Rodrigo Fresán, "El detective salvaje," in *Roberto Bolaño: Una literatura infinita*; Mario J. Valdés and Djelal Kadir, eds., *Literary Cultures of Latin America: A Comparative History*, 3 Vols (New York: Oxford University Press, 2004); and Roberto González Echevarría, *Myth and Archive: A Theory of Latin American Narrative* (Durham, NC: Duke University Press, 1999).

3. Baudelaire, OC 53–54 and 129–134; Howard, 58–59 and 151–157; OC 301–303; LV 32–34; KW 33–35. See Bolaño, "Literature + Illness = Illness," in *The Insufferable Gaucho*.

4. Freud, *The Interpretation of Dreams, Jokes and Their Relationship to the Unconscious, Beyond the Pleasure Principle*, and *The Ego and the Id* in *The Standard Edition of the Complete Psychological Works of Sigmund Freud*, vols. IV and V, VIII, XVIII, and XIX; Friedrich Nietzsche, *The Will to Power* (*Der Wille zur Macht*, 1901), trans. Walter Kaufman (New York: Random House, 1967); Jorge Luis Borges, "La trama," in *El hacedor, obras completas*, vol. 1, 180–181.

5. LDS, 151; SD, 154.

6. Baudelaire, OC 275–276; LV ix and KW 3–4. On poets and poetry in *The Savage Detectives*, see Roberto Bolaño: *Muchachos desnudos bajo el arcoiris de fuego (once poetas Latinoamericanos)* (Mexico City: Editorial Extemporáneos, 1979); "La nueva poesía latinoamericana. ¿Crisis o renacimiento?" *Revista Plural* (1977): 41–49; "El estridentismo," *Revista Plural* 61 (1976): 48–50; "Tres estridentistas," *Revista Plural* 62: 48–60; Roberto Bolaño, "Déjenlo todo, nuevamente. Primer

manifiesto del movimiento infrarealista," *Revista Infra 1. Revista menstrual del movimiento infrarealista* 1 (October/November 1977): 5–11; Claude Fell, "Errancia y escritura en *Los detectives salvajes*: viaje a los confines de la poesía," in *La experiencia del abismo*; Javier Campos, "El 'Primer Manifiesto do los Infrarealistas' de 1976: su contexto y su poética en *Los detectives salvajes*"; Andrea Cobas Carral and Verónica Garibotto, "Un epitafio en el desierto: poesía y revolución en *Los detectives salvajes*," in *Bolaño salvaje*; Monserrat Maldariaga Caro, *Bolaño infra: 1975–1977, los años que inspiraron* Los detectives salvajes (Santiago, Chile: RIL, 2010); Philip Derbyshire, "*Los detectives salvajes*: Line, Loss and the Political," *Journal of Latin American Cultural Studies* 18, no. 2–3 (2009): 167–176; Sam Anderson, "Prose Poem: Roberto Bolaño's Brilliant, Messy, Everything Novel," *New York Magazine*, November 7, 2008, http://nymag.com/arts/books/review/; Florence Olivier, "El honor y el deshonor de los poetas en la obra de Roberto Bolaño," in *Les Astres noirs*; and Manuel Jofré, "Bolaño: romantiqueando perros, como un detective salvaje," in *Territorios en fuga*.

7. Bakhtin, *The Dialogic Imagination* and *Speech Genres and Other Late Essays*.

8. LDS, 13; SD, 3.

9. LDS, 17; SD, 7.

10. SD, 7; LDS, 17.

11. SD, 5; LDS, 15.

12. Bolaño, "Fragmentos de un regreso al país natal," in *Entre paréntesis*; "Fragments of a Return to the Native Land," in *Between Parenthesis*; James Joyce, *Ulysses* (1922, New York: Vintage, 1990); Aimé Césaire, *Cahier d'un retour au pays natal* (1939, *Notebook of a Return to the Native Land*), bilingual edition, trans. Clayton Eshleman and Annette Smith, in *Aimé Césaire: The Collected Poetry* (Berkeley: University of California Press, 1983); Derek Walcott, *Omeros* (New York: Farrar, Strauss, and Giroux, 1992).

13. See Amy King, "Dilatory Description and the Pleasures of Accumulation: Toward a History of Novelistic Length" in *Narrative Middles*, ed. Caroline Levine and Mario Ortiz-Robles (Columbus: Ohio State University Press, 2010).

14. SD, 4.

15. *Ibid.*, 6.

16. SD, 6; LDS, 16.

17. Marjorie Perloff, *Unoriginal Genius: Poetry by Other Means in the New Century* (Chicago: University of Chicago, Press, 2010).

18. SD, 8; LDS, 17.

19. LDS, 21–22; SD, 12.

20. Baudelaire, "Le Vampire," *OC* 33–34. See Daniel Tiffany, *My Silver Planet: A Secret History of Poetry and Kitsch* (Baltimore: Johns Hopkins University Press, 2014).

21. Rimbaud, *Une Saison en Enfer* and *Illuminations, Oeuvres de Rimbaud,* 188–189.

22. Rimbaud, "Le Coeur volé" ("The Stolen Heart") and "Alchimie du verbe" ("Alchemy of the Word"), in *Oeuvres de Rimbaud; Une Saison en Enfer* and *Illuminations,* in *Complete Works, Selected Letters,* 80–83 and 192–201. See my "Narrative, History, Verse Undone: The Prose Poetry of Arthur Rimbaud," in *A Poverty of Objects*; Kristin Ross, *The Emergence of Social Space: Rimbaud and the Paris Commune* (Minneapolis: University of Minnesota Press, 1988, rpt. London and Brooklyn: Verso, 2008); Alain Badiou, *La Commune de Paris* (Paris: Conférences du Rouge-Gorge, 2003); Rancière, "Rimbaud: Voices and Bodies," in *The Flesh of Words: The Politics of Writing* (*La chair des mots: Politiques de l'écriture,* 1998), trans. Charlotte Mandell (Stanford, CA: Stanford University Press, 2004); and Kristin Ross, "Historicizing Untimeliness," in *Jacques Rancière: History, Politics, Aesthetics,* 15–29.

23. See Friedrich Schlegel, *"Lucinde" and the Fragments,* trans. Peter Firchow (Minneapolis: University of Minnesota Press, 1971), 174. See my *"Universalpoesie* as Fragment: Friedrich Schlegel and the Prose Poem," in *A Poverty of Objects,* 45; and Philippe Lacoue-Labarthe and Jean-Luc Nancy, *L'absolu littéraire* (Paris: Seuil, 1978), 141.

24. SD, 157–159.

25. SD, 588; LDS, 554; NC, 148–150; BNC, 128–130.

26. DS, 639–640; LDS, 602.

27. Baudelaire, OC 275–276; LV i-x and KW 3–4.

28. Efrén Rebolledo, "El vampiro" ("The Vampire"), *Caro victrix* (1916), in *Obras completas,* ed. Luis Mario Schneider (1968) and *Obras Reunidas* (Madrid: Consejo Nacional para la Cultura y las Artes, 2004). Edgar Allan Poe, "The Raven" and "The Bells," *Poems and Essays on Poetry.*

29. Paulo Freire, *Pedagogy of the Oppressed: 30th Anniversary Edition* (Bloomsbury, 2014); Jacques Rancière, *The Ignorant Schoolmaster: Five Lessons in Intellectual Emancipation* (*Le Maître ignorant: Cinq leçons sur l'émancipation intellectuelle,* 1987). trans. Kristin Ross (Stanford, CA: Stanford University Press, 1991).

30. SD, 632.

31. *Ibid.,* 3.

32. SD, 587–588; LDS, 553.

33. LDS, 374–377, 398–401, 553–554 and SD, 397–398, 421–424, 588.

34. DS, 587–588; LDS, 553.

35. José Lezama Lima, *Muerte de Narciso* (1937; Madrid: Alianza, 2007), also in *Poesía completa* (Mexico City: Sexto Piso, 2016); *Paradiso* (1966; Havana,

Cuba: Ediciones Era; Madrid: Catedra, 2006); *Paradiso*, trans. Gregory Rabassa (New York: Farrar, Straus & Giroux, 1974, 2000, Normal, IL: Dalkey Archive, 2000, 2005).

36. Borges, "La trama," *Obras Completas*, 180–181. See Christopher Domínguez Michael, "Roberto Bolaño y la literatura Mexicana," in *La experiencia del abismo*; Oswaldo Zavala, "*Los detectives salvajes* y el mescal 'Los suicidas,'" in *Roberto Bolaño: Ruptura y violencia*; and Ricardo Cuadros, "La escritura y la muerte en *Los detectives salvajes*," in *Roberto Bolaño: Una literatura infinita*.

37. *Ibid.*, 164. Parra, *Poemas y antipoemas; Obra gruesa*; and *Artefactos*, in *Obras completas; Antipoems: How to Look Better and Feel Great*.

38. SD, 4–5.

39. LDS, 557–558; SD, 591–593.

40. LDS, 18; SD, 7. See Bakhtin, "Discourse in the Novel," in *The Dialogic Imagination*, 289.

41. LDS, 562–563; SD, 597–598.

42. Bakhtin, *Speech Genres and Other Late Essays*; Volosinov, *Marxism and the Philosophy of Literature*.

43. See Andés Neuman, "La fuente y el desierto," in *Roberto Bolaño. Estrella cercana*; Debra A. Castillo and María-Socorro Tabuenca Córdoba, *Border Women: Writing from La Frontera* (Minneapolis: University of Minnesota Press, 2002).

44. David Foster Wallace, *Infinite Jest* (1996; Back Bay Books, 2006). See Hungerford's "On Not Reading DFW," in *Making Literature Now*.

45. SD, 19–21; LDS, 28.

46. *Ibid.*, 21, 50.

47. SD, 638–639; LDS, 601.

48. SD, 166.

49. *Ibid.*, 145.

50. *Ibid.*, 494.

51. *Ibid.*, 609–613.

52. SD, 646–648; LDS, 608–609. See also Walkowitz, *Born Translated*, 17–20; Fernando Saucedo Lastra, "Forma y función del discurso visual en la novela *Los detectives salvajes* de Roberto Bolaño," *Ciberletras* 22 (August 2009); Carlos J. Labbé, "Cuatro mexicanos velando un cadáver. Violencia y silencio en *Los detectives salvajes* de Roberto Bolaño," *Taller de Letras* 32 (2003); Cristián Gómez, "Qué hay detrás de la ventana? (Roberto Bolaño y el lugar de la literatura)," Ricardo Martínez, "Más allá de la última ventana. Los 'marcos' de *Los detectives salvajes* desde la poética cognitiva," and Grinor Rojo, "Sobre *Los detectives salvajes*," in *Territorios en fuga*; Carlos Rincón, "Las imágines en el texto: Entre García Márquez y Roberto Bolaño, de la alegoría del tiempo al universo de las imágines," *Revista de Crítica Literaria Latinoamericana* 28, no. 56 (2002): 19–37.

53. ED, 143, 141; DS, 135, 132. Jacques Rancière, *Hatred of Democracy* (*La Haine de la démocratie*, 2005), trans. Steve Corcoran (London and New York: Verso, 2006); Ben Lerner, *The Hatred of Poetry* (New York: Farrar, Straus, Giroux, 2016).

Chapter 7   Making Visible the "Non-Power" of Poetry

1. Bolaño and Álvarez, "Positions Are Positions and Sex Is Sex," in *The Last Interview*, 69–91, 79; Roberto Bolaño, *Amuleto* (Barcelona: Anagrama, 1999); *Amulet*, trans. Chris Andrews (New York: New Directions, 2007), hereafter cited in the text as AMs and AM.

2. Christopher Domínguez Michael, "El arcón de Roberto Bolaño; *Prólogo*," in Roberto Bolaño, *El espíritu de la ciencia-ficción* (Barcelona: Alfaguara, 2016; New York: Vintage Español, 2017), 9–16; *The Spirit of Science Fiction*, trans. Natasha Wimmer (New York: New Directions, 2019).

3. See Jaime Concha, "Amuleto," in *Roberto Bolaño: La experiencia del abismo*; Myrna Solotorevsky, "*Amuleto* de Roberto Bolaño: expansión de un hipotexto," in *Roberto Bolaño: Ruptura y violencia en la literatura finisecular*; Celina Manzoni, "Recorridos urbanos, fantasmagoria y espejismo en *Amuleto*," in *Roberto Bolaño: Una literatura infinita,* and "Reescritura como desplazamiento y anagnórisis en *Amuleto*," in *Roberto Bolaño: La escritura como tauromaquia*; and Aguilar Gonzalo, "Los amuletos salvajes de un novelista," *Suplemento Cultura y Nación* (Buenos Aires, 2001).

4. See Adriana Castillo-Berchenko, "Roberto Bolaño y la poesía del héroe desolado," *La experiencia del abismo*.

5. See Juan Antonio Sánchez Fernández, "Bolaño y Tlatelolco," *Études Romanes de BRNO* 33, no. 2, (2012): 133–143; and Lepage, "Littérature et Dictature: lecture croisée de trois romans de Roberto Bolañó (*Estrella distante – Amuleto – Nocturno de Chile*)," in *Les Astres noirs,* 67–90.

6. AM, 17, 20.

7. AM, 1, 22; AMs 11, 27. See Alejandro Palma Castro, "Un poeta latinoamericano en el DF," *Roberto Bolaño: Ruptura y violencia en la literatura finisecular;* Jaime Blume, "Roberta Bolaño poeta," *Territorios en fuga,* 166; Bolaño, *Reinventar el amor* (México: Taller Martín Pescador, 1976); Bolaño, *Muchachos desnudos bajo el arcoiris de fuego.* México D.F.: *Extemporáneos* (1979).

8. AM, 13–14; 4–5. See Raymond Williams' "Hegemony," "Traditions, Institutions, and Formations" and "Dominant, Residual, and Emergent," in *Marxism and Literature*, 108–114, 115–120, and 121–128; Judith Butler, *Notes Toward a Performative Theory of Assembly* (Cambridge, MA: Harvard University Press, 2015), *Giving an Account of Oneself* (New York: Fordham

University Press, 2005), and *The Psychic Life of Power: Theories in Subjection* (Palo Alto, CA: Stanford University Press, 1997).

9. AM, 151; AMs, 129; AM, 12–13; 3–4.
10. AM, 3–4.
11. AM, 15–16; AMs, 22–23.
12. AM 1, 21, 25–27; AMs, 11, 27, 3–32.
13. AM, 5.
14. Appearing three years after *Amuleto* and two years after *Nocturno de Chile*, a year before Bolaño's death in 2003, Bolaño's late novella *Una novelita lumpen* (Barcelona: Anagrama, 2002; *A Little Lumpen Novelita*, trans. Natasha Wimmer [New York: New Directions, 2014]) is narrated in the first-person, like the former, by a central female character, in this case the sympathetically drawn Italian high school dropout and salon worker Bianca. Set in Rome in the context of "economic conditions … deteriorating … in Europe or Italy" (36), with a pervasive emphasis on popular culture and a conspicuous absence of Bolaño's usual allusions to poets and poetry, to Chile and Mexico, it suggests the full extent to which Bolaño understands himself to be a writer of both Europe and the Americas. Describing herself at the time of the novella's retrospective narration as a "mother and a married woman" who rarely read but studied "video cases as if they were books," the TV-obsessed Bianca is far removed, both geographically and in her relation to reading, from *Amulet*'s Uruguayan-Mexican "mother of all poets," yet as each tells her own story a common struggle emerges of both class and gender, a struggle against poverty and for self-determination. Through Bianca's first-person narrative, the novella insistently attests to literature's subordination at the turn of the millennium to video stores and TV game shows, celebrity culture and mass media.
15. *Ibid.*, 9–10.
16. *Ibid.*, 9–10.
17. AM, 10; Baudelaire, OC 277; LV 1 and KW 5.
18. See Rory O'Bryen, "Mourning, Melancholia, and Political Transition in *Amuleto* and *Nocturno de Chile* by Roberto Bolaño," *Bulletin of Latin American Research* 30, no. 4 (2011): 473–487.
19. Raúl Rodríguez Freire, "La traición de la izquierda en *Amuleto* de Bolaño," *Guaraguao* 15, no. 37 (2011): 33–45; Adrianna Castillo de Berchenko, "Una novela en busca de su género: *Amuleto* de Roberto Bolaño," in *Roberto Bolaño: Una literatura infinita*. See also Bruno Bosteels, "The Dialectic of the Dialectical and the Nondialectical," in *Badiou and Politics* (Durham, NC: Duke University Press, 2011), 331–336.
20. AM, 32.
21. *Ibid.*, 59.

22. AM, 67; AMs, 61. The second chapter describes the suicide of a professor of classics within the "intricate, hierarchical world of the academy" ("el intricado mundo de las jerarquías universitarias"); the sixth chapter alludes to the "Nerudian apocalypse" ("apocalípsis nerudiano"); Lacouture frequently voices a concern with going mad (AM, 23–24; AMs, 27–29).

23. AMS, 37, 39, 55–58; AM, 35, 38, 60–65, 57. William Carlos Williams, "Asphodel, That Greeny Flower," *The Collected Poems of William Carlos Williams, vol. 2*; Pound, "A Retrospect," in *Literary Essays of Ezra Pound*, 3; *ABC of Reading*, 29, 44; *Literary Essays*, 91; and *Selected Prose, 1909–1965* (New York: New Directions, 1973), 37.

24. AM, 44; AMs, 43.

25. AMs, 55, 57–58; AM, 59, 62.

26. AM, 68; AMs, 62.

27. AM, 80, 86.

28. *Ibid.*, 95, 103.

29. AM, 105, 40, 108, 113; AMs, 90, 41, 92, 97.

30. AMs, 124; AM, 146, 120, 151–154. See Eric Mécvhoulan, "Sophisticated Continuities and Historical Discontinuities, Or, Why Not Protagoras?" and Gabriel Rockhill, "The Politics of Aesthetics: Political History and the Hermeneutics of Art," in *Jacques Rancière: History, Politics, Aesthetics*; Ernesto Laclau, "The Time is Out of Joint," in *Emancipation(s)* (London and New York: Verso, 1996).

31. AMs, 131–135; AM, 156–161. See Agamben, "What Is the Contemporary?" in *What Is an Apparatus?*; Bakhtin, *Speech Genres and Other Late Essays*.

32. AM, 397, 156–161; AMs, 131–135. Benjamin, "On the Concept of History," in *Selected Writings*, vol. 4, 397.

33. AMs, 154, 131–135; AM, 172–175, 156–161. See María Martha Gigena, "La negra boca de un florero: Metáfora y memoria en *Amuleto*," in *La fugitiva contemporaneidad: Narrativa latinoamericana (1990–2000)*, ed. Celina Manzoni (Buenos Aires: Corregidor, 2003).

34. See Moretti, "The Slaughterhouse of Literature," *Distant Reading;* and Bolaño, "Encuentro con Enrique Lihn," in *Cuentos*, 408; "Meeting with Enrique Lihn," in *The Return*, 192; Bloch, *Traces, The Principle of Hope, The Spirit of Utopia*. Arguably the key that more than any other unlocks Bolaño's entire *oeuvre*, the final line of the final poem of *Les Fleurs du Mal*, "Le Voyage" (*OC* 134)—the poem with which Baudelaire literally closes the book on his own verse poetry before turning to the *Petits poèmes en prose* of *Le Spleen de Paris*—resonates throughout Bolaño's work in multiple, pivotal ways, among others as 1) the sole epigraph at the beginning of *2666*, 2) the source of the title of his collected poems, *The Unknown University*, and 3) the centerpiece of his affirmation of the enduring legacy of Baudelaire and mid-

nineteenth-century French poetry and its continuing impact—both in general and on his work in particular—in Bolaño's indispensable late essay in *The Insufferable Gaucho,* "Literature + Illness = Illness."

Chapter 8 Poetry, Politics, Critique

1. Roberto Bolaño, *Nocturno de Chile* (Barcelona: Anagrama, 2000); *By Night in Chile,* trans. Chris Andrews (New York: New Directions, 2003), hereafter cited in the text as NC and BNC; Bolaño, *Amuleto,* 11, 27; *Amulet,* 1, 22; Bolaño and Boullosa, "Reading Is Always More Important than Writing."
2. Leo Tolstoy, *The Death of Ivan Ilyich* (1886), trans. Richard Pevear and Larissa Volokhonsky (New York: Vintage, 2012); Rancière, "On the Battlefield: Tolstoy, Literature, History," in *The Politics of Literature*; Borges, "The Aleph," *The Aleph and Other Stories*; Poe, "How to Write a Blackwood Article," in *Complete Tales and Poems.*
3. BNC, 1; NC, 11.
4. NC, 15; BNC, 4.
5. BNC, 56, 60, 118; NC, 70, 74, 147.
6. BNC, 22.
7. NC, 23–24; BNC, 13–14.269 Baudelaire, OC 277; LV 1 and KW 5; J.K. Huysman, *Là-bas* (1891); *The Damned,* trans. Teresa Hale (London and New York: Penguin, 2002). See Paula Aguilar, "Pobre memoria la mía. Literatura y melancolía en el contexto de la postdictadura chilena," in *Bolaño salvaje*; Antonio Gómez, "Roberto Bolaño: literatura y política después del fin del exilio," in *Escribir el espacio ausente: Exilio y cultura nacional en Díaz, Wajsman y Bolaño* (Providencia, Santiago: Editorial Cuarto Propio, 2013); Patrick Dove, "The Nights of the Senses: Literary (Dis)orders in *Nocturno de Chile,*" *Journal of Latin American Cultural Studies* 18 (2009; Amy K. Kaminsky, *After Exile. Writing the Latin American Diaspora* (Minneapolis: University of Minnesota Press, 1999); Stéphanie Decante-Araya, "Mémoire et mélancolie dans *Nocturno de Chile*: éléments pour une poétique du fragmentaire," in *Les Astres noirs*; Eugenia Brito, *Campos minados (literatura post-golpe en Chile)* (Santiago, Chile: Editorial Cuarto Propio, 1990).
8. Ezra Pound, *Hugh Selwyn Mauberley: Contacts and Life* (London: The Ovid Press, 1920), in *Ezra Pound, New Selected Poems and Translations,* ed. Richard Sieburth (New York: New Directions, 1957), 111–123. See Cristián Gómez Olivares, "Bolaño, su poesía y los derechos humanos (el poeta y su significado para la poesía chilena)," in *Roberto Bolaño: Ruptura y violencia en la literatura finisecular*; Caroline Lepage, "Littérature et dictature: lecture croisée de trois romans de Roberto Bolaño" in *Les Astres noirs,* 67–90.

9. Bolaño, *NC*, 35, 34–37, 140; *BNC*, 22, 21–25, 120. See Adolfo De Nordenflycht, "La paciencia del Dios de los críticos. Alegorías de la crítica en *Nocturno de Chile*," in *La experiencia del abismo*; Milagros Ezquerro, "Sebastián Urrutia Lacroix alias H. Ibacache," in *Les Astres noirs*; María José Bruña Bragado, "Roberto Bolaño: Formas del mal y posiciones intelectuales," in *Ruptura y violencia*; Gutiérrez Giraldo and Rafael Eduardo, "De la literatura como un oficio peligroso: Crítica y ficción en la obra de Roberto Bolaño" (Pontifícia Universidade Católica de Rio de Janeiro, 2010), hwww2.dbd.puc-; Ignacio López-Vicuña, "The Violence of Writing: Literature and Discontent in Roberto Bolaño's 'Chilean' Novels," *Journal of Latin American Cultural Studies* 18, no. 2 (2009): 155–166; Karim Benmiloud, "Figures de la mélancolie dans *Nocturno de Chile*" and Milagros Ezquerro, "Sebastián Urrutia Lacroix alias H. Ibacache," in *Les Astres noirs*.

10. BNC, 29.

11. *Ibid.*, 42–43.

12. *Ibid.*, 48, 51–53.

13. *Ibid.*, 55–56; NC, 69–70.

14. NC, 72–74; BNC, 56–60.

15. BNC, 66, 68. See Thomas O. Beebee, "'More Culture': The Rules of Art in Roberto Bolaño's *By Night in Chile*," in *Roberto Bolaño as World Literature*; and Ignacio López-Vicuña, "Malestar en la literatura: Escritura y barbarie en *Estrella distante* y *Nocturno de Chile*," *Revista Chilena de Literatura* 75 (2009).

16. BNC, 73, 76, 69.

17. *Ibid.*, 81, 83.

18. BNC, 84–85; NC, 101. See O'Bryen, "Mourning, Melancholia, and Political Transition in *Amuleto* and *Nocturno de Chile* by Roberto Bolaño," *Bulletin of Latin American Research*; Pablo Berchenko, "El referente histórico chileno en *Nocturno de Chile* de Roberto Bolaño," in *La memoria de la dictadura: Nocturno de Chile, Roberto Bolaño; Interrupciones* 2, Juan Gelman, (Paris: Ellipses, 2006); Fernando Moreno, "La memoria de la dictadura. *Nocturno de Chile*," in *Roberto Bolaño; Interrupciones 2*, ed. Juan Gelman (Paris: Ellipses, 2006); Cecilia Manzoni, ed., "Roberto Bolaño, entre la historia y la melancholia," in *Roberto Bolaño: La escritura como tauromaquia*; Idelber Avelar, *Alegorías de la derrota: La ficción postdictatorial y el trabajo de duelo* (Santiago, Chile: Cuarto propio, 2000).

19. BNC, 87, 95.

20. BNC, 99–100; NC, 115–118.

21. BNC, 101–105; NC, 120–123.

22. See Ximena Briceño and Héctor Hoyos. "'Así se hace la literatura': Historia literaria y políticas del olvido en *Nocturno de Chile* y *Soldados de Salamina*."

Revista iberoamericana 76, no. 232–233 (2010): 601–620; Sebastian Faber, "Zapatero, a tus zapatos: La tarea del crítico en un mundo globalizado," in *América Latina en la "literatura mundial,"* in *Instituto Internacional de Literatura Iberoamericana*, ed., Ignacio M. Sánchez-Prado (Pittsburgh: 2006).

23. BNC, 105.

24. *Ibid.*, 111, 114.

25. *Ibid.*, 112, 121–123.

26. *Ibid.*, 125, 127. See Hannah Arendt, *Eichmann in Jerusalem: A Report on the Banality of Evil* (New York: Penguin Classics, 2006); Emil Latin Volek, ed., *America Writes Back: Postmodernity in the Periphery* (New York: Routledge, 2002); Nelly Richard and Alberto Moreiras, *Pensar en/laPostdictadura* (Santiago, Chile: Cuarto Propio, 2001); Nelly Richard, ed., *Políticas y Estéticas de la Memoria* (Santiago, Cuarto Propio, 2000).

27. See Jameson, *The Political Unconscious*, ix, 62; Alan Pauls, "La solución Bolaño," in *Bolaño salvaje*; Idelber Avelar, *The Untimely Present: Postdictatorial Latin American Fiction and the Task of Mourning* (Durham, NC: Duke University Press, 1999); and Paula Moya, *The Social Imperative: Race, Close Reading, and Contemporary Literary Criticism* (Stanford, CA: Stanford University Press, 2016).

28. BNC, 128–130; NC, 148–150.

29. See Juan E. De Castro, "Politics and Ethics in Latin America: On Roberto Bolaño," Finchelstein, "On Fascism, History, and Evil in Roberto Bolaño," and Zavala, "The Repoliticization of the Latin American Shore," in *Roberto Bolaño as World Literature*. See also Rancière, "The Poets' Lesson" and "The Community of Equals" (in "Reason Between Equals") and "The Society of Contempt," in *The Ignorant Schoolmaster*; and "The Community of Equals" and "Democracy Corrected," in *On the Shores of Politics* (*Aux bords du politique*, 1990), trans. Liz Heron (London: Verso, 1995/2007).

Chapter 9   Literary Taxonomies after the Wall

1. Roberto Bolaño, *Los sinsabores del verdadero policía* (Barcelona: Anagrama, 2011); *Woes of the True Policeman*, trans. Natasha Wimmer (New York: Farrar, Straus and Giroux, 2012).

2. See Ignacio Echevarría, "'Bolaño. Penúltimos sinsabores de un novelista convertido en leyenda,'" *El cultural. Libros* (January 21, 2011) and "Bolaño internacional: Algunas reflexiones en torno al éxito internacional de Roberto Bolaño," *Estudios públicos* 130 (Fall 2013): 175–202; and Antonio Gómez, "El boom de Roberto Bolaño: Literatura mundial en un español nuevo," *Insula* 787 (July 2012): 34–36.

3. See my "Philosophy, Poetry, Parataxis," in *Philosophy as a Literary Art: Making Things Up*, ed. Costica Bradatan (New York and London: Routledge, 2014), 89–102; Rancière, "Sentence, Image, History" and "The Sentence-Image and the Great Parataxis," in *The Future of the Image*.

4. See Thomas E. Yingling, "The Homosexual Lyric," in *The Lyric Theory Reader*, ed. Virginia Jackson and Yopie Prins (Baltimore and London: Johns Hopkins University Press, 2014); Lauren Berlant and Lee Edelman, *Sex, or the Unbearable* (Durham, NC: Duke University Press, 2013); Lee Edelman, *Homographesis: Essays in Gay Literary and Cultural Theory* (New York: Routledge, 1994); Antony Easthope, *Poetry as Discourse* (London: Methuen, 1983).

5. Roberto Bolaño, *Consejos de un discípulo de Morrison a un fanático de Joyce*.

6. See my "Genre," in *Literature Now: Key Terms and Methods for Literary History*, ed. Sascha Bru, Ben De Bruyn, and Michel Delville (Edinburgh: Edinburgh University Press, 2015), 252–264. See also *Remapping Genre*, ed. Wai Chee Dimock and Bruce Robbins, special issue, *PMLA* 122, no. 5 (2007); Stephen Heath. "The Politics of Genre," in *Debating World Literature*, ed. Christopher Prendergast (London: Verso, 2004); Hayden White. "Anomalies of Genres: The Utility of Theory and History for the Study of Literary Genres," in *Theorizing Genres 2*, special issue, *New Literary History* 34, no. 3 (2003): 597–615.

7. TP, 3–5; SVP, 21–24.

8. *Ibid.* See Judith Butler, "Gender Politics and the Right to Appear" and "Bodily Vulnerability, Coalitional Politics," in *Notes Toward a Performative Theory of Assembly*; Bakhtin, *Speech Genres and Other Late Essays*; Volosinov, *Marxism and the Philosophy of Literature*.

9. See Judith Butler, *"Competing Universalities"* and *"Restaging the Universal: Hegemony and the Limits of Formalism,"* in *Contingency, Hegemony, Universality: Contemporary Dialogues on the Left*, ed. Judith Butler, Ernesto Laclau and Slavoj Žižek (London and New York: Verso, 2000).

10. TP, 18.

11. *Ibid.*, 46; 24. See David Harvey, *A Brief History of Neoliberalism* (Oxford: Oxford University Press, 2005); Michael Hardt and Antonio Negri, *Empire* (Cambridge, MA: Harvard University Press, 2000); Hans Magnus Enzensberger, *Civil Wars: From L.A. to Bosnia* (New York: The New Press, 1995); Francis Fukayama, *The End of History and the Last Man* (New York: The Free Press, 1992).

12. TP, 34–35; SVP, 61.

13. 2666, 209; 2666s, 268.

14. TP, 85.

15. *Ibid.*, 88.2

16. SVP, 131–134; TP, 89–91.
17. Sianne Ngai, *Our Aesthetic Categories: Zany, Cute, Interesting* (Cambridge, MA: Harvard University Press, 2012).
18. TP, 94.
19. *Ibid.*
20. TP, 102; SVP, 146. Breton, *Manifestoes of Surrealism.*
21. TP, 35; SVP, 61.
22. TP, 132; SVP, 185. Rimbaud, "Le Coeur volé" ("The Stolen Heart"), *Complete Works,* 80–83.
23. See Hungerford, *Making Literature Now*; Caroline Levine, *Forms: Whole, Rhythm, Hierarchy, Network* (Princeton, NJ: Princeton University Press, 2015). Departing from Bolaño's characteristic deployment of the novel as fictive literary history by other means, *A Little Lumpen Novelita* prefaces its sixteen chapters, each an average length between prose poem and short story, with an epigraph from Antonin Artaud that signals literature's devalued currency in contemporary culture: "All writing is garbage / . . . / All writers are pigs. Especially writers today" ("Toda escritura es una marranada. / . . . / Todos los escritores son unos cerdos. Especialmente los de ahora"). Reclaiming her dignity by leaving the house of the blind former bodybuilder and star of gladiator movies who has been paying her for sex (and keeps his money in the Seychelles), a house in which he keeps next to his in-house gym a "bookless library," Bianca returns in the end to her own low-rent apartment filled with "the echoes of thousands of hours of television" (95, 91). Recalling the letters to North American writers of seventeen-year-old "Jan Schrella" ("alias Roberto Bolaño") in *The Spirit of Science Fiction*—each of which resembles in its purpose and prose-poem length Baudelaire's sales-pitch as preface to Arsène Houssaye—the concluding paragraph's description of Bianca's TV watching conjoins the genre Bolaño would soon largely abandon with the one that would prove to be his signature investment, the detective genre: "from the screen of our TV set . . . killers and victims . . . a storm not located in the skies of Rome, but in the European night or the space between planets . . . another world . . not even the satellites in orbit around the Earth could capture . . ." (109).
24. Umberto Eco, *The Name of the Rose*, trans. Richard Dixon (New York: Harcourt Brace Jovanovich, 1980, 1983, 2014).
25. SVP, 257–258; TP, 195–196.
26. See Wendy Brown, "The Vanquishing of *Homo Politicus* by *Homo Oeconomicus*," *Undoing the Demos*, 107–111; Judith Butler, "Subjects of Sex/ Gender/Desire," in *Gender Trouble* (New York: Routledge, 1990).
27. Bolaño and Boullosa, "Reading Is Always More Important than Writing" in *The Last Interview*, 63, 53–68. See Michael D. Snediker, *Queer Optimism:*

Lyric Personhood and Other Felicitous Persuasions (Minneapolis: University of Minnesota Press, 2009).

28. SVP, 310–311; TP, 241–242.
29. TP, 242; SVP, 312. Édouard Glissant, *Poetics of Relation* (*Poétique de la relation,* 1990), trans. Betsy Wing (Ann Arbor: University of Michigan Press, 1997).
30. TP, 248.
31. *Ibid.*, 86, 237, 243; *SVP*, 127–128, 305, 313. See also Bolaño, "Fragmentos de un regreso al país natal," in *Entre paréntesis,* 59–70; "Fragments of a Return to the Native Land," in *Between Parentheses,* 61–74; and Sartre, "Black Orpheus," in *"What Is Literature?"* 289–322.
32. TP, 196; SVP, 259. See Sara Ahmed, *Queer Phenomenology: Orientations, Objects, Others* (Durham, NC: Duke University Press, 2006); and Moretti, "Style, Inc.: Reflections on 7,000 Titles (British Novels, 1740–1850)," in *Distant Reading,* 179–210: "'Literature is the fragments of fragments', wrote Goethe in *Wilhelm Meister's Years of Wandering* ... the 'fossils' of literary evolution are often not lost, but carefully preserved in some great library ... we have never really tried to read the entire volume of the literary past. Studying titles is a small step in that direction" (210).

Chapter 10   "What a Relief to Give Up Literature"

1. T. S. Eliot, "Burt Norton," *Four Quartets,* in *The Complete Poems and Plays of T.S. Eliot* (New York: Harcourt Brace, 1969).
2. Bolaño, *Los detectives salvajes,* 17; *The Savage Detectives,* 8. Harold Bloom, *The Anxiety of Influence: A Theory of Poetry. Second Edition* (Oxford: Oxford University Press, 1997).
3. 2666, 74.
4. *Ibid.*, 80. Baudelaire, "Assommons les pauvres!" OC 357–359; "Beat Up the Poor," LV 101–103; "Knock Down the Poor!" KW 94–95.
5. See Spivak, *Death of a Discipline,* 73; Mariano Siskind, *Cosmopolitan Desires: Global Modernity and World Literature in Latin America* (Chicago: Northwestern University Press, 2014); Rebecca L. Walkowitz, *Cosmopolitan Style: Modernism beyond the Nation* (New York: Columbia University Press, 2006).
6. 2666, 26, 37.
7. Bolaño calls Kafka, in "Literature + Illness = Illness," not just "the greatest German writer," but "the twentieth century's greatest writer" (*The Insufferable Gaucho,* 144).

8. *2666*, 117–118. See Wolfgang Iser's focus on what he calls "Leerstellen" in *Der Akt des Lesens* (Munich: Wilhelm Fink, 1976); *The Act of Reading* (London: Routledge and Kegan Paul, 1978).

9. See Manuel Asensi Pérez, "Atreverse a mirar por el agujero: Lo real y lo político en *2666* de Roberto Bolaño," in *Roberto Bolaño: Ruptura y violencia en la literatura finisecular.*

10. 2666, 206; 2666s, 264–265.

11. 2666s, 265; 2666, 207.

12. 2666, 209.

13. Bolaño, 2666s, 268; 2666, 209; Bolaño, *Nocturno de Chile*, 34, 140; *By Night in Chile*, 22, 120; Baudelaire, OC 277; LV 1 and KW 5.

14. 2666, 212.

15. *Ibid.*, 219.

16. *2666s*, 288–289; 2666, 226.

17. See Slavoj Žižek, *Welcome to the Desert of the Real* (New York and London: Verso Books, 2002).

18. Baudelaire, OC 275–276; LV i–x and KW 3–4.

19. Bakhtin, *The Dialogic Imagination* and *Speech Genres and Other Late Essays.*

20. 2666, 266–267; 2666s, 338–339.

21. 2666, 314–315.

22. *Ibid.*, 287–291.

23. *Ibid.*, 348.

24. Poe, "The Poetic Principle," *Poems and Essays on Poetry*, 88–95, 92; "The Philosophy of Composition," *Poems and Essays on Poetry*, 138–150.

25. 2666s, 446; 2666, 355.

26. 2666s, 447; 2666, 356.

27. See Jean Franco, "Apocalypse Now," in *Cruel Modernity*; and "Questions for Bolaño"; Sergio González, *The Feminicide Machine*, trans. Michael Parker-Stainback (Boston: MIT Press, 2012); Jorge Volpi, "Los crímenes de Santa Teresa y las trompetas de Jericó. Bolaño y la escritura fronteriza," in *Bolaño salvaje*; Grant Farred, "The Impossible Closing: Death, Neoliberalism, and the Postcolonial in Bolaño's *2666, Modern Fiction Studies* (Winter 2010): 689–670; Marcela Valdes, "Alone among the Ghosts: Roberto Bolaño's *2666*," *Nation*, December 8, 2008; Carlos Burgos Jara, "Los crímenes de Santa Teresa: Estado, globalización y mafia en *2666*," in *Ruptura y violencia*; Paz Balmaceda García-Huidobro, "La violencia del norte: dos aproximaciones a las muertas sin fin," in *Ruptura y violencia*; Camps, "'Con la cabeza en el abismo': Roberto Bolaño's *The Savage Detectives* and *2666*. Literary Guerrilla, and the Maquiladora of Death," in *Less Distant Star*; and Claudio Lomnitz, *Death and the Idea of Mexico* (Brooklyn: Zone Books, 2005).

28. See Bakhtin, *The Dialogic Imagination* and *Speech Genres and Other Late Essays;* Volosinov, *Marxism and the Philosophy of Language.*

29. See Sartre, *Search for a Method,* 30; "Question de Méthode," *Critique de la raison dialectique,* vol. 129.

30. See Debarati Sanyal, *The Violence of Modernity: Baudelaire, Irony, and the Politics of Form* (Baltimore: Johns Hopkins University Press, 2006).

31. *2666,* 458, 576, 488, 499.

32. *2666s,* 868–869; *2666,* 694–696.

33. *2666s,* 891; *2666,* 713.

34. See Bolaño, "The Last Interview," in *The Last Interview,* 118.

35. *2666,* 785, 787; *2666s,* 984, 986. See Moretti, "The Slaughterhouse of Literature," in *Distant Reading*: "The majority of books disappear forever . . .. I don't really believe that professors can change the canon . . .. Reducing the unreads from 99.5 per cent to 99.0 percent is no change at all. / My model of canon formation is based on novels for the simple reason that they have been the most widespread literary form of the past two or three centuries and are therefore crucial to any social account of literature (which is the point of the canon controversy, or should be)" (66–68).

36. *Ibid.,* 850. See Friedrich Kittler, *Gramophone, Film, Typewriter* (*Grammophon Film Typewriter,* 1986), trans. Geoffrey Winthrop-Young and Michael Wutz (Stanford, CA: Stanford University Press, 1999).

37. *2666,* 861, 864, 868.

38. Bolaño and Maristain, "The Last Interview," 117.

39. *2666,* 891–892; *2666s,* 1116–1118.

40. TP, 88, SVP, 131; Wallace Stevens, "The Emperor of Ice-Cream," in *The Collected Poems* (New York: Alfred A. Knopf, 1954), 64; Baudelaire, "Perte d'aurole," OC 352; LV 94; KW 88. See among others "La Soupe et les nuages," "Les Bons Chiens," OC 350 and 360–363; "The Soup and the Clouds," "The Faithful Dog," LV 91 and 104–107; "Soup and Clouds," "Good Dogs," KW 88 and 96–99; *2666,* 863; *2666s,* 1081.

41. Baudelaire, "Un plaisant," OC 279; "A Wag," LV 4; "A Joker," KW 8.

Conclusion

1. Benjamin, "On the Concept of History," in *Selected Writings,* vol. 4, 389. Bolaño, *Amuleto,* 135; *Amulet,* 161. On the novel's literary-historical hegemony, see Moretti, "Figure 9: British novelistic genres, 1740–1900" and "A Note on the Taxonomy of Forms," in *Graphs, Maps, Trees,* 19 and 31–33; and Mads Rosendahl Thomsen, "Franco Moretti and the Global Wave of the Novel," in Theo D'haen, David Damrosch, and Djelal Kadir, eds., *The Routledge Companion to World Literature* (New York: Routledge, 2012).

2. Poe, "The Man of the Crowd," *Complete Tales and Poems*, 475, 481. Baudelaire, "Les Foules," OC 291–292. Benjamin, "The Paris of the Second Empire in Baudelaire," in *Selected Writings*, vol. 4, 27.

3. See Moretti, *Distant Reading*; Stephen Best and Sharon Marcus, "Surface Reading: An Introduction," *Representations* 108, no. 1 (Fall 2009); Virginia Jackson, *Dickinson's Misery: A Theory of Lyric Reading* (Princeton, NJ: Princeton University Press, 2005); Rita Felski, *The Limits of Critique* (Chicago, University of Chicago Press, 2015), 1–21; *The Uses of Literature* (Oxford: Blackwell, 2008); and Elizabeth Anker and Rita Felski, eds., *Critique and Postcritique* (Durham, NC: Duke University Press, 2017).

4. N. Katherine Hayles, "Combining Close Reading and Distant Reading: Jonathan Safran Foer's Tree of Codes and the Aesthetic of Bookishness," *PMLA* 128, no. 1 (2013): 226–231; Walkowitz, *Born Translated*.

5. Bolaño, *2666*, 815; *2666*, 653.

6. Benjamin, "On the Concept of History," in *Selected Writings*, vol. 4, 391; Bolaño and Boullosa, "Reading Is Always More Important than Writing," in *The Last Interview*.

7. Erich Auerbach, *Mimesis: The Representation of Reality in Western Literature*, trans. Willard R. Task (Princeton, NJ: Princeton University Press, 2013); Benjamin, "Unpacking My Library," in *Selected Writings*, vol. 2; Bolaño, "Un paseo por la literatura" / "A Stroll through Literature," in *Tres*.

8. Bolaño, *2666*s, 1118; *2666*, 892. On speculation that Auerbach and Benjamin met in Berlin in the 1920s, see Emily Apter, "Global *Translatio*," "Global *Translatio*: The 'Invention' of Comparative Literature, Istanbul, 1933," in *The Translation Zone: A New Comparative Literature* (Princeton, NJ: Princeton University Press, 2006), 261 n.36. See also Andrew Parker, "Impossible Speech Acts: Jacques Rancière's Erich Auerbach," in *Jacques Rancière: History, Politics, Aesthetics*; Alex Woloch, "Form and Representation in Auerbach's *Mimesis*," *Affirmations of the Modern* 2, no. 1 (2014); and James I. Porter, ed. *Time, History and Literature: Selected Essays of Erich Auerbach*, trans. Jane O. Newman (Princeton, NJ: Princeton University Press, 2014).

9. Nietzsche, *On the Uses and Disadvantages of History for Life*, in *Untimely Meditations*. See Lisa Gitelman, *Always Already New: Media, History, and the Data of Culture* (Cambridge, MA: MIT Press, 2006); Peter Boxall, *Twenty-First Century Fiction and The Value of the Novel* (Cambridge: Cambridge University Press, 2015).

10. Hoyos, *Beyond Bolaño*, 201; and Moretti, *The Bourgeois*.

11. Benjamin, "Commentary on Poems by Brecht," in *Selected Writings*, 539. On poetry's "untimely," redemptive importance, see Agamben, "What Is the Contemporary?" in *What Is an Apparatus?*

12. Bolaño, "Literature + Illness = Illness," *The Insufferable Gaucho,* 128. See Toril Moi, "'Nothing Is Hidden': From Confusion to Clarity: or, Wittgenstein on Critique and Postcritique," in *Critique and Postcritique.*

13. Bolaño, *Los detectives salvajes,* 484–500; *The Savage Detectives,* 513–530.

14. See Rancière, "Dialectical Montage, Symbolic Montage," in *The Future of the Image*; Bosteels's "On the Subject of the Dialectic," in *Marx and Freud in Latin America*; "Introduction: Elements of Dialectical Materialism," "Logics of Change," and "Conclusion: The Speculative Left," in *Badiou and Politics*; Gabriel Rockhill, "For a Radical Historicist Analytic of Aesthetic and Political Practices" *Radical History and the Politics of Art* (New York: Columbia University Press, 2014).

15. See Moretti, "Evolution, World-Systems, *Weltliteratur*," in *Distant Reading*; Héctor Hoyos and Librandi Rocha, eds. "Theories of the Contemporary in South America." Dossier. *Revista de Estudios Hispánicos* 48, no. 1 (March 2014).

16. Bakhtin, *The Dialogic Imagination* and *Speech Genres and Other Late Essays.*

17. Roberto Bolaño, "Fotos," in *Putas asesinas*, rpt. in *Cuentos*, 389–397, 393–394; "Photos," in *The Return*, 181–190, 181, 185, 188.

18. "Photos, 189; "Fotos," 396.

19. Bolaño, SVP, 310–311; TP, 241–242. Spivak, *Death of a Discipline* (published in Bolaño's last year, 2003); see also her *An Aesthetic Education in the Era of Globalization* (Cambridge, MA: Harvard University Press, 2012); Joel Nickels, *World Literature and the Geographies of Resistance* (Cambridge: Cambridge University Press, 2018); Neil Lazarus, *The Postcolonial Unconscious* (Cambridge: Cambridge University Press, 2011); Jahan Ramazani, *A Transnational Poetics* (Chicago: University of Chicago Press, 2009).

20. Bolaño, "Fotos," 397; "Photos," 190. See Valeria De los Ríos, "Mapas y fotografías en la obra de Roberto Bolaño," in *Bolaño salvaje.*

21. Baudelaire, "Le Voyage," OC 134. On the Unknown University's "many secret faculties ... scattered around the world" ("las tantas facultades esparcidas por el mundo de la Universidad Desconocida"), see *The Spirit of Science Fiction*, 9 (ECF, 25), and passim. *The Spirit of Science Fiction* contains a powerful example of roads less taken in Bolaño's work in more capaciously postcolonial directions in its memorable story within a story of two missionaries in the Belgian Congo, "the Chiapas priest Sabino Gutiérrez ... and his friend Pierre Leclerc" (134). Proving over the course of Bolaño's career to have been a rich seedbed for the development of much of his later work, including *The Third Reich, Distant Star, The Savage Detectives, Amulet,* and *Woes of the True Policeman, The Spirit of Science Fiction* reveals to a striking degree the global, planetary, even extraterrestrial scale of Bolaño's early imaginary, encompassing indigenous and hemispheric, national,

transnational, and trans-Atlantic cultures; the Cold War, the space race, and the threat of nuclear war between the United States and the former Soviet Union; questions of race and ethnicity, of gender and sexuality, of literature and other media; both North–South and Global South, historical and literary-historical, socio-economic and geopolitical contexts.

22. Ernst Bloch, *Spuren*, 151; *Traces*, 151.

23. Gertrude Stein, *Tender Buttons* (1914, San Francisco: City Lights; Rpt., Centennial Edition, 2014); William Carlos Williams, *Kora in Hell: Improvisations* (1920, San Francisco: City Lights, 1957); and *Spring and All* (1923), in *The Collected Poems of William Carlos Williams, Volume I: 1909–1939*, ed. Walton Litz and Christopher MacGowan (New York: New Directions, 1991); Claudia Rankine, *Don't Let Me Be Lonely: An American Lyric* (Minneapolis: Graywolf Press, 2004) and *Citizen: An American Lyric* (Minneapolis: Graywolf Press, 2014). On the prose poem's legacy in Stein and Rankine, see my "The Violence of Things: The Politics of Gertrude Stein's *Tender Buttons,*" in *A Poverty of Objects* and "Genre," in *Literature Now*. Sam Anderson's use of the term prose poem in the title of his brief review of *The Savage Detectives*, "Prose Poem: Roberto Bolaño's Brilliant, Messy, Everything Novel," though gestural, is serendipitous. The same is true of the grouping of the two concluding essays of López-Calvo's *Roberto Bolaño, a Less Distant Star*, by Luis Bagué Quílez and Enrique Salas Durazo on *Distant Star* and *Antwerp*, respectively, under the rubric "Prose Poetry and Poetry in Prose." For sustained inquiry into these terms in the United States in particular, see also Michel Delville, *The American Prose Poem: Poetic Form and the Boundaries of Genre* (Gainesville, FL: University Press of Florida, 1998); and Stephen Fredman, *Poet's Prose: The Crisis in American Verse* (Cambridge: Cambridge University Press, 1983, 1990).

24. Rimbaud, *Une Saison en Enfer, Oeuvres de Rimbaud;* also in *Rimbaud: Complete Works,* 208–209.

25. See Moretti, "Style, Inc.: Reflections on 7,000 Titles (British Novels, 1740–1850)," in *Distant Reading*; Jacques Rancière, "The Ethical Turn of Aesthetics and Politics," in *Aesthetics and Its Discontents* (*Malaise dans l'esthétique*, 2004), trans. Steven Corcoran (London: Polity Press, 2009).

Index

Lightning Source UK Ltd.
Milton Keynes UK
UKHW011850080821
388503UK00001B/29